For my Father and Mother

THE RUSSIAN REVOLUTION AND THE BALTIC FLEET

STUDIES IN RUSSIAN AND EAST EUROPEAN HISTORY

Phyllis Auty and Richard Clogg (editors)
British Policy towards Wartime Resistance in Yugoslavia and Greece

Elisabeth Barker
British Policy in South-East Europe in the Second World War

Richard Clogg (editor)
The Movement for Greek Independence 1770–1821

Olga Crisp
Studies in the Russian Economy before 1914

D. G. Kirby (editor)
Finland and Russia 1808–1920: Documents

Martin McCauley
The Russian Revolution and the Soviet State 1917–1921: Documents (editor)
Khrushchev and the Development of Soviet Agriculture
Communist Power in Europe 1944–1949 (editor)

Evan Mawdsley
The Russian Revolution and the Baltic Fleet

Further titles in preparation

THE RUSSIAN REVOLUTION AND THE BALTIC FLEET

War and Politics, February 1917 – April 1918

EVAN MAWDSLEY

BARNES & NOBLE

BOOKS

10 East 53d St., New York 10022
(a division of Harper & Row Publishers, Inc.)

First published 1978 by
THE MACMILLAN PRESS LTD
London and Basingstoke

Published in the USA 1978 by
HARPER & ROW PUBLISHERS, INC.
BARNES & NOBLE IMPORT DIVISION

Printed in Hong Kong

Library of Congress Cataloging in Publication Data

Mawdsley, Evan, 1945–
  The Russian Revolution and the Baltic Fleet.
  (Studies in Russian and East European history)
  Bibliography: p.
  Includes index.
  1. Russia – History – Revolution, 1917–1921 – Naval
operations. 2. Russia (1923–   U.S.S.R.). Voenno-
morskoĭ flot. Baltiiskii flot. 3. Russia – Politics
and government – 1917–1936. I. London. University.
School of Slavonic and East European Studies.
II. Title.
DK265.35.B3M38 1978   947.084′1   77–17554

ISBN 0-06-494665-7

Contents

List of Illustrations   ix

Preface   xi

List of Abbreviations   xiii

1 THE FEBRUARY REVOLUTION   3
   The Baltic Fleet   3
   Petrograd and Kronstadt   12
   The Active Fleet   14

2 POLITICISATION   22
   The Political Setting   22
   The Socialist-Revolutionaries   24
   The Social Democrats   28

3 NAVAL DEMOCRACY: MARCH–JUNE 1917   36
   Reform from Above   36
   Revolution from Below   41
   Admiral Verderevsky   46

4 THE GOVERNMENT CHALLENGED: MAY–JULY
  1917   51
   The Kronstadt Republic   51
   The July Days and Kronstadt   55
   The July Days in the Active Fleet   59

5 EBB AND FLOW: JULY–SEPTEMBER 1917   67
   Reaction   67
   Kornilov   76
   Resurgence   79

6 NAVAL OPERATIONS   84
   Preparations   84
   Revolutionaries at War   86
   The Battle of Moon Sound   89

7 THE OCTOBER REVOLUTION 97
  Attack 97
  Motivation 100
  Organisation 106
  Assessment 112

8 CIVIL WAR: POLITICS AFTER OCTOBER 116
  The Centre 116
  The Periphery 119
  Political Mood 122

9 THE RED FLEET: ORGANISATION AFTER OCTOBER 128
  Naval Revolution 132
  Sovietisation 132
  Sovkombalt 134

10 THE ICE CROSSING: OPERATIONS AFTER OCTOBER 141
  Invasion 141
  Exodus 146

CONCLUSION 153

APPENDICES
1 Baltic Fleet Personnel 157
2 Baltic Fleet Order of Battle 160
3 Democratic Organisations 163

Bibliography 171

Index 207

List of Illustrations

1 Dreadnoughts frozen into Helsingfors North Harbour, March 1917
2 A meeting on the ice of Helsingfors Harbour, 4 March 1917
3 Kadet F. I. Rodichev speaks to Helsingfors sailors, March 1917
4 Executive Committee of Helsingfors Soviet, spring 1917
5 S. G. Roshal', a leading Bolshevik agitator at Kronstadt
6 P. E. Dybenko, first chairman of Tsentrobalt
7 A. G. Zhelezniakov, the anarchist sailor who closed the Constituent Assembly
8 Rear-Admiral A. V. Razvozov, C.-in-C., Baltic Fleet, 1917–18
9 Demonstration in Railway Station Square, Helsingfors, 18 June 1917
10 The crew of Kronstadt training ship *Okean*
11 The dreadnought *Sevastopol'* at Reval
12 The battleship *Slava* after Moon Sound battle
13 *Pobeditel'*, a 'Novik' type destroyer
14 The minelayer *Amur*
15 Revolutionary sailors at Gatchina
16 HQ ships in Helsingfors South Harbour, winter 1917–18
17 Helsingfors North Harbour from a German reconnaissance plane, 31 March 1918
18 A ship of the 5th Destroyer Flotilla leaving Helsingfors

Preface

Sixty thousand Baltic sailors had an importance in 1917 out of all proportion to their numbers. The most violent episodes of the whole February Revolution were at the Kronstadt and Helsingfors naval bases. In the eight-month life of the Provisional Government the sailors, especially those at Kronstadt, occupied the extreme left flank of the popular movement. The shot from the cruiser *Avrora* is part of the legend of October – and it highlighted the fleet's prominent role in the uprising. And after 25 October the sailors were again conspicuous, this time in the campaign to spread Soviet power throughout Russia. Any assessment of Bolshevik success in seizing and keeping power should take into account the actions of the Baltic ratings.

There are other reasons why the Baltic Fleet is so interesting. One shortcoming of Western research on the revolution until recently has been an emphasis on the centre, on the leadership of the government and of the political parties, on the mechanics of the power struggle in the capital. Little attention has been paid to the 'grass roots', and the revolution will only be properly understood when local studies are available. This book, then, looks at developments not only at the centre, but also in a 'provincial' area. The Baltic Fleet cannot serve as a microcosm of the Russian Revolution; no area of Russian life could be taken as typical, and in some respects the fleet was quite *a*typical. But some insights may be provided here into the revolutionary process as a whole.

Part of this process was a general politicisation, and here the book is concerned with all the parties which were active locally, not just with the Bolshevik victors. It also studies another neglected area, the attempted democratisation of life, the transfer of administrative power from the ex-tsarist authorities to – for want of a better term – the masses; in the fleet this transfer took the form of the replacement of the officer corps by elected committees. Finally, to assess the effect of this transfer, there is an examination of the 'conventional' military operations of the fleet. This last point is of more than incidental importance, as the ships, mines, and shore batteries of the Baltic Fleet were vital to the defence of the Russian capital.

The book ends not in October 1917 but in April 1918. This is partly because the real end of the 'pre-Soviet' Baltic Fleet came only at the later date, when the fleet was evacuated from its Finnish bases and almost completely demobilised. In addition, the Bolshevik Revolution created, in the navy and elsewhere, as many problems as it solved. The extent of these problems and the first – faltering – steps toward their resolution became evident in the six months after October.

The transliteration system used is a simplified version of the Library of Congress system. Contemporary Russian spelling of place names is used (e.g. Gange rather than Hanko or Hangö), with exceptions for well-known towns (Helsingfors rather than Gel'singfors, Reval rather than Revel', Kronstadt rather than Kronshtadt). All dates, unless otherwise noted, are those used in Russia at the time; that is, 'old style' until 1/14 February 1918 and 'new style' thereafter.

I would like to express my gratitude to those who helped me. Professor J. L. H. Keep provided advice and encouragement for an embryonic version of this work. Mr George Taube of the Association of Former Russian Naval Officers in America first showed me the value of émigré materials. Dr David Kirby provided invaluable information on sources available in Finland. Viktor Vasil'evich Petrash, the leading Soviet authority on the revolutionary Baltic Fleet, gave me some of his views on the subject. Various people read all or part of the manuscript and offered useful advice of an historical or technical nature; in the latter connection I am particularly grateful to Margaret Liston. And, finally, especial thanks are owed to Jean Fyfe, who produced the typescript and who made many helpful suggestions.

Research in Russian history is virtually impossible without aid from learned institutions. My thanks go to the University of London Central Research Funds Committee, the Carnegie Foundation, the University of Glasgow, and the British Council, who paid for research trips to Leningrad and Paris and to places directly connected with the Baltic Fleet: Helsinki, Tallin, Hanko, and Turku (but not, unfortunately, Kronstadt). My research in Leningrad was facilitated by guidance and advice from fellow specialists at the Historical Institute of the Academy of Sciences.

July 1977 E.M.

List of Abbreviations

1. In the text

C.C.	Central Committee
C.C.B.F.	Central Committee of the Baltic Fleet (Tsentrobalt)
C.E.C.	(All-Russian) Central Executive Committee
C.-in-C.	Commander-in-Chief
E.C.	Executive Committee
M.N.S.	Main Naval Staff
M.O.	(Bolshevik) Military Organisation
M.R.C.	Military-Revolutionary Committee
M.T.C.	(Kronstadt) Military-Technical Commission
N.G.S.	Naval General Staff
N.R.C.	Naval Revolutionary Committee
P.S.R.	Party of Socialist-Revolutionaries
R.S.D.W.P.(b.)	Russian Social-Democratic Workers' Party (Bolsheviks)
S.D.	Social Democrat
Sovkombalt	Council of Commissars of the Baltic Fleet
Sovnarkom	Council of People's Commissars
S.R.	Socialist-Revolutionary
Tsentrobalt	Central Committee of the Baltic Fleet
Tsentroflot	Central Committee of the All-Russian War Fleet
Vobalt	Military Section of Tsentrobalt

2. In the notes

Adm.	Admiralty Papers in the P.R.O.
BFORGV	A. K. Drezen (ed.), *Baltiiskii flot v Oktiabr'skoi revoliutsii i grazhdanskoi voine*
BMBVS	A. L. Fraiman (resp. ed.), *Baltiiskie moriaki v bor'be za vlast' sovetov*
BMPP	R. N. Mordvinov (ed.), *Baltiiskie moriaki v podgotovke i provedenii Velikoi Oktiabr'skoi sotsialisticheskoi revoliutsii*
EMS	*Ezhenedel'nik Morskogo sbornika*
F.O.	Foreign Office Papers in the P.R.O.

HSSS	Meeting of Helsingfors Soviet Sailors' Section
IGS	*Izvestiia Gel'singforsskago Soveta*
IKS	*Izvestiia Kronshtadtskago Soveta*
IRS	*Izvestiia Revel'skago Soveta*
OSh	P. F. Kudelli (ed.), *Oktiabr'skii shkval*
Ostsee	E. von Gagern (ed.), *Der Krieg in der Ostee*
PLKF	*Piat' let Krasnogo flota*
Prikaz Komflota	Prikaz Komanduiushchago flotom Baltiiskago moria
Protokoly	D. A. Chugaev (ed.), *Protokoly i postanovleniia TsKBF*
PVRK	D. A. Chugaev, *et al.* (eds), *Petrogradskii V – RK*
RDR . . .	*Revoliutsionnoe dvizhenie v Rossii* . . . *;* volumes in the series *Velikaia Oktiabr'skaia sotsialisticheskaia revoliutsiia: Dokumenty i materialy*
RPG	R. P. Browder and A. F. Kerensky (eds), *The Russian Provisional Government 1917*
SS	*Svobodnoe slovo soldata i matrosa*
TShSV	D. A. Chugaev (resp. ed.), *Triumfal'noe shestvie Sovetskoi vlasti*; in same series as *RDR* . . .
VK	Venäläinen Kokoelma; Russian Collection of the Finnish Military Archives

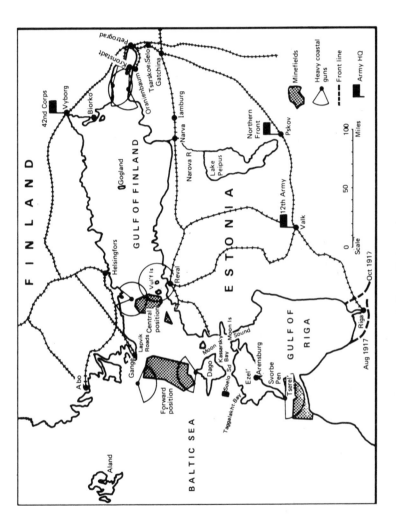

Russia's Baltic Defences, 1917

1 The February Revolution

Mutiny in *Andrei*, *Pavel*, and *Slava*. Admiral Nebol'sin killed. Baltic Fleet does not now exist as a fighting force. Will do what I can.

Vice-Admiral Nepenin to M. V. Rodzianko, 3 March 1917

THE BALTIC FLEET

The third week of February 1917 was the last normal week. From the deck of his flagship, the *Krechet*, Vice-Admiral Nepenin could see the nucleus of his battle fleet, seven battleships, frozen into the North Harbour at Helsingfors (now Helsinki). With a few exceptions, the rest of the 'Active Fleet' – cruisers, destroyers, submarines, mine ships, and auxiliaries – was divided between the two main bases of Helsingfors and Reval (now Tallin). Nepenin felt no particular problems in this fleet he had commanded for five and a half months. Men and ships were going through their January-April hibernation just as they had in the two previous winters. The frozen Gulf of Finland made it impossible for them to put to sea, but it also prevented a Germal naval attack on Petrograd (now Leningrad). Nepenin's main concern was an early attack on the Gulf of Riga, but against this contingency he had left a battleship and a cruiser in Moon Sound. The situation in the rear also seemed satisfactory, for at Kronstadt and Petrograd the winter training courses were ending, promising an influx of trained men.

The calm was deceptive. In most of the 700 ships and in the shore installations there were latent tensions, and in some instances the situation was explosive. Many of the Baltic ratings were prepared to rise against their officers and their government.

Prince Liven, a leader of the post-Tsu-shima reforms, once said that Russian naval officers could have no idea of what their men were thinking: 'Normally they are for us absolutely inscrutable. Officers who imagine they know the physiognomy of their people, outside service matters, are sadly mistaken'.[1] What was hard for the officer on the spot should be doubly hard for the historian, looking back over half a century later. However, to understand what happened in February and March (and in the months that followed) it is vital to try to find out what the Russian naval rating felt about his everyday life and his government.

The Russian citizen was subject to military conscription at the age of twenty-one (in 1916 some were called a year early); a man assigned to the navy was obliged to serve for five years, two years longer than an infantryman. That the Imperial Navy was manned by conscripts, not volunteers, was a fundamental problem. In the Baltic Fleet, career sailors (warrant officers, extended-enlistees, and volunteers) made up only 5 per cent. The war aggravated this problem, because service was involuntarily extended and reservists were recalled. By January 1917 a third of Baltic ratings had been kept beyond their normal term: 15 per cent had been serving since 1909–11, and 17 per cent were reservists originally called up in 1904–8.[2] Prolonged involuntary service bred resentment. To add insult to injury, warrant officers and extended-enlistees received more pay than involuntary re-enlistees with the same length of service. Also the Navy Department did not give older men priority for higher-paid and less dangerous shore service.

The Russian sailor was poorly paid, and wartime inflation put him in an increasingly difficult financial position, especially if he had a family living on a serviceman's allowance; the fact that the sailor was often a townsman made pay for his family a more important consideration than it was for the self-sufficient family of the peasant soldier. The sailor's provisions were poor; there was real trouble over food in 1915 and a number of *pretenzii* (hunger strikes) later. On the whole however food was not the central grievance that it was in the German Navy after the 'Turnip Winter' of 1916–17. Russian warships were not prisons, but leave was limited. During the 'campaign' (ice-free season) a sailor from a battleship or cruiser could count on getting ashore on one weekday in eight from 1 p.m. to 6.30 p.m.; during the winter he could occasionally stay out until 10 p.m.[3] The situation with regard to longer annual leave was also unsatisfactory.

How a sailor spent his time differed from base to base and depended on his unit and on the stage of his career. A new conscript was assigned to the Baltic Fleet at a local recruiting centre and then was sent to a naval depot (*ekipazh*) in the capital. If he was in outstanding physical condition with a clear political record he went to the Naval Guards; most conscripts however were assigned to a training company in one of two other depots, the 1st Baltic Fleet Depot being at Kronstadt and the 2nd at Petrograd. The first six months of naval life, from October to March, were spent in barracks, where the conscript was isolated; he spent his time learning military discipline, marching, and riflery. Early in March he took an oath to the Tsar and was allowed to leave the barracks for the first time. Some men were sent directly to the Active Fleet at this point. Others however stayed at Kronstadt until November or even until March of the following year, learning some special skill in one of the training detachments. The most able men might spend yet another year training as petty officers; other experienced sailors would return to Kronstadt from the Active Fleet for similar training.

Life at Kronstadt (and at the Petrograd depot) was not really naval. The trainee went to sea (to Biorko Sound) only for a few summer months and in one of the old training ships. By the end of February 1917 the Kronstadt sailors, including the conscripts of the class of 1917, had spent a winter in barracks and classrooms. The sedentary life at Kronstadt was bad for morale, for there was no way of creating a fighting spirit and no proper units existed around which morale could be built.

The nature of service in the Active Fleet also hurt morale. The *Stavka* (G.H.Q.) had assigned to it the primary task of protecting the sea approaches to Petrograd. This meant a concentration of strength at the Central and Forward Positions, two formidable complexes of minefields and coastal batteries, one between Helsingfors and Reval and other at the mouth of the Gulf of Finland. It made sense to fight a superior enemy from behind prepared defences, but the corollary was that until the Germans attacked no risks should be taken, especially by the six most modern battleships. As a result, three of these ships never left the gulf, and none took part in prolonged operations. Furthermore, from the summer of 1916 a serious U-boat threat led the C.-in-C. to report that 'the combat training of large fleet units had been reduced to a minimum'; 'This situation and the tasks confronting the fleet do not allow it to carry out any sort of exercises in the eastern part of the Gulf of Finland'.[4] Many smaller ships however saw more action, particularly in the Gulf of Riga; the morale of these active ships, which were based at Reval, was considerably better.

The first wartime C.-in-C., Admiral fon-Essen, kept to the basic strategy but sent submarines and a few destroyers and cruisers to raid German communications in the southern Baltic. Fon-Essen's successor, Admiral Kanin, was much more cautious. In the 1915 and 1916 'campaigns' the fleet was inactive, and morale suffered. One result was a mutiny aboard the new dreadnought *Gangut* in October 1915; her captain explained that part of the cause lay 'in our (our brigade) constantly lying at anchor, and in the lack of combat action for our ships'. One of the Tsar's naval adjutants considered Kanin a desk man who made a poor fleet commander; under Kanin's administration 'the Baltic Fleet quickly began to break down, which everyone felt and was conscious of'. The senior naval officer at the Stavka finally called for Kanin's replacement, charging that his inactivity might lead to 'the extinction of the fighting spirit of the personnel'.[5]

When Nepenin took over in September 1916 he saw it as his task to resuscitate the dying morale of his men. Plans for the 1917 'campaign' included greater activity for the fleet and even the use of the dreadnoughts in the open Baltic.[6] In the short term however he could do nothing, since it was so late in the year. Winter arrived, and even the active ships were consigned to months in port.

Morale reached low ebb in the winter months. The climate made life unpleasant. For the ships in the frozen harbours day followed day with monotonous regularity. The rating's existence was full of *polundra* or make-work, each new activity heralded by the 'archangel', the bosun's pipe. This was the situation in all ships, and in the worst it aggravated the effect of previous years of inactivity. Ironically, Nepenin was the first C.-in-C. who tried to do something about this problem; he encouraged football and other teams and even began to plan a Sailors Club in Helsingfors.[7] In the winter of 1916–17 however this was too little and too late.

These factors – involuntary service, low pay, inactivity – do not necessarily add up to incipient mutiny. Conditions in all armed forces contain similar elements. The Russian navy however was probably worse than other services in its discipline and in the relations between officers and men.

From the time he arrived at the depot in Petrograd the Russian sailor was forced to live within a stringent system of discipline which emphasised his low status. There were no up-to-date Naval Regulations, so each ship operated on a set of rules drawn up by the captain. Individual officers had the power to award summary punishment, and this led both to more arbitrariness and to animosity towards those officers who were known as 'dragons' (*drakony,* disciplinarians). As officers served long terms in one ship there was a further reduction in uniformity; some ships became well-disciplined and others slack.[8]

The general level of discipline was determined by the local commander. All sources agree that the Governor-General of Kronstadt, Admiral Viren, was a severe disciplinarian. One rating, writing in 1917, recalled that over the island 'like an evil genius and like the curse of Hell, ruled Admiral Viren, to whose terroristic activity whole volumes could be devoted'. Another remembered that Viren's very name was 'like the crack of a cossack's whip'.[9] No doubt these comments betray a certain revolutionary hyperbole, but the 61-year-old admiral, who had been in overall charge of Kronstadt for eight years, was both very strict and very unpopular.

One reason for the strictness was that Kronstadt was a training establishment where the normal naval regime did not obtain. There were no combat units and only one naval officer for every 45 ratings, as compared to one for 18 in the rest of the Baltic Fleet. Much of the training was supervised by auxiliary officers from the merchant marine or the army. Another problem was that many of the fleet's 'unreliables' had been drafted to the depots and prisons at Kronstadt. The size of the depots had greatly expanded during the war to contain men sent back from the Active Fleet. The island was nicknamed the 'sailors' Sakhalin' because of the number of detention centres – several prisons, a punitive company in the 1st Depot, and the prison hulk *Volkhov*. Viren was unhappy about this situation, and in September 1916 he requested the tranfer of the Kronstadt sailors to the White Sea and Siberian Flotillas. The Stavka felt that there was no point in spreading the Kronstadt 'infection' all over Russia, so the situation remained unchanged. The presence of so many discontented men and the release of the prisoners – one of the first acts of the February uprising – must have had considerable influence on the massacre which followed.[10]

Admiral Nepenin too was something of a martinet. Rear-Admiral Timirev, then captain of the cruiser *Baian*, a perceptive man and in no way sympathetic to the revolution, recalled that Nepenin

> began to demand model military bearing and saluting, strictly punishing guilty officers and sailors alike. Such pedantry, in questions to which no special significance was attached in wartime, made, from the very beginning, an unfavourable impression among the personnel and created more than a few enemies of Nepenin among the younger officers and especially among the sailors.

Of particular significance was Nepenin's order of November 1916 imposing stiff penalties for failure to salute. The admiral's behaviour during inspections was also tactless. In the *Baian* he unjustly criticised first the captain and then the whole crew: 'The ship is in complete disorder! Dirt, loathsomeness!' During a visit to the *Gangut* he announced that had *he* been C.-in-C. in 1915 the mutinous dreadnought would have been sunk. Yet another confrontation took place in the *Diana*.[11] It was not surprising that when the revolution came Nepenin was condemned as a 'tyrant'.

Closely connected with the problem of discipline were the relations between officers and men. As Prince Liven wrote:

> The sailor comes from the lower, underdeveloped and poor levels of the population, the officer, on the other hand, belongs to the more educated and propertied classes, to the so-called privileged order. Between the two there exists a gulf from birth which is difficult to cross from one side to the other.

As in all the Russian armed forces, the menial status of the 'lower ranks' was emphasised, and exaggerated subservience was demanded. Officers were called 'Your Excellency' or 'Your Honour', and used the familiar 'thou' with ratings. Sailors were forbidden to enter restaurants or taverns, to ride inside trams, to smoke in the street, or to be anywhere in a theatre except the gallery. Kronstadt was particularly bad for these petty regulations; one sailor recalled that 'without exaggeration it can be said that . . . there was everything to lower, insult, and kill all human dignity and honour in military personnel'. A famous sign stood at the entrance to Petr Park: 'No admittance to lower ranks and dogs'. Sailors were forbidden to walk down one side of Nikolai Prospekt, the main street. They could not enter inns, restaurants, or private homes.[12]

Despite a relaxation of entry regulations in 1907 and 1913 the name 'blueblood' (*belaia kost'*) could still be applied to most officers. Of 1,128 youths entering the Naval Cadet Corps between 1910 and 1915, 1,033 belonged to the hereditary gentry, 17 were children of the 'personal' gentry, and in all only 78 – less than 7 per cent – came from other parts of society. Even the small proportion of non-noble officers came from affluent families and were well-educated. Many officers were *ostzeiskie* – from the German Baltic nobility. The hostility of the Slav sailors to these officers was increased by wartime Germanophobia. The unpopularity of the *nemtsy* was one cause of 1915 trouble in *Gangut*; during the mutiny the cry 'Beat the Germans!' was heard.[13]

The ranks of the army's officer corps – less aristocratic to begin with – were thinned out by the fighting. Replacements came from lower levels of society, the officer corps became less exclusive, and the gap between officers and men was reduced. In the navy no democratisation took place, even though at the beginning of 1917 the Baltic Fleet was nearly 600 officers below its establishment (owing to new construction, not war losses).[14] Because prospective sea-going officers had to be taught so much they could not be produced quickly. The Detached Naval Cadet Classes were a new source of regular officers, but the first graduates finished only in 1916.

The warrant officer problem showed that 'upward mobility' would not have solved everything. The Corps of Warrant Officers comprised men risen from the ranks who wore uniforms similar to the officers'. The institution was, in part, a means of keeping technically-trained men in the navy, but it also had a political function after 1905, since the warrant officers acted as a buffer between officers and men, supplying information and enforcing discipline. Because of this, and because of their privileges, the 'lower ranks' seem to have disliked the 'skins' (*shkury*) as much as the commissioned officers.[15] One of the first post-revolutionary demands was for the abolition of the corps.

The life of the Russian rating had many unpleasant aspects. Some could be found in other armed services – in Russia and elsewhere – but not, perhaps, all together. The most significant appear to be the inactivity of some parts of the fleet and the relations between officers and men. Nevertheless, these conditions do not in themselves explain the mutinies. Although the 'system' was important as an underlying element which kept morale low in many units and bred resentment, the direct causes of rebellion lay elsewhere.

The officials at the recruiting centres did not pick at random the conscripts who were to go to the fleet. Mechanisation meant that the nineteenth-century rating, an uneducated peasant or fisherman, was no longer satisfactory, and in 1898 the Navy Department began drafting men from the more industrialised provinces. After the mutinies of 1905–6 some people questioned the political wisdom of this, but the logic of *mashiniza-tsiia* was against them; as a government commission reported in 1912, 'in view of the special complexity of the modern warship the Russian peasant cannot go immediately from the plough to become a sailor, and the worker element is rather better prepared to handle machinery'. Of the 'classes' (*sroki sluzhby*) of 1904–16 only one quarter belonged to the dominant Russian social group, the peasantry. More numerous were factory workers, who made up nearly a third. The remainder, a little less than one-half, were of various professions – unskilled workers, boatmen, employees, artisans, men from the building trades. Peasants were much more important in the army; in the infantry of 1913 only 4 per cent were factory workers while 61 per cent were peasants. What was important was not so much the factory worker element (and two-thirds were *not* factory workers) as the large urban working-class element. This meant that the ratings were relatively well-educated; 84 per cent of the men of 1904–16 were literate, and a further 10 per cent were classed as 'semi-literate'. (In addition, the year or more of education which was common in the fleet must have added to the literacy of all elements.) These figures should be contrasted with those for the 1913 infantry, where only 49 per cent were literate and 23 per cent were semi-literate.[16] A literate person was more politically-conscious; he could deal better with complicated political ideas, and he was more receptive to revolutionary leaflets and newspapers (both before and after the revolution). The revolutionary movement was largely an urban phenomenon and a sailor-townsman was more likely to have participated in it. A sailor of the class of 1912 would have been fourteen or fifteen during the Revolution of 1905; a sailor drafted in 1914 could have taken part in the upsurge of political activity in the last two years before the war. Because of the nature of the service and the predominance of the working class even the peasant-rating, one of the 20,000 in the fleet, would be losing his traditional mentality; he had, after all, served in warships for several years.

Another point, which has not been brought out by Soviet research, is that the typical Baltic rating was quite young. Nearly half were twenty-three and under, and the average age was considerably below the average age in the army (where more reservists were called up).[17] The effect of this factor is difficult to pin down, but it might be suggested that younger men were more inclined to be hot-headed, more ready to take risks.

It was hardly surprising that among 80,000 sailors, many from the working class, there were active members of the revolutionary parties, the S.D.s (Social Democrats) and the S.R.s (Socialist-Revolutionaries). This underground however was small and ineffective in the years of the World War. I will discuss the particular appeal of the various parties in the following chapter. However, to briefly describe the situation before 1917, it should be said that the socialist parties, and especially the S.R.s, were influential during the 1905 Revolution. They co-ordinated several naval mutinies in 1905 and 1906. Afterwards the socialists (particularly the émigrés) continued to agitate. Literature of both parties was discovered hidden in warships. Fresh mutinies were planned; the biggest incident came in 1912, when 72 sailors were arrested. On the whole however the revolutionaries never recovered the influence and success that they enjoyed in 1905–6. Moreover, when war came, the anti-government movement was temporarily stilled by a wave of patriotic feeling and by a government clamp-down.

During the war the feeble centre of S.D. activity was Kronstadt. In 1915 several ratings tried both to make contact with the Bolshevik Petersburg Committee and to establish links with the Active Fleet. Owing to war-time conditions civilian agitators could not function at Kronstadt, and organisation was left to the sailors themselves. They were amateurs at conspiracy, and the Okhrana was able to arrest the ringleaders. Nineteen were brought to trial, and long prison sentences were received by several men (among them three prominent in 1917: Ivan Sladkov, Nikolai Khovrin, and Kirill Orlov). A second attempt was made in 1916, but the so-called 'Main Collective of the Kronstadt Military Organisation of the R.S.D.W.P.' was broken up in September, having been unable to establish a lasting connection with the Petersburg Committee. So, although there were doubtless a number of S.D. sympathisers (and many surfaced in March 1917) there was no fleet-wide Bolshevik organisation. One recent Soviet source admitted that the 1915 group represented only the 'beginning phase of the creation of an organisation' and that the Kronstadters had practically no links with Party members in 'the basic force of the fleet' at Helsingfors, Reval, etc.[18]

The S.D. sailors furthermore were not sure what to do. Talking about his group in the battleship *Imperator Pavel I*, Nikolai Khovrin recalled that he found it 'difficult to say what its political colouration was'. No one knew how revolution would come about, and 'we confined ourselves to obtaining "tendentious" books and brochures'. Armed uprisings were not the style of the Social Democrats. One Petersburg Committee leaflet (a major piece of evidence against the 1915 group) concluded: 'Long live the democratic republic! Long live the confiscation of land! Down with tsarist autocracy! Down with the bloody Romanov monarchy!' Nevertheless the only practical steps recommended were the organisation of unit committees, the reading of literature, and general preparation for action *along with* the working class. In a 1916 leaflet the Main Collective stressed the need for organisation and for close links with the workers:

> All sorts of unorganised uprisings, isolated riots, and outbreaks are fatal to us. They are doomed in advance to failure and death. They play into the hands of our enemies, for it is easy for them to grapple with us in a completely unequal battle.[19]

The S.R.s, for their part, were divided over the war and even less likely than the S.D.s to provoke uprisings. They too had connections in the fleet. One Bolshevik recalled that the 1915 group used them as allies: 'We were ready to turn to the S.R.s in order to grasp some thread with the rest of the world'. Kronstadt received some literature from the Petrograd S.R.s, and in October 1915 an S.R. sailor-deserter came out to establish contact. There is no evidence of an extensive S.R. underground, however, and the Helsingfors S.R.s later admitted that the revolt there was wholly spontaneous; 'revolutionary organisations were completely absent from the town'.[20]

Neither party had anything to do with the *Gangut* mutiny. Recent Soviet research admits that 'there was no uprising but [rather] there took place spontaneous, unplanned, and unorganised disturbances of sailors whom . . . no one led'. The Kronstadt Gendarme Administration was correct in reporting on 8 February 1917 that 'the collective of the Kronstadt Military Organisation does not in reality exist'. The same could be said of an organised S.D. or S.R. underground anywhere in the fleet. Many Soviet sources assert that a Bolshevik underground led the February mutinies, some émigré historians share this view, but they have not produced any convincing evidence, and there was no such evidence in the 1917 press.[21] Even had organised S.D. and S.R. groups existed, there was no 'centre' to direct them. In fact, organised left-wing groups appeared in the fleet only after the February Revolution (and after a considerable delay). There were certainly isolated revolutionaries, but they were important not as instigators of mutiny but as symptoms of a more general malaise.

Not only were just a small minority active members of left-wing parties, but there were a large number who were simply not politically conscious. In March 1917, when Lieutenant D. N. Fedotov of the destroyer *Strashny* asked his men what they thought of the revolution they replied, 'The same as you, your honour'. One of the Helsingfors mutineers recalled that only a quarter of his comrades realised the importance of the February crisis.[22] Even after the February Revolution, when politics became a feature of everyday life, many ratings did not participate. On the other hand, a large number of sailors *were* politically conscious and did not belong to an underground. They were the ones who joined the socialist parties after February. Their political attitudes were of fundamental importance.

One Russian sailor, Nagorny, stayed with the imperial family until the very end, but there is no reason to think that the autocracy was popular. Nikolai 'the Bloody' (as he was called in 1917) was the man responsible for the repression of the Revolution of 1905. His government clearly did not intend to make any concessions to democracy or even to court popularity. Moreover the war had brought a general deterioration in the standard of living, especially in the towns, and this could be blamed on the regime.

A high proportion of ratings were patriotic, but this did not imply support for Nikolai II. On the contrary, the obvious military failures and the rumours about Rasputin and Germanophiles in high places must have turned even the patriots against the imperial family. The war was a central factor, but also a very complicated one. It was responsible for the rating being in the fleet in the first place and for the hardships of his family. Nevertheless the average sailor was probably not a defeatist; the Bolsheviks found this out in the first months after February, when their anti-war line was widely attacked. The dominant opinion seems to have been that the Germans were aggressors led by the government of Wilhelm II, a government as obnoxious as the Russian autocracy. The rating was prepared to defend his motherland against 'Wilhelm' until a reasonable peace could end the bloodshed. The war aims of the autocracy, however, were quite different, as the Tsar's Order to the Army and Navy of 11 December 1916 showed; he announced that the war's tasks, the first of which was the capture of Tsar'grad (Constantinople), had not been achieved and that, as a result, the situation did 'not allow even a thought of peace before the final victory' over the enemy'.[23] Thus, while the rating supported the war he opposed the Tsar's war aims.

To the mass of politically-conscious ratings, and not just to the underground 'card-carrying' S.R.s and S.D.s, revolution seemed the only way to democracy and a just peace. (It might even be argued that some of the organised radicals were more cautious than their unorganised fellows; hence the warnings of the need to observe restraint.) The Russian political system offered no alternative. A tradition of rebellion reinforced this feeling. The *Potemkin* mutiny followed the initial stages of the 1905 Revolution. The riots at Kronstadt and the Sevastopol Uprising were a response to the Tsar's October (1905) Manifesto granting a Duma (Parliament). The closing of the first Duma in the summer of 1906 led to risings at Helsingfors, Kronstadt, and in the cruiser *Pamiat' Azova*. Even the abortive 1912 plot was a response to the Lena Massacre. The risings were important as a precedent (although there were few veterans of the movement in the Active Fleet). Equally significant were the autocracy's reprisals. Dozens of ratings were killed during the mutinies or executed after trial. Thousands of men were arrested, and hundreds received long sentences. Probably as consequential were the myths that grew up – of iron barges full of prisoners being sunk by shell-fire or of forgotten ratings rotting in underground dungeons. The memory of 1905–6 was a major theme in the naval press after February; the memory must have been alive before February as well. Potential rebels were made aware of the price of failure, and when they decided to act they would strive for complete victory.

Another important consideration was the political outlook of the officer corps. The Baltic officers were not black reactionaries, and many were genuinely concerned about the situation in Russia. The commander of a Reval destroyer flotilla, for example, said that he would not fire on the people 'for Protopopov and Co.' A circle of officers on Nepenin's staff were critical of the 'camarilla' (the Empress's circle), if not of the institution of monarchy. Commander Zhitkov, editor of the naval journal *Morskoi sbornik*, used his offices to print and distribute censored Duma speeches. Individual officers, like Engineer Commander Filippovsky (significantly however a wartime officer), actively participated in the February struggle against the autocracy.[24] After the revolution most officers were willing to work with a republican government, and a number even served on under the Communists.

It would be wrong however to say, as Aleksandr Kerensky did on the night of 3–4 March, that 'the great majority of citizen officers are on the side of the people'. Most were apolitical or monarchist. As the (monarchist) Commander Graf of the destroyer *Novik* put it, naval officers 'grew up and were educated in the traditions of the monarchy, they took an oath of loyalty to the Tsar and the motherland and never became involved in politics'.[25] The officer corps did have a professional aversion for politics, but in Russia political passivity was the same as tacit support for autocracy. Even if some officers had political doubts, the officer corps appeared to the sailors to be a bastion of the old regime. The officers – with a few notable exceptions – had remained loyal to the autocracy in 1905–6. They were obviously 'blue-bloods' with a hereditary commitment to the system.

In the February Revolution the officers made no serious attempt to oppose the 'movement'. This was partly because they had no opportunity (had the autocracy been stronger, had the men been more passive, the officers might well have supported the Tsar as they did in 1905–6). Also, what most concerned the officers in the winter of 1916–17 was the continuation of the war and the maintenance of their own authority, and it is possible that many were prepared to sacrifice the 'camarilla' to these ends. By the time the revolution neared Helsingfors (Kronstadt mutinied too early) the movement had the blessing of a number of senior army commanders and 'reputable' centrist politicians, and this helped assure the neutrality of the officers (although Graf felt that if the officers 'had known that the Provisional Government seized power forcibly most of them would have continued to stand firmly behind the Tsar').[26]

By the first days of March the revolution was victorious and many officers were prepared to accept it as a necessity. Thus the officers were not really a threat. The point is that they were *seen* as a threat by the ratings, and they suffered as a result. As one junior officer, Dmitry Fedotov, put it, 'the mine had been prepared for explosion but there was nothing to explode – the enemy had dismantled their own walls'; nevertheless, the 'inertia of revolution had its way'.[27]

PETROGRAD AND KRONSTADT

It was in the third winter of the war and the coldest month of the year that the edifice of tsarist Russia collapsed. Its foundations had proved too weak for the twentieth century and total war, its last steward too feeble.

Revolution began in Petrograd, suddenly and unexpectedly, on Thursday, 23 February 1917, with worker demonstrations against the bread shortage. The action of the masses spread rapidly as an expression of their grievances. World War had worsened the people's economic position, and they found autocracy increasingly hateful. Decisive change came on Monday, when the garrison began to go over to the rebels. By Tuesday morning the last loyalist stronghold – the Admiralty – had been abandoned.

The spontaneous and unorganised activity of the workers and soldiers who took and kept control of the streets of the capital was one aspect of the revolution. Another was the appearance of a rebel government which could capitalise on the people's uprising. Monday evening brought the formation of a Soviet (Council) of Workers' and Soldiers' Deputies. A few hours later part of the State Duma decided to act unconstitutionally and form a new cabinet, the Provisional Committee of the State Duma.

Emperor Nikolai II was away from his capital, at the Stavka. On Thursday, 2 March, under pressure from the Provisional Committee and senior generals, he abdicated in favour of his brother Mikhail Aleksandrovich. The next day Mikhail declined the throne, and the three-century old Romanov dynasty came to an end.

The Baltic Fleet did not play a very important part in the Petrograd uprising. It produced no leaders. Basically the fleet provided foot-soldiers for revolution, and small detachments at that, because there were only about 10,000 sailors in a garrison of 180,000. The largest units were the 2nd Depot, the Naval Guards Depot, and the cruiser *Avrora*. All three were within half an hour's march of the capital's administrative heart, but they did not act until Tuesday, after the decisive moment. The commander of the 2nd Depot was killed, and there was violence aboard the *Avrora*. The cruiser was refitting at the Franco-Russian Shipyard, and a mob of workers dragged the captain and senior officer ashore, killing the former and seriously injuring the latter. On the same day the crew elected the first ship committee of the revolution.[28]

Twenty miles from the capital, across frozen St Petersburg Bay, was the eastern tip of Kotlin Island, and here the naval town of Kronstadt was located. The Governor-General, Admiral Viren, was acutely aware of the dangers of the political crisis. There had been two Kronstadt mutinies during the previous revolution, and in a letter to the Stavka of 16 September 1916 he had reported a new revolutionary situation:

I honestly say that one tremor from Petrograd would be enough and Kronstadt, together with all ships now in Kronstadt Port, would rise against me, the officers, the government, and anyone else. The fortress is a powder magazine in which a wick is burning down, in a minute the explosion will be heard.

On 14 and 15 February, 1,400 men staged a hunger strike against bad food and in favour of the Progressive Bloc in the Duma.[29] Then came the 'tremor from Petrograd', the February Revolution.

Vice-Admiral Kurosh, the Kronstadt Commandant, refused a Stavka request that two Kronstadt army regiments be assigned to a punitive expedition which General Ivanov was trying to organise; he explained that no units were sufficiently trustworthy. Viren and Kurosh did everything to isolate the island, but it was physically impossible. On Monday, 27 February, everyone could hear shooting and see the smoke from fires at Oranienbaum on the mainland; in the evening the news arrived that the Petrograd garrison had gone over to the rebels. On Tuesday the workers in the Steamship Shipyard and the port workshops went on strike, and the sailors abandoned their training courses.

Viren was in an impossible situation. Having been in the Tsar's service for forty years he could not readily join the Duma rebels. He did not know that the revolution was already victorious and that opposition was pointless. The old order had collapsed and the new one was too busy consolidating its own position to worry about the periphery, so no instructions arrived. Kurosh received from the rebels' Military Commission the message, 'are you with us or against us?'; his answer was noncommittal. Viren and Kurosh could only wait and hope that the disturbances would either abate or be crushed. In the meantime Viren ordered all alcoholic spirits destroyed and promised to meet the striking workers' delegates in Anchor Square on Wednesday morning. According to some accounts the Governor-General prepared for this meeting by putting machine-guns in a cathedral overlooking the square. True or not, the rumour was accepted by many people, and it must have inflamed the situation.

Kronstadt mutinied on Tuesday night. Like the rising in Petrograd it was spontaneous. The rebellion began in the northern part of town among the barracks on Pavel Street. First to act was an army regiment, the 3rd Kronstadt Fortress Infantry. Out of their barracks the soldiers marched, with the regimental band playing the Marseillaise. After killing one of their officers the sailors of the Torpedo and Mining Training Detachment followed. They rallied the 1st Baltic Fleet Depot. Soon the whole garrison was on the streets. Exuberant sailors and soldiers exchanged caps. Then the training ships in the frozen harbour mutinied.

The commanders were helpless. Kurosh reported: 'Do not find it possible to take measures for pacification with personnel from the garrison because there is not one unit I can rely on'.[30]

During the night Kronstadt was visited by the exterminating angel of the revolution. Some officers died at their posts in the first struggles for control. Others were taken to a ditch in Anchor Square and executed. In the small hours of Wednesday Viren was brought there and bayoneted to death. A number of other senior officers perished: Viren's chief of staff; the heads of the 1st Depot, the Torpedo and Mining Training Detachment, the Artificers School, and the Boys School; the captain of the old battleship *Imp. Aleksandr II.* Altogether, 24 naval officers and probably about 10–15 naval n.c.o.s were killed. In addition, 162 naval officers and many naval n.c.o.s were arrested; others fled for their lives.[31]

Wednesday morning was devoted to mopping up the last supporters of the old regime. A six-inch naval gun cracked open the local gendarme headquarters in Nikolai Prospekt, where six policemen were killed. The threat of similar action convinced the officer-cadets of the Naval Engineering Academy that they must surrender.

It is important to see the situation as the Kronstadt sailors did on the night of 28 February–1 March. It was certainly not clear that the revolution was victorious. No one anticipated that the autocracy would prove to be so weak. On Wednesday the whole town expected that loyal troops would try to put down the rising–just as they had in 1905 and 1906.[32] The Kronstadters were *making* a revolution, not just taking advantage of one to settle old scores. To them the struggle for power was still going on, and everything possible – including the killings and arrests – had to be done to assure victory.

If the old regime died in its sleep in most of Russia, it was battered to death at Kronstadt. Of the officers who survived, a large proportion were thrown into prison and others fled. Discipline could not (and would not) be restored. One ratings' memory of that night was very significant: at the foot of the Makarov monument Viren warned his tormentors that two loyal regiments were coming from Finland to put down the rebellion. 'This is not a mutiny, comrade admiral', replied the sailor, 'but a revolution!'[33] He was right; the loyal regiments would never arrive, the old regime would never return. Red Kronstadt had been born.

THE ACTIVE FLEET

It was early on Tuesday, 28 February, that Nepenin learned that Petrograd was 'in the hands of the mutineers'. Unlike Viren he did not try to black-out all news, but he minimised the crisis; he ordered his captains to reassure the men that the new ministers could resolve everything. On Wednesday, when M. V. Rodzianko informed him that the Provisional Committee had taken 'governing power', Nepenin replied that he considered the Committee's intentions 'worthy and correct' and went on to request recruits and war supplies. Nepenin was the first important commander to accord the new – tsarist – ministry *de facto* recognition. The exchange was circulated as a printed order.[34]

The fact was that, in terms of the Russian officer corps, Nepenin was relatively progressive. There is evidence that he shared the doubts of much of the Russian élite regarding the competence of the autocracy. Early in 1916 he asked one of his subordinates, 'Is it possible that only a revolution can save Russia?' In a later coversation with another officer he admitted great concern over the course the nation was taking. He had some contacts with the Duma.[35] Nevertheless, the C.-in-C. was acutely aware of the dangers of the situation (especially after the Kronstadt massacre), and this led him to act – publicly, at least – with the greatest caution.

When, on Thursday morning, the hard-pressed Reval Commandant begged for advice about which side to take, Nepenin replied, 'If the situation demands a categorical answer at any cost, then announce that I am united with the Provisional Government.' Later on in the day he told his flag-officers that he would openly recognise the Provisional Committee ('I will answer with my head, but I have firmly decided') 'if the circumstances demand it'. This last was the operative phrase. Nepenin's behaviour was conditioned not by diehard loyalty but by a desire to keep politics out of the fleet. There was still no trouble at Helsingfors, and releasing the news might stir up his ratings and even the Finnish population. So, it was not until some time on Friday, evidently after a minor local demonstration, that the admiral announced, 'I openly, with the whole fleet entrusted to me, have taken sides with the Provisional Government as the only power upholding order.' He was also late in announcing Nikolai II's abdication in favour of Mikhail Aleksandrovich. He approved the abdication on Thursday evening, received the abdication manifesto very early on Friday, but did not release it until 3.30 p.m.; the reason was that Rodzianko had asked him to hold it up. In addition Nepenin released no news about the course of the Petrograd uprising or about the Kronstadt and Reval events. The communications problem was made worse by the fact that even Nepenin was not aware of the latest events; in particular, he did not know that on Friday morning Mikhail Aleksandrovich had declined the throne. In addition, technical delays and the attitude of individual captains slowed the spread of information. The news of Nikolai's abdication did not reach the sailors until 5–8 p.m., and it would appear that in some important ships, like the *Andrei Pervozvanny*, it was not announced formally at all.[36]

All this looked bad. Nepenin had not been as candid as possible. Preoccupied with maintaining military discipline, he restricted the crew's movements, forbade any demonstrations, and made no attempt to meet delegates (until too late). Meanwhile the men were learning through the 'forecastle bulletin' that something was happening in Petrograd. At best, as the perceptive Timirev pointed out, the men received the impression 'that the commanders were bowing to the unavoidable course of events but did not want to sympathise with them'. At worst, the C.-in-C.'s silence bred rumours that the officers secretly planned to send help to the counter-revolution, that they wanted to put down the Kronstadt uprising, and that the various announcements were merely tactical concessions. Vice-Admiral Verderevsky later recalled that 'the basic reason for those horrors in Helsingfors was the habit of concealing the truth from the command – a habit to which we who have spent our entire military service under the old regime have become accustomed; this habit, this concealing [of the truth], was the fundamental cause of all the horrors'.[37]

In any event, the initiative now passed to the crews.

The difference of attitudes between the men and even the 'progressive-minded' officers must be stressed. When Commander I. I. Rengarten, one of Nepenin's staff officers, learned (early on Friday) of the abdication he noted in his diary, 'What a glorious memorable night of the conclusion of the Great Russian revolution.' To many ratings, however, the revolution did not seem to have been concluded. The position of the monarchy was a central point, and even those who knew of the first abdication thought that Emperor Mikhail II was on the throne. The Provisional Committee might be issuing decrees, but who knew what the 'dark forces of the old regime' were up to? Something had to be done to support the Provisional Committee and prevent a repetition of 1905–6. To be sure, only a part of the lower deck was politically aware; for the active minority, however, 'the moment demanded active support'.[38]

Some informal meetings between sailors took place in the outskirts of the town, but there is no evidence of conspiracy; the Helsingfors uprising began spontaneously. The first signs of trouble appeared on Friday afternoon in the Mine Defence Depot (*Beregovaia rota minnoi oborony*) where the men gathered in the courtyard and prepared to march out into the town. Nepenin drove up and by threatening the assembled sailors made them disperse. The real epicentre however was to be the *Andrei Pervozvanny* and *Imp. Pavel I* of the 2nd Battleship Brigade. The 'wharf-rats', as they were called, had seldom been to sea, and their morale was low. In November 1916 there had been a hunger-strike aboard the *Pavel* (which led Nepenin to criticise her captain for being too lax).

The *Andrei* was evidently the first to act – at about 7 p.m. Her crew believed their captain was hiding something and learned through a telegraphist that there was trouble at Kronstadt. They became excited. Then the officer of the watch arrested some ratings who had been signalling to the *Slava*, and that set the mutiny off. Guns were seized, shooting began. The officer of the watch and a warrant officer were killed, and then Rear-Admiral Nebol'sin, the brigade commander. Men ran amok, firing through skylights into the officers' cabins. After about 45 minutes order of a sort was restored, but with the crew in control. A petty officer was elected captain. The surviving officers were arrested. Unpopular warrant officers were also dealt with (one was hunted through the bowels of the ship all Friday night until he was killed). Red navigation lights were switched on at the masthead.

The *Pavel* rose at about the same time and with similar carnage. This ship was evidently the first to raise the red flag, usually raised only in battle. The crew trained her turrets on neighbouring ships. Minor disorders also broke out in the third ship of the brigade, the *Slava*.

Red lights appeared everywhere in the darkness of the North Harbour. Sailors bellowed through megaphones. Cheers echoed from ship to ship. The vessels which had mutinied sent messages to the others. '*Andrei* has risen. Join us comrades.' The *Pavel* signalled the *Petropavlovsk*: 'Deal with the officers you dislike, our officers have been arrested.' Hundreds of armed men began to run about on the ice, trying to rally other ships and, in some cases, killing officers from the smaller ships. Altogether, about 40 naval officers and at least a dozen n.c.o.s were killed, mostly on Friday night.[39]

The men of the mutinous battleships were now fighting for their lives, for if the officers regained control they would be doomed. Pro-government forces might arrive at any moment. The crew of the *Andrei* stayed up all Friday night mounting machine-guns and searchlights; they had heard that two loyalist regiments were on the way. Even in the relatively calm *Petropavlovsk* the crew demanded 4.7 in. primers, in case 'infantry come from the shore to pacify the ships'.[40]

It was a nightmare, but not as bad as at Kronstadt three nights before, where the officer corps had been effectively liquidated. Only in the *Andrei*, the *Pavel* and one or two smaller ships did the crews kill their own officers. The other killings were by outsiders, probably from the 2nd Battleship Brigade. On most ships there were no murders. The officers were simply disarmed and temporarily arrested; revolution demanded their neutralisation, not their deaths. So, by 1.30 a.m. the C.-in-C. could report, excluding the *Pavel*, the *Andrei*, and the cruiser *Rossiia*, 'subordination gradually being restored'. An *ad hoc* 'revolutionary committee' was set up in the dreadnought *Petropavlovsk*. After ordering red lights lit it sent the signal: 'Officers to be disarmed but not killed.' One officer recalled that without the *Petropavlovsk* committee 'the number of the revolution's victims would have been much greater'.[41]

In the *Krechet* the C.-in-C., as he promised Rodzianko, was doing what he could. 'Delegates', a new term in the fleet, were summoned, and Nepenin spoke to a hundred of them at about 10 p.m. Their first demands were simply to be allowed to smoke in the street and wear galoshes. A little earlier a *Poltava* sailor, Adam Sakman, had been allowed to speak by 'Hughes' teletype machine with one of the brilliant figures of the revolution, Aleksandr Kerensky. Sakman minimised the disorders and stressed that there were no special demands, just a desire for better living conditions: 'The comrade sailors want that they should feel free outside service and an improvement in the food, if that is possible.' The essence of Kerensky's advice was that the revolution had already gone far enough: 'Stop immediately the destruction of the Russian Fleet'. Nepenin had recognised the new power, therefore he was to be obeyed:

> Remember that for the first time in our history soldiers and officers and sailors fought together for the overthrow of the Tsarist order. I announce to You that in reality the great majority of citizen officers are on the side of the people. . . .

Seven months later the fleet would send 'curses' to 'the traitor to the revolution, Bonaparte-Kerensky'; now Nepenin reported to the Stavka that this conservation had reduced the bloodshed. (It was through Kerensky that the fleet learned of Mikhail Aleksandrovich's abdication.)[42]

Another hub of activity was an ephemeral committee in the *Pavel*. Early on Saturday morning it radioed: 'Do not believe the tyrant [i.e. Nepenin]. Remember the order about saluting [of November 1916]. No, we will not receive freedom from the vampires of the old order.' The concluding words were 'death to the tyrant . . . !' Later on this organisation told the C.-in-C. to stop issuing orders.[43]

A fourth centre was on the other side of town, in the Sandviks Harbour, where the Mine Defence ships were based. The men there elected their own commander, Vice-Admiral Maksimov, as the new revolutionary C.-in-C. When Maksimov presented himself in the *Krechet* at 11.40 a.m. Nepenin decided to resign.

On Saturday afternoon a crowd of sailors came to the *Krechet* and demanded that Nepenin go with them to meet delegates from Petrograd. He did so, hesitantly, and partly because he did not want the flagship boarded and secret papers compromised. As the group reached the gates of Sveaborg Port, just before 1.45 p.m., Vice-Admiral Nepenin was shot and killed by a sailor.[44] It was unnecessary – like the mutiny as a whole – as the C.-in-C. had already resigned. No one ever claimed credit for the assassination, and no enquiry was held; most likely it was the act of one disgruntled sailor. Given the mass hysteria, the murders of the previous night, and the victim's reputation, it was not so surprising.

Years of isolation ended, as the Baltic sailors entered Free Russia. The first two emissaries of the revolution, Fedor Rodichev, a Kadet from the Provisional Government, and Matvei Skobolev, a Menshevik from the Petrograd Soviet, arrived at the Helsingfors station within hours of Nepenin's death. Thousands of sailors and soldiers gathered in Railway Square to meet them. Maksimov appeared, wearing a red ribbon and escorted by a lorry-load of jubilant ratings. The delegates rushed directly from their train to a makeshift podium in the middle of the square. Rodichev recalled that 'the first of the main commanders-in-chief who supported our people's power was the noble Admiral Nepenin' and, pointing with his hat at Maksimov, said, 'Look after him!'[45] It was a symbol for the future. The authorities were running contrary to the sailors' mood and backing a power that was doomed. Rodichev had endorsed a dead man.

Nevertheless with the support of the two – undoubtedly popular – delegates, the new C.-in-C. was able to complete the restoration of order. Red flags were lowered and all hands returned to their normal duties. After touring the fleet on Saturday, Rengarten reported to Captain Al'tfater of the Naval General Staff that a calmer mood now prevailed. Al'tfater said, 'Thus, if I understand you correctly, it is possible to hope, thank God, that the fleet is saved.' Rengarten replied, 'We must hope; that is the way it seems, that is the way the men talk, that is the morale situation at the present moment.'[46]

The other major base for the Active Fleet was Reval. Wintering in the harbour were four of the best cruisers (the *Baian*, *Bogatyr'*, *Oleg*, and *Riurik*), many destroyers, most submarines, and numerous auxiliaries and mine ships. Morale was higher than elsewhere. The ships had seen a good deal of action. Also the spirit tended to be better on small ships where officers and men were well acquainted and shared the same – often difficult – conditions.

At Helsingfors and Kronstadt the February Revolution was made by sailors and soldiers; at Reval the Estonian workers initiated it. Strikes began on Wednesday, 1 March, and on Thursday 30,000 people demonstrated in Market Square. The biggest threat to the local Commandant, Vice-Admiral Gerasimov, was not his crews, but the crowds of workers who marched down to the harbour demanding that the fleet join them. On Tuesday Gerasimov had declared that he would allow 'no sort of action and demonstration' and warned the population not to force him 'to resort to extreme steps'. It was probably fortunate that the admiral was seriously wounded by a workman's bayonet at the provincial prison, because the subordinates who replaced him, Rear-Admirals Leskov, Pilkin, and Verderevsky, showed much greater flexibility. They saved the situation on Thursday by – on their own initiative – ignoring Nepenin's orders and allowing the men ashore. The next morning Rear-Admiral Pilkin, the cruiser brigade commander, explained his action:

Categorical demands not to allow crews ashore cannot be executed and greatly complicate problem, as they create risk of crowds breaking on to ships. Situation more serious than you imagine. Exceptional times need exceptional measures, therefore I foresee necessity of involuntarily breaking your orders and, perhaps, of taking part in festive demonstration of unity of fleet with new government and with people.

In addition, an order was released on Thursday to the effect that Nepenin was on the side of the new government.

The Pilkin formula worked where those of Viren and Nepenin failed. There were a few deaths in the army, but the fleet at Reval entered the revolutionary era peacefully.[47]

At the smaller bases, events followed the Reval pattern. At Nikolaishtadt (now Vaasa), Gange (Hanko), and Abo (Turku) there was little violence. Order was maintained in Moon Sound, where the battleship *Tsesarevich* and the armoured cruiser *Admiral Makarov* were wintering.

Kerensky once wrote that even without the February Revolution he was 'quite certain there would have been a great mutiny in the fleet before the end of the summer'.[48] Definite conclusions can never be reached on this sort of speculative question, but I find Kerensky's statement difficult to accept (in 1917 he betrayed no particular gift of prescience). The situation in the Active Fleet was not so bad that a general and *independent* explosion could be expected. Kronstadt was worse, but the same might be said of it – despite Viren's apprehensions. There were few revolutionaries in the Baltic Fleet, they were unorganised, and they were not planning an uprising. The mutinies were actually a spontaneous reaction to the February Revolution in Petrograd.

Why was this reaction so violent? The various factors discussed in this chapter predisposed Russian sailors to radical action once the revolution had begun. The Russian revolutionary experience had shown that half-measures were not enough. There was a tradition of violence – on both sides; Khovrin called the February–March massacre 'child's play' compared to the repression in the fleet after the mutinies of 1905–6, and there is some truth in this.[49] Furthermore officers and men were packed together in a ship, and ships and other naval units were in close proximity to one another at the naval bases. This made it difficult for officers to hide and easy for violence to spread.

These factors applied to the whole Russian Navy, yet violence was largely confined to Kronstadt and Helsingfors. How can this be explained? Geography was certainly important. Petrograd made the revolution and knew when it was victorious. Distant towns, armies, and fleets were insulated and learned of the revolution when it was demonstrably victorious; local officials and commanders could readily vow sub-ordination, and the masses felt no need to participate. The Baltic Fleet was in the middle, because it joined the movement between the collapse of the old order and the consolidation of the new; the Baltic sailors were unable to see that their rebellion was superfluous.

The sailors at Kronstadt and Helsingfors – who were under a parti-cularly rigorous system of discipline – were the most inactive in the fleet. The Reval sailors had at least been to sea the previous autumn. In the

Black Sea, in contrast, the fleet was still operating in mid-February, and at the critical moment Admiral Kolchak, the C.-in-C., could take his ships to the Bosphorus for a demonstration – and a distraction.

The role of chance should not be forgotten. The *Pavel* and the *Andrei* were the core of the battle-fleet uprising, and under somewhat different conditions they might not have mutinied. If they had not mutinied, or if they had been refitting at Kronstadt or Petrograd, there might have been no rebellion at Helsingfors. Of course, luck works both ways, and given the situation at Reval on 2 March there could have been more killings there.

What was the effect of the mutinies? At Kronstadt the naval hierarchy was destroyed; one eyewitness later recalled that here it was a case of 'October in February' – in other words, power changed hands eight months earlier than in the rest of Russia.[50] The same could not be said of the Active Fleet. Most ships at Helsingfors, including five out of seven battleships and all three cruisers, were not greatly affected; action was confined to disarming and briefly locking up the officers and setting up proto-committees. At Reval the officers were not even imprisoned. It seems fair to say, then, that the backbone of the fleet had not been broken.

On the other hand, the mutinies clearly were important. Referring in October 1917 to the killings, Admiral Verderevsky (then Navy Minister) noted; 'If to this day there is still a gulf between [officers and men], it is a gulf at the bottom of which lies the blood that was shed in vain'.[51] The mutinies destroyed much of what *camaraderie* had existed. Also there would be occasions in 1917 when the threat of renewed violence would force new C.-in-C.s to make concessions.

It was however the February Revolution *as a whole* which led ultimately to the collapse of the Baltic Fleet. From the point of view of *matériel* alone the navy was doomed; even with the most loyal crews it could not have survived the exhaustion of naval stockpiles caused by revolutionary chaos. Politically also, February doomed the old order. Conditions in the fleet were unsatisfactory, and changes would be demanded. The legalisation of the revolutionary parties and their freedom to propagandise permitted agitation for aims directly contrary to those of the naval authorities. The coming of the new order made the disintegration of the navy inevitable, and the Baltic mutinies merely accelerated this.

2 Politicisation

1. All servicemen have all the rights of citizens. . . .
2. Every serviceman has the right to be a member of any political, national, religious, economic, or professional organisation, society, or union.
3. Every serviceman has the right, outside the hours of duty, to freely and openly state and confess, orally, in writing, or in the press, his political, religious, social, or other views.

From the Declaration of Servicemen's Rights, 11 May 1917

There had been little political life in the fleet before February; the fate of the Marseillaise during the first Helsingfors demonstrations was symbolic – 'the sailor masses tried to sing, but almost no one knew the words'. Things quickly changed. Within a few months an admiral could complain that 'politics were everywhere: nearly every day there were meetings of ships' delegates, eternal conversations by semaphore and signal lamp, frequent meetings on shore'.[1] And this was among the relatively calm ships in the Gulf of Riga; at the main bases new democratic institutions held power, and thousands of ratings poured into the radical parties. The new interest in politics affected the democratisation of the fleet and led to the appearance of some Baltic sailors in the all-Russian political arena, but these two themes will be pursued in Chapters 3 and 4. The object here is to see how politicisation began and developed.

THE POLITICAL SETTING

Within a week of the mutinies there were soviets of workers' and soldiers' deputies at all three major Baltic bases. Sailors made up about 40 per cent of the Helsingfors Soviet, soldiers a slightly higher percentage, and workers and merchant seamen the remainder. Perhaps a third of the delegates to the Kronstadt and Reval Soviets were from the fleet; at both places the soldiers formed the largest group. Despite this the soviets became the first major channel for the political expression of the fleet.

Before discussing the major fleet parties, the S.R.s and Bolsheviks, and their activities in the soviets and elsewhere, it is important to note the limits of politicisation. Not everyone was interested in politics, even in the midst of a revolutionary earthquake. Some ratings were immersed in their duties. To others 'revolutionary freedom' meant the freedom to devote their new-found leisure time to drinking, gambling, and mastering the 'Windsor', the

'Matelot', and the 'Petrograd Tango' (as one Kronstadter put it, 'These dances deflect the thoughts of our comrades from political questions').[2]

The Bolshevik rating Nikolai Khovrin mentioned another limitation: 'until the July events the whole mass of sailors, or more correctly, the vast majority, very poorly understood the meaning of political parties'. There predominated a kind of populism which was the child of revolutionary euphoria and political inexperience; a populism which coupled a naive belief in 'the people' with a feeling that partisan squabbles were not only meaningless but – in view of the danger of counter-revolution – positively dangerous. This mood was well expressed by a sailor from the battleship *Respublika* (formerly the *Imp. Pavel I*):

> If you want the Russian people to move by quick leaps to socialism, if you want to unite in one whole all the toiling class of many millions, then do not break it into separate groups, arguing among themselves on the basis of some programmes which you regard as immutable laws. Combine your agitation, unite all your separate groups into one united people's party. The programme for this great party will not be some little booklet, but the multi-faceted whole of Russian life.

Or, to quote from a declaration of the 1st Patrol Boat Flotilla: 'there must exist only one party uniting all, the "Free Russian People" '.[3]

In the early sessions of the Kronstadt Soviet the 'non-partisan' group held from a quarter to a third of the seats; the non-partisans vacillated from moderate to extreme left, and the Bolsheviks called them the 'Swamp' after the *Marais* of the French Convention. Non-partisans made up a large part of the Helsingfors Soviet, and there were also some in Reval, but in neither case were they as well organised as in Kronstadt.

Gradually the non-partisans lost ground. Late in June the Kronstadt Soviet advised the population not to vote for the non-partisans in the Town *Duma* (municipal council) elections; in July the non-partisan chairman of the Kronstadt Soviet was replaced. More significantly, the non-partisans themselves became more party-conscious, and this was surely sign of politicisation. In August the 'non-partisan party' 'Republic of Labour' (*Trudovaia respublika*) was formed, with 'the goal of uniting all the labouring people . . . around their soviets'.[4] The last stage came shortly afterwards when many members of this group joined the semi-anarchist S.R.-Maximalist party. At Helsingfors and Reval the process was less clear-cut, as the non-partisans were absorbed by other groups.

The anarchists were not non-partisans, but in their rejection of 'conventional' political forms they were similar. They were unsuccessful in the Baltic Fleet, winning over individuals but not securing mass support. Even at Kronstadt their delegates never constituted more than 6 per cent of the soviet, and their Helsingfors organisation did not appear until after October. This is a little surprising, given that their short-term views and activities were not very different from those of the Bolsheviks; they favoured ultra-democratic reform and were uncompromisingly hostile to the Provisional Government. But the anarchists had not been important in the recent revolutionary tradition, and they were not prominent in 1917 national (i.e. Petrograd) politics. They may have seemed too ideological – and, in fact, were split into Anarcho-Syndicalist and Anarcho-Communist factions. And they lacked a national organisation which could act as a focus and which could channel funds and agitators to local bases; anarchist agitators from Petrograd went no farther than Kronstadt, and the one anarchist base newspaper, *Vol'nyi Kronshtadt* (Free Kronstadt), was started only in August.

Another characteristic of Baltic politicisation was the weakness of the centre-right parties. The sailors saw the Octobrists and Kadets (Constitutional Democrats) as the parties of the bourgeoisie (and later of the counter-revolution). The Octobrists provided the first Navy Minister, and the Kadets provided the first head of the commission for naval reform and the first government commissars in Kronstadt, Reval and Finland, but these parties made no attempt to agitate, except for the desultory mailing of propaganda. They had no newspapers – aside from the short-lived quasi-Kadet *Obshchee delo* (Common Cause) at Helsingfors – and their local civilian organisations were very weak. The centre-left Trudoviks and People's Socialists also had practically no following in the fleet, even though both Kerensky and the fleet Commissar-General belonged to the former party; neither group was represented in the base soviets. (At Kronstadt the Trudoviks did publish a newspaper, *Trud i zemlia* (Labour and Land), and they enjoyed some civilian support.)

Naval officers might have been expected to support the centre parties, but this was not the case. Some still felt bound to the Tsar, while others were professionally apolitical. The minority who decided to dabble in politics believed that they saw which way the wind was blowing and either held to a vague 'republican' position or supported the Right S.R.s. The slogans of the Helsingfors officers' group were typical: 'War to Victory for Free Russia' and 'Democratic Republic'. The officers pledged themselves to 'educate' the lower deck politically, but they made little headway. The sailors learned their political lessons elsewhere.

THE SOCIALIST-REVOLUTIONARIES

The Party of Socialist-Revolutionaries was the most popular political group in Russia for most of 1917; not surprisingly, it was also the strongest party in the Baltic Fleet in the first months. The P.S.R. was the heir to the great populist tradition; it had acted heroically in 1905, and it was regarded as the party of such heroes of early 1917 as Kerensky, Breshko-Breshkovskaia, and Chernov. The S.R.'s promise of land reform and their support for 'revolutionary defensism' (i.e., for continuation of the war) matched the popular mood of that spring. And while other parties appeared to represent narrow social groups – the bourgeoisie or the urban working class – the S.R.s were the party of the mass of the population – the peasantry.

S.R. organisations appeared at the three bases at the end of March or the beginning of April; the S.R.s were a little slower off the mark than the Bolsheviks, but they soon outran all rivals. In May the Helsingfors S.R.s boasted that 'the young organisation is growing not from day to day but from hour to hour, and its influence both among the wide masses and in the Soviet . . . is unique'; they claimed 15,000 members. In late May the Kronstadt S.R.s claimed 2,500 dues-paying members, and in August there were 6,000 S.R.s in Reval. The P.S.R. dominated the first session of the Kronstadt Soviet and was only slightly behind the Bolsheviks in the second; with 40 per cent of the vote the S.R.s were slightly ahead of the Bolsheviks in the July Town Duma election. When firm party lines were drawn in the Reval Soviet in May, the S.R.s held nearly half the seats (the other half being shared by three groups). The Helsingfors Soviet was not divided into political factions, but the Bolshevik Zalezhsky recalled that the S.R.s ruled unchallenged there in April;[5] the balance in June may be judged from the fact that all three of the soviet's delegates to the 1st Congress of Soviets were S.R.s.

Part of the S.R. local success can be explained by the presence of thousands of soldier-peasants. According to the Mensheviks, the local P.S.R. won its basic support at Kronstadt from the soldiers; the S.R.s themselves admitted that they predominated among the soldiers and workers, while the Bolsheviks held the sailors, and the Town Duma elections confirm this. And as for Helsingfors, the Bolshevik leader Antonov-Ovseenko reckoned that in May the S.R.s dominated the garrison, while the Bolshevik stronghold was the fleet. But the P.S.R. was undoubtedly very strong in the navy as well, particularly during the spring. In Helsingfors the first organisational meeting of the party was called on the initiative of the sailors. One Bolshevik sailor recalled – acidly – that there 'the fleet was completely dominated by the S.R.s. The party swelled up, like the body of a drowned man, from an influx of new members. Young and old alike joined – the sailor, the boatswain, the officer . . .'; several other Bolshevik sources confirm this early S.R. predominance. The Bolshevik Raskol'nikov reported that in June the P.S.R. was dominant among the sailors at Reval; this would fit in with the pro-government and pro-war attitudes of the ships based there – the 1st Cruiser Brigade, the Destroyer Division, and the Submarine Division. There were at least two sailors in the first nine-man S.R. Reval Committee. Only at Kronstadt were the fleet S.R.s weak; they received a mere third of the naval votes in the Town Duma elections.[6]

From this position of strength the P.S.R. suffered a relative decline. By the autumn the party held only a quarter of the seats in the Kronstadt Soviet, and two-fifths in the Reval Soviet and the Finnish Regional (*Oblast'*) Committee. In the November elections for the Constituent Assembly in the Baltic Electoral District the two S.R. lists (Left and Right) received only 40.5 per cent of the naval vote. How can this fundamentally important shift be explained?

It was partly due to organisational weaknesses. First, the S.R. leadership tended to be local, and it included some individuals who had only joined after February, 'March S.R.s' or – as one Bolshevik put it – 'revolutionary dandelions'. A radical Kronstadt S.R. condemned the Helsingfors S.R.s with a pun: 'Comrades, what sort of S.R.s are these? They are March S.R.s. They aren't S.R.s (*es-ery*), but inexperienced (*serye*), comrades.' Secondly, S.R. agitation was not all it might have been; the Bolshevik Zalezhsky felt that in the early months they concentrated on 'high politics' in the Helsingfors Soviet at the expense of mass propaganda. Significantly, their press was much weaker than that of the Bolsheviks. *Narodnaia niva* (People's Field) appeared in Helsingfors only on 25 April; Kronstadt's *Za zemliu i voliu* (For Land and Freedom) came out on 19 May and was short-lived; there was no Russian-language S.R. newspaper in Reval until December. Thirdly, the P.S.R. was as interested in agitating in the distant countryside as in building up a local power base; in Kronstadt, for example, the S.R.-backed Peasant Soviet had by June sent out 248 agitators at a cost of 6,000 rubles.[7] Another important organisational weakness was a result of the growing friction between the base S.R.s and their more conservative Central Committee and, in Helsingfors at least, of the division of effort between rival S.R. factions.

Even more important was the programmatic weakness of the P.S.R. The party was hamstrung by its early success, and its actions belied its slogan, 'In struggle you will attain your rights'. Rather than calling for Soviet power, the P.S.R. entered a coalition in early May, and thereafter it found itself supporting the Provisional Government. The leader of the Helsingfors S.R. centrists defended this line in late June ('the first order of the day is the organisation of the provinces and the countryside. Any attempt at the immediate transfer of power [to the soviets], if it might lead to civil war, we reject and condemn'), but a local Left S.R. put it another way: the socialist ministers became 'the captives of the bourgeoisie'. One of the Reval S.R. leaders concluded on the eve of the October Revolution that 'we made the greatest mistake when we did not take power in the spring'. The party's national centre temporised on the land question, continued to favour defensism after it fell out of favour with the masses, and was reluctant to criticise the Provisional Government. In November a Kronstadt S.R. declared that the local party organisation could only be saved by a complete rejection of the C.C., a body which the Kronstadters had long regarded as 'almost counter-revolutionary'.[8]

Kerensky (a Trudovik, but linked to the S.R.s) was Navy Minister from

May to September, and the ultra-Right S.R. Vladimir Lebedev was Director of the Navy Department, so service dissatisfaction could be directed against the P.S.R. Some of the 'March S.R.s' were officers, drawn to the party by its early moderation. In Helsingfors several of the more popular of these were actually made members of the local committee. The radically-minded ratings were driven away; one, from the *Diana*, decided to join the Bolsheviks, for 'if the officer goes to the S.R.s, then I shan't go with him'.[9]

The S.R. attempt to be a party of the broad centre, rejecting 'both the hurrah-patriots and the hurrah-socialists', was doomed to failure. From mid-summer the local organisations swung increasingly to the left. At Helsingfors this took the form of an open split, probably because of the existence of strong personalities on both sides. The leaders of the left were Prosh Prosh'ian and Aleksei Ustinov, intellectuals fresh from emigration – via Petrograd. After a few weeks with *Narodnaia niva* they left over the government's 18 June offensive and put out their own successful daily, *Sotsialist-revoliutsioner*. The new paper proposed a seven-point programme which included no co-operation with the bourgeoisie, putting revolution before war, and an armistice on all fronts. At the 'Balto-Finnish Congress' in mid-June the centre was still dominant ('the left wing was powerless and small in numbers'), but by the '2nd Regional Congress' at the end of September the situation was reversed; as *Sotsialist-revoliutsioner* put it, 'from defensism and patriotism to international socialism, from a passive temporising policy to an active and creative one, from Menshevism to S.R.-ism, from compromise with the bourgeoisie to class struggle – such is the path that party thought has followed in Finland'.[10]

Elsewhere the left predominated without a split. As early as May the Kronstadt S.R.s declared their adherence to the 'internationalist tendency'; 'the new young Kronstadt does not want to know any compromise on the question of the [defensist "Liberty"] "loan", on the participation of socialists in the coalition ministry, on the secret treaties, on land, on an "offensive" '. The disgruntled local Trudoviks complained that 'our Socialist-Revolutionaries differ from the Bolsheviks only by the "sign" on their "club" '. At Reval the party moved from a centre-left to a left position in the course of the summer, and the 2nd Town Conference resolved in August that the party 'must rid itself of all responsibility for the policy of the Provisional Government as a whole and of its Socialist-Revolutionary members in particular'.[11]

In the end the left was victorious within the fleet P.S.R., receiving three and a half times as many votes as the right in the Constituent Assembly elections. But although local Left S.R. organisations could break loose from the moderate centre and retain much of their local following, they did not develop a national organisation until November. And they appeared to lack an independent policy, simply following in the wake of the

Bolshevik initiatives – they seemed to be sterile hybrids between the P.S.R. and the Bolsheviks. Ultimately they became mere auxiliaries of the Bolsheviks.

THE SOCIAL DEMOCRATS

The Russian Social-Democratic Workers Party was also divided. On the right were the Mensheviks, who achieved early prestige by the participation of their leaders in the Petrograd Soviet, the second Provisional Government, and the Central Executive Committee. At first they formed the strongest Marxist group at Kronstadt, and at all three bases they produced early leaders; the first chairmen of the Helsingfors and Reval E.C.s were Menshevik workers. By late spring however the Mensheviks were clearly in decline, and they never received much support from the fleet. They did not even put up candidates in the Constituent Assembly elections.

Self-conscious Menshevik (as opposed to mixed Social-Democratic) organisations appeared only in April and May, and Menshevik local newspapers were late and short-lived. The Mensheviks were basically pessimistic (at Kronstadt they argued that from the point of view of scientific Marxism further revolution was impossible – 'the proletariat is a minority, it is a small group of five million, and if we carry out a socialist revolution now this dictatorship would fail just as our offensive [of 18 June] failed');[12] this view had little appeal in the heady days of revolution. Moreover the Mensheviks, like the S.R.s, compromised themselves by entering the government. Menshevik leaders like Tseretelli, Skobolev, Sokolov, and Chkheidze were sent on minatory visits to the Baltic bases. Local organisations tended to a Menshevik-Internationalist position, but this compromise was not enough to win support.

It is of course the other Social Democrats, the Bolsheviks, who really attract the attention. They were able to use the fleet as a political instrument in July and October and in the consolidation of Soviet power. How were they able to get so much support?

One advantage of the Bolsheviks lay in the quality of their cadres and organisation. The other parties had no lack of well-known speakers whom they sent on flying visits around the bases. The Bolsheviks were actually behind with regard to agitation by party leaders; none of the senior Bolsheviks like Lenin, Zinoviev, Kamenev, or Stalin spoke openly at the naval bases (Trotsky and Lunacharsky did speak at Kronstadt before they joined the party, and Kollontai spoke several times at Helsingfors). But in other respects the Bolsheviks had the advantage, because they were able to send from the centre a large number of experienced junior party workers who stayed permanently in the base towns.

There is some value in a detailed look at three such party workers, the three key local leaders before July. The head of the Kronstadt Bolsheviks was Fedor Fedorovich Raskol'nikov (born Il'in), the son of a priest. He was only 25 in 1917, but had been a Social Democrat since 1910, becoming involved while a student at the St Petersburg Polytechnical Institute (along with the young Molotov). He had worked as a secretary on the party newspaper *Pravda* in 1912 and was imprisoned (he was released on account of a nervous breakdown and the 1913 amnesty). When the war broke out Raskol'nikov opted for naval service 'having long been drawn to the poetry of the sea', and it says something about the tsarist government that with his record he was accepted for the Detached Naval Cadet Corps. The course ended shortly after the February Revolution, but Sub-Lieutenant Il'in did not attend his graduation ceremony – he was already carrying out party work for the Petersburg Committee in Kronstadt. He soon became chairman of the Kronstadt Committee. The Menshevik diarist Sukhanov thought him remarkable, 'not only an unusually amiable, sincere, honest, "attractive" man, a devoted revolutionary and fanatic for Bolshevism, but also a man much involved conscientiously – and originally – with revolutionary-socialist culture'.[13]

Raskol'nikov's right-hand man was Semen Grigorovich Roshal', who was 23 and from a Jewish middle-class St Petersburg family. He had been politically active while in secondary school and was arrested at the age of 18. At this time, and until 1914, he was a Menshevik. He was called up in 1915, after a short term at the Psychoneurological Institute (hence, presumably, his party name – 'the Doctor'). Invalided home, he was arrested in Petrograd in December 1915 and spent the following 14 months, until the February Revolution, in the Kresty prison. Then, as a government report put it, 'One of the first orators to appear in Kronstadt [from Petrograd] was the student . . . Roshal'. Hitherto unknown in Kronstadt and presenting as personal credentials a mandate from the Vyborg District Committee of the R.S.D.W.P., Roshal' very quickly won the sympathy of the Kronstadters'. He was a popular and effective agitator; 'Comrade Roshal' always gets the soup going,' grumbled one S.R., 'and the Soviet . . . has to clean up the mess'.[14]

Most important of all was Vladimir Antonovich Antonov-Ovseenko (born Ovseenko), the Helsingfors party leader. He was the son of an army doctor and was 33 in 1917. With his long greying hair and homely face he looked, so one sailor recalled, 'more like a book-keeper than a re-volutionary', but he had been totally committed to the revolutionary movement since 1901 and was even sentenced to death in 1906; during the 1905 revolution he had agitated among the garrisons of Kronstadt and Sevastopol. Abroad from 1910 to 1917, he was a Menshevik at least until 1914, and during the war he was involved in Paris with Trotsky's newspaper *Nashe slovo*. Antonov-Ovseenko arrived back in Russia in May 1917, embraced the Bolshevik cause, and set off for Helsingfors with credentials from the C.C. He was a popular and vigorous agitator who took a special interest in the fleet. With his long hair and singing voice he was nicknamed 'the priest from the *Respublika*' by the S.R.s[15]

The characteristics of these three were important. They were not sailors or local 'March Bolsheviks', but outsiders sent by the party's central organisations to organise the bases. They were from bourgeois back-grounds and, with the exception of Raskol'nikov, had no professional connection with the base populations. They were fairly young, yet had considerable underground experience, and each had spent some time in prison. Their popularity was based largely on their effectiveness as agitators, on personal charisma (one Menshevik recalled that Roshal' would have been the 'perfect leader of a teenage gang').[16]

Among the Bolshevik local leadership, men with such qualities pre-dominated. Roshal', N. K. Antipov, B. A. Breslav, I. P. Flerovsky, V. E. Kingissepp, K. N. Orlov, I. T. Smilga, and V. N. Zalezhsky had been in prison or administrative exile during the war. A. L. Sheinman, like Antonov-Ovseenko, was a returned émigré. Other veterans were Ia. Ia. Anvel't, L. A. Bregman, and I. V. Rabchinsky. And there were 'youngsters' with considerable underground experience, including Raskol'nikov, his brother A. F. Il'in-Zhenevsky, P. I. Smirnov, and B. A. Zhemchuzhin. These men – and others about whom information is lacking, V. I. Berliand, V. I. Deshevoi, and S. L. Entin – were nearly all sent to the bases at the behest of the C.C. or the Petersburg Committee. A study of the situation at Kronstadt, Helsingfors, and Reval indicates that no other party was able to deploy so much revolutionary ability and experience. The men on the spot in February, whom Zalezhsky termed 'provincial Bolsheviks', did not dominate the local organisations after the first month. The party workers from the centre played a disproportionate role. They provided the key leadership at the bases (Raskol'nikov, Roshal', Flerovsky at Kronstadt; Antonov-Ovseenko, Zalezhsky, Smilga, Sheinman at Helsingfors; Kingissepp at Reval). The 'outsiders' accounted for over a third of the delegations sent to central party gatherings.[17] Of the 25 members of the Kronstadt Committee at the end of June at least nine – including the chairman and his two assistants – were intellectuals or professionals, most of whom had not been in Kronstadt before February. And in July the Reval Organisation admitted that agitational work was led by 'intellectuals (about 10 persons) released from hard labour and from emigration'.[18]

The Baltic sailors did not play the leading role here, but they were still important. The Bolsheviks were unique in having the sailor-defendants of the 1916 trial, including N. A. Khovrin, I. D. Sladkov, S. G. Pelikhov, and T. I. Ul'iantsev; these veterans of the revolutionary struggle enjoyed great prestige in 1917. And within the naval *milieu* – if not in overall leadership – individual Bolshevik sailors were quick to assert themselves. P. E. Dybenko was the first chairman of the Central Committee of the Baltic Fleet,

Sladkov was Kronstadt delegate to the 1st Congress of Soviets, I. N. Kolbin was an early Kronstadt delegate to the Petrograd Soviet, and even at Reval the ratings Boitsov and Shushara were the leaders of the sailors' club 'Unity'.

Another sign of Bolshevik organisational vitality was the prompt appearance of their press. Their first newspaper in the Baltic area was the Kronstadt *Golos pravdy* (Voice of Truth), which came out on 15 March; the Helsingfors *Volna* (Wave) was begun soon afterwards (30 March); only at Reval was the party's Russian–language paper–*Utro pravdy* (Morning of Truth) – delayed until mid-May. At each town these were the first Russian-language party newspapers to be published. (Kronstadt had the eighth Bolshevik paper in Russia, Helsingfors the fourteenth; both had papers before such major towns as Baku, Minsk, and Odessa.) The Kronstadt and Helsingfors papers were both the result of the efforts of the centre, which was aware of the power of the press and sent young agitators out for this purpose. By contrast, in May the Helsingfors S.R.s were bemoaning 'the lack of forces from the intelligentsia' which was leading to a decline in their newspaper and their propagandists school.[19]

The level of Bolshevik organisation should not be exaggerated however. Kronstadt was the only case of an early pure-Bolshevik committee having strong links with the centre. Most likely this is explained by Kronstadt's proximity to Petrograd and by its revolutionary reputation; on 18 March the Petersburg Committee recognised the island as fertile ground for agitation and resolved, 'in view of the special importance of the Kronstadt organisation, to send more comrades there'. The organisations at Reval and Helsingfors appeared more slowly, and were at first mixed. The Bolshevik Zalezhsky recalled that Finland was ignored in the first months; 'In the heat of the burning issues of the day, we, who were guiding the workers of the Petersburg Committee, somehow completely forgot about it.' And when many new party members joined the party they did not automatically constitute an efficient organisation. A delegate to the April party conference remarked, apropos of Helsingfors, that 'from the point of view of organisation there is still more and more to be done. It is easier to summon the masses to the most radical revolutionary acts than to organisation.' At a meeting of the Kronstadt Committee on 5 June it was revealed that there were only eight collectives on the island, and that liaison and agitation were weak.[20] The men who controlled the organisations were young and had in some cases strayed from Leninism. All these factors made the local party groups something less than a well-oiled political machine. The Bolsheviks did have a certain organisational advantage, but this was – especially before July – relative and potential rather than absolute.

The Bolshevik Party had another advantage, more valuable than its organisational superiority, and this was its ideology. The essence of

Bolshevik political thought was contained in the very first issue of *Volna*:

> The wave of revolution has risen. Boldly it rushed at the dark sombre
> rock, with one blow it brought down its eroded, shaky foundation.
>   It pulls back for a moment and again, with still greater strength, falls
> upon the dense pile of fragments, washes them away and carries them off
> to the depths of the sea.
>   And the wave will not fall, it will not become calm, rather it will grow,
> absorbing in itself new strengths until it has finished its task, the task of
> truth.[21]

But Baltic sailors who took an interest in politics could have been
excused for any confusion about the position of the Bolsheviks in the first
two months of the revolution. Those who read *Pravda* would have noticed
that the party was taking a somewhat ambiguous position with respect to
the war and the governemnt. The Bolshevik Duma deputy Muranov spoke
at Kronstadt in mid-March and called for unity with the Provisional
Government. The local organisations did not take a definite stand against
the Provisional Governemnt. At Helsingfors and Reval there were mixed
S.D. organisations following a relatively moderate line. The first leader of
the Helsingfors Bolsheviks was the captain of the despatch vessel *Sekret*,
Admiralty Ensign Sergei Garfil'd (Garin); at a conference of party workers
in Petrograd at the end of March he, following the resolutions of the
Helsingfors Section, urged support for the government and provisional
support for the war; he also spoke against petty demands which might erect
barriers between government and people. Even after a more radical line
was adopted, there were some Bolsheviks who were slow to accept it. Kirill
Orlov (born Ivan Egorov), the senior Bolshevik sent first to Kronstadt and
then to Helsingfors, disagreed with Lenin's call for struggle with the
government, and this view was at first supported by one of the leading
Bolsheviks at Kronstadt, the worker M. D. Lebedev.[22]

In March and April, then, the Bolsheviks did not seem so different from
the other socialists; indeed, on 11 April their Helsingfors Committee
decided to co-operate with the S.R.s and others 'to consider the question of
joint work for the fortification of the conquests of freedom and for struggle
with the counter-revolution'.[23] This early muddled line earned toleration
for the Bolsheviks – among those who had actually heard of this small
splinter party. It was hardly a formula for success, however, since the S.R.s
and Mensheviks were saying roughly the same thing.

The return of Lenin from emigration and the publication of his 'April
Theses' in *Pravda* changed all that. The idea of a continuing revolution,
which had only been accepted by some Bolsheviks, was now adopted by
the whole party (albeit after considerable debate). The Bolsheviks now
possessed a political line distinct from and to the left of all the other major
parties: no support for the imperialist war or the capitalist Provisional

Government, not a parliamentary republic but a republic of soviets, fraternisation with the enemy, a militia army with elected officers, nationalisation of the land and the banks, and soviet control of industry.

In the short term, the new Bolshevik policy – combined with Lenin's return in a 'sealed train' through Germany and his contempt for the Allies – had a negative effect in the fleet. The Bolsheviks turned from being a little-known party into an infamous target of hatred for the nationalist masses. Even the naval honour guard sent to the Finland Station later declared that, 'having learned that Mr Lenin returned . . . at the supreme pleasure of his Majesty, the Emperor of Germany and King of Prussia', it expressed 'deep regret' for participation in his welcome. The effect was particularly marked in the bases of the Active Fleet; one leading Bolshevik recalled that in mid-April his party was an 'impotent pariah'. Men selling *Volna* were beaten up, and the paper's offices received a stream of messages such as 'Go back to Germany!'. 'The sailors . . . tore up [our] paper in the streets of Helsingfors,' recalled another Bolshevik, 'they trampled it in the dirt'. Formerly revolutionary ships threatened to physically liquidate their Bolshevik collectives, and there were even conversations between the battleships *Petropavlovsk* and *Sevastopol'* on towing the pro-Bolshevik *Respublika* out to sea and sinking her.[24]

Extreme hostility to the Bolsheviks was an hysterical reaction to the 'sealed train' incident and to the first breach of inter-party peace. The physical danger passed in a few weeks, as moderate socialists sprang to Lenin's defence and other moderates returned from emigration 'at the supreme pleasure of H. M. the Kaiser'. But the Bolsheviks were still widely criticised. The Helsingfors S.R.s accused them of sowing 'disorder in the friendly common work of the whole revolutionary democracy'. A Reval newspaper called them the '*anarkho-ksheshintsy*' (the Ksheshinskaia Mansion was the Bolshevik H.Q.). The Helsingfors Mensheviks complained: 'in place of a carefully planned organisation of the masses [there were] disorganised meetings (*mitingi*); in place of cultural and educational propaganda – agitation saying "down with everything!" ' In the first half of 1917, when there was still wide confidence in the moderate socialists, the following comment by a Reval sailor was typical:

No, comrades, it is shameful to talk about Kerensky and Lenin in the same breath. The first, with all his strength, not sparing himself, is trying to fortify for us the dear freedom which was achieved by suffering and blood, but the other only fantasies, and these fantasies are so destructive for Freedom that they are close to treason. In other words, Wilhelm knew well to whom he granted a favour.

This last note of patriotism was an important factor in hostility to Bolshevism, especially on the part of the men closest to the fighting. 'I do not know, comrades,' said a destroyer sailor, 'what the Bolsheviks & Co.

would say if flying over *their* heads were birds of prey – German aeroplanes.' Another sailor, from the cruiser *Oleg*, had nothing but contempt for the Bolsheviks, who 'all consider the Allies as enemies and the Germans as brothers'; 'it is clear just who the Bolshevik is, the serviceman who has a factory job (*uchetnik*), the young soldier in the rear'; 'now they see that the motherland demands the fulfilment of duty for the sake of the defence of freedom, and they have all become Bolsheviks, crying "down with the war".'[25]

The collective effect of all these criticisms was most evident at Reval, where on 2 June angry sailors tore down a Bolshevik banner inscribed with the slogan "Workers of the World Unite'. The following week a Bolshevik sailor named Radzikovsky wrote an open letter to his naval comrades, sadly noting that they had turned their backs on *Pravda* and had become unable 'to tell your friends and enemies apart'. In reply, an S.R. sailor noted that Radzikovsky, who called for 'fraternisation and a separate armistice', was 'aware that his voice remains the voice of one crying in the wilderness'.[26]

On the whole, however, the new Bolshevik line was a success. If the slogan 'All Power to the Soviets' temporarily cost the support of the patriots, it was popular with the growing ranks of the dissatisfied. Because the Bolsheviks were uncompromised they were able to make capital out of the failure of the Provisional Government – and of the S.R.s and Mensheviks associated with it – to do anything about the war, the land, the capitalists, or the economic crisis.

From virtually no members in the Baltic area in February, the party expanded quickly. By late April it claimed 3,000 members at Kronstadt and 3,000 at Helsingfors, and only at Reval was it weak (in mid-June there were only 2,100 Bolsheviks, of whom only a minority were ethnic Russians). By May the Bolsheviks were the largest party in the Kronstadt Soviet, and by August they occupied a similar position at Reval. An early chairman of the Helsingfors E.C. was at least a self-styled Bolshevik (S. A. Garin), and in September A. L. Sheinman was elected to that post; at about the same time the Bolsheviks gained a majority in the Finnish Regional Committee. Perhaps more important, the Bolsheviks also became the most influential party in the fleet. The Helsingfors Committee relied on the sailors from the beginning; as Zalezhsky put it, 'the basic core of the . . . organisation was the sailors'; in April collectives were claimed aboard 22 ships, with 1,400 members. In the Kronstadt Town Duma election the Bolsheviks received 58 per cent of the naval vote. Only at Reval was the party weak among the sailors – in August a mere 209 members out of 3,182 were from the armed forces.[27] The final test for the party, however, was the Consituent Assembly elections, where the party received 50.1 per cent of the naval vote at Reval, 54.4 per cent at Helsingfors, and 80.3 per cent at Kronstadt.

Politicisation did not happen overnight, and the level of political organisation and consciousness should not be exaggerated. The dominant 'mood' (as contemporaries termed it) was subject to considerable fluctuation. The Helsingfors S.R.s 'expressed apprehension regarding the masses, noting the instability of their mood and orientation', and even Antonov-Ovseenko recalled 'the sailor youth, especially numerous on the dreadnoughts', who introduced 'many unexpected zig-zags into the political activities of the fleet'.[28] It was no easy task to channel discontent into political action. But the key point was that the number of the discontented and frustrated grew with each passing week, and the Bolsheviks were the only organised party able to profit from this.

3 Naval Democracy: March–June 1917

I say that Russia is now the freest state, the Russian fleet the freest one.

Kerensky in Helsingfors, 10 May 1917

REFORM FROM ABOVE

Commander F. N. A. Cromie, R.N., responsible for British submarines, reported just after the revolution that even in Reval 'discipline has disappeared and the ships are run by Committees of sailors. The real Captain on the *Dwina* [i.e. the submarine depot ship *Dvina*] is the man who used to get my bath ready every morning.'[1] The *Dvina* was an exceptional case, but on all ships committees were formed, and the officers lost much of their old authority.

The officer corps was forced to find some way of regularising the situation. One faction urged a return to the *status quo ante*, carried out by force if necessary. 'Urgent planned actions on the part of the government are necessary for the restoration of the prestige and power of the command and officer staff, for the restoration of discipline,' declared Admiral Rusin, Chief of the Naval Staff at the Stavka, 'otherwise in June or July the enemy will take Petrograd'. At a less exalted level, Sr Lieutenant Aldaisky of the destroyer *Iziaslav* stood at the foot of the gang-plank with a revolver and a bulldog and forbade his men to go to meetings. Another larger group of officers, perhaps the majority, simply sank into passivity. Cromie found them 'terribly depressed and pessimistic'. As Admiral Stanley, the head of the British naval mission put it, the Russian officers 'have never taken any interest in the welfare of their men and can hardly be expected to make a start now'. The general frustration with this world-turned-upside-down was expressed by a Lieutenant Dmitriev in the Gulf of Riga: he interrupted a general meeting waving his arms, cursing, and shouting: 'Go away, all of you, we'll get Chinamen and go on without you'.[2]

But there were also officers who saw the need to swim with the current. From Reval Rear-Admiral Verderevsky (soon to become C.-in-C.) and Rear-Admiral Pilkin reported that the main task was actually the *organisation* of ship committees and ship courts – albeit with limited powers:

The continuing and deepening of the normalisation of ship life on a new basis, the continuing of creative organisational work, in which the elected officers and sailors participate, open to our naval force the bright horizons of a new life, based on the mutual confidence of leaders and subordinates and on the mutual recognition of individual rights.

With this course of action, and with quick reforms which would retain the confidence of the lower deck, the Reval ships would be ready for battle by the beginning of navigation.[3]

Kapnist, the Assistant Chief of the Main Naval Staff, accepted the principle of limited reform:

The general goal is to preserve the battle-readiness of the ships, to which end it is tactically essential to make all necessary social concessions to the crews. The most important thing is to preserve complete confidence in the officers and the unity of officers and men and the complete consciousness of officers and men alike that there will be no return to the old regime.

The predominant feeling at the Admiralty was that a restoration of the pre-February situation was impossible. As one – critical – officer put it: 'The road of endless compromise, of gradual concessions, with the hope of recanting them later – this was the position of the Naval Staff'.[4]

The need for concessions was also recognised by many 'rank and file' officers. It was necessary, resolved some 400 of them in Reval on 24 March, 'to forget all offences which took place during the period when the crews had misgivings about the sincerity of the officers' coming over to the side of the people'. What was needed now was discipline based on mutual confidence. To maintain an effective fleet 'the authority of elected committees must be supported and recognised by their crews'. 'Energetic measures must be adopted through the . . . committees to curb those sailors who, as a result of their lack of consciousness, do not want to submit to any kind of regulations.'[5]

Vice-Admiral Maksimov, C.-in-C. by popular acclaim, had been a heroic destroyer captain at Port Arthur and commander of the 1st Battleship Brigade and of Baltic Sea Mine Defence during the World War. 'Poika' Maksimov was popular among the ratings, partly because he was widely believed to have shielded his men from the gendarmes before the war. After February he was attentive to the demands of the lower deck and later wrote to the Helsingfors E.C. that 'Three months of creating a free strong fleet with you were the best days of my life'.[6]

Maksimov's Order No. 3 required officers to use the polite form of address with their men; they themselves were to be called 'Mr Senior Lieutenant', etc., instead of some more honorific title. The same order permitted smoking in the street. In March the C.-in-C. also permitted beards and longer hair, relaxed dress regulations, and reduced inspections, as well as increasing leave and releasing men for the spring sowing. He accepted the end of the hated shoulder-straps in April, and also 'democratised' the uniforms of his officers. Two of Maksimov's reforms were more fundamental. First, he encouraged the organisation of committees. A special commission for this purpose was set up, as well as a 'Committee Section' of the Baltic Staff, and provisional regulations for committees were worked out in March. Maksimov even began the organisation of a fleet central committee in early April. And second, he accepted a resolution of the Helsingfors Soviet which ended warrant officers, sub-ensigns, and extended-enlistees. This was of particular importance. Prince Liven had written before the war that on the question of such senior ratings 'hangs not only our position in wartime, but even our existence in time of peace. Until it is satisfactorily resolved the fate of the fleet will be in the hands not of its commanders but of the haphazard mood of the sailor masses.'[7]

The Provisional Government also favoured a policy of concession. The portfolios for War and Navy were given to Aleksandr Guchkov, an Octobrist industrialist and a prominent politician who had long been interested in military affairs; his technical adviser was Rear-Admiral M . A. Kedrov. Guchkov's early Navy Department orders eliminated many of the irritating petty restrictions on the ratings. A more significant step was his order of 16 April making official unit committees and elected disciplinary courts. The committees were assigned a limited role: the supervision (*kontrol'*) of supply work (*khoziaistvennaia deiatel'nost'*), legal appeal against unfair commanders, deciding questions of the 'internal mode of life' (*byt*), and work in education and recreation; moreover the committees were to assist the officers in maintaining 'discipline and order'.[8]

At the end of April Guchkov resigned from the Government. His replacement was one of the outstanding figures of the revolution, Aleksandr Fedorovich Kerensky. If he lacked Guchkov's military expertise, the 36-year-old Trudovik made up for it by his radical reputation and genuine popularity. Admiral Maksimov received a stormy affirmation when he asked a general meeting, 'Are you able to promise the minister without epaulettes, the minister from the workers, that you will execute his orders better than you executed the orders of the ministers, the adjutant-generals, of the Tsar? '[9]

A week after his appointment Kerensky released the 'Declaration of Servicemen's Rights', which Guchkov had refused to sign. It recognised full political and civil freedom for servicemen, abolished saluting and, more important, stated that 'the right of internal self-administration, the imposing of punishments and supervision in precisely defined instances [as defined by Guchkov's 16 April decree] belongs to elected military organisations, committees, and courts'. On the other hand the officers alone could give orders regarding the 'combat activity and preparation for battle of a unit, its training, its special duties, duties in [the spheres of] inspection and supply'. And, on Kerensky's insistence, the officers were given the right to use force against enlisted men in battle and to appoint their own officer-subordinates. The declaration, which would have seemed wildly liberal three months before, or in any other armed forces, was not well received. It caused explosive scenes in Helsingfors, where the soviet finally watered down the point about the use of force and rejected the appointment of officers from above. The Kronstadt Soviet voted to 'wholly reject' the Declaration and stood firmly for the Petrograd Soviet's Order No. 1, which left the position of the officers much more vague.[10]

Kerensky's appointment also affected reforms which were specifically naval. A 'Commission for the Working Out of Regulations Concerning Naval Life (*byt*)', comparable to the army's Polivanov Commission, had been set up on 15 March, but the first working meeting was held only on 12 April, and little had been accomplished by the time the first chairman, the Kadet N. V. Savich, resigned (in sympathy with Guchkov). After further delay a new chairman began work on 16 May; this was Vladimir Ivanovich Lebedev, an old comrade of Kerensky's who stood on the extreme right of the P.S.R. A colleague summed him up as 'an émigré, a revolutionary political figure, a participant in the Japanese War, and a lieutenant in the French Army'. (One officer described him less charitably as 'a short swarthy little gentleman of about thirty, dressed in the decidedly frayed uniform of a French officer'.) Although he was later named to be Director of the Navy Ministry, Lebedev's naval experience had been confined to agitating among Russian sailors on foreign cruises.[11]

Whatever his professional shortcomings, Lebedev produced quick results. On 22 May two decrees on naval life were passed. The 'Definition of the Spheres of Influence of Commanders and Committees' divided responsibilities into three groups: (1) the officers alone were in charge of operations, training, communications, and orders 'for the performance of work necessary for the military life of the ship'; (2) the committee maintained discipline, looked after education and health, administered meals and public funds, and supervised finances, materials and supply; (3) the officers and committee together supervised general work, recommended promotions, and assigned leave. The 'Regulations for Ship Committees' formalised the structure of these organisations and stipulated that all orders of the committee – in its legitimate sphere – were legally binding; they also permitted the appeal to the next highest committee of conflicts between the officers and the committee. Another important product of the Lebedev Commission was the naval pay rise of 6 June, which was stimulated by an army pay rise and by growing pressure from the lower deck. The rise was backdated to 1 May, but it still provoked protests from a number of unsatisfied crews. It was significantly inferior to the proposals of the Helsingfors Sailors' Section; total monthly pay for a senior specialist ranged from 85r. to 45r. (compared to 75r. –60r. in the Helsingfors proposals), for a junior specialist from 69r. to 30r. (67r.50k. – 52r.50k.), and for a seamen 30r. (52r.50k.); in addition, the Sailors' Section had advocated backdating the rise to 1 March.[12]

The Lebedev Commission was not the only source of reform from above. The day after his appointment, Kerensky published an order on Provisional Naval Courts, similar to the new army regimental courts. (In fact, mixed army-navy courts were elected; the one at Helsingfors began to function late in July, the Reval court in August, and the Petrograd court at the end of September.) Officer selection and training was reformed. 'Wartime' officers were granted rights equal to those of regulars; in addition, petty officers could now become junior commissioned officers. Kerensky declared that the cadets at the Naval Academy should learn the life of the sailor by participating in manual labour. Later, the government announced that the two naval academies at Petrograd and Sevastopol were to be dissolved and replaced by the more democratic Detached Naval Cadet Classes, which would be moved to Sevastopol.[13]

Kerensky was personally dissatisfied with the central institutions of the navy (one of his decrees urged a streamlining of paper work through the omission of formal phrases like 'I have the honour . . .' and 'I humbly request . . .'). He wanted to a fight bureaucracy by bringing in fresh blood from the Active Fleet. The proposals of the minister included, ultimately, a 'Naval Council', but at the time he confined himself to appointing energetic assistants. The '1st Assistant Navy Minister' – overlord of the N.G.S., the M.N.S., and other organs – was Boris Dudorov, a 35-year-old captain who had been the head of the Aviation Division and chairman of the Reval Naval Officers Union; the '2nd Assistant Minister' – in charge of the various technical departments – was Sergei Kukel', a 32-year-old commander who had been Torpedo Officer of the Submarine Division. Two weeks later, on 13 June, Lebedev was placed between these officers and Kerensky as the acting Director (*upravliaiuschii*) of the Navy Department.[14]

A final development was the assignment of a 38-year-old Trudovik, Fedot Onipko, as Commissar-General of the Baltic Fleet. The appointment was, as Kerensky put it, 'for the establishment of direct and close links between myself and the sailor and officer staff of the Baltic Fleet, for supervision of the correct execution of my orders, and for the regularisation, on the spot, of misunderstandings which may arise'. The new Commissar-General was a veteran revolutionary, a member of the 1st Duma, who has helped to organise the 1906 Kronstadt and Sveaborg uprisings. (Onipko, as one defender said during a meeting, 'was serving the revolution when many of the comrades sitting here could not pronounce the word "revolution" '.)[15] He was also a staunch defensist and had served as a volunteer with the French Army.

By June the Russian Navy had been much reformed. But the changes had been some time in coming – by revolutionary standards, of course – and they did not go far enough. Even the main vehicle of reform, the Lebedev Commission, became unpopular. The Helsingfors Sailors' Section withdrew its representatives, 'recognising the composition of the Lebedev Commission [as] extremely unsatisfactory and all its previous work as not corresponding to the interests of the sailors'; the Baltic congress came to a similar conclusion.[16] The lower deck, it was clear, would no longer be satisfied with a modification of the traditional structure; it wanted a throughgoing democratisation which would put decisive power in its hands. As a result, the final form of the Baltic Fleet was determined not by reform from above but by revolution from below.

REVOLUTION FROM BELOW

The first sailors' organisations were the ship committees. These had an important but limited role, as they only spoke for individual ships. Next to appear were the local soviets of workers' and soldiers' deputies which, for want of any naval professional organisation, became the main institutions pressing for reform. The Helsingfors Soviet was particularly active; on 13 April, for example, it voted to allow 5 per cent leave for spring sowing and to abolish warrant officers and extended-enlistees. The Helsingfors Sailors' Section, a consituent part of the soviet, also made important decisions on its own initiative. At Kronstadt a Naval Section of the soviet was not set up until September, but the soviet felt competent to decide naval matters; it too ruled on leaves and warrant officers. At Reval the Local Naval Committee, also part of the soviet, worked out its own regulations on ship committees, and the Reval Soviet set set up a Military Committee to deal with all non-operational questions.[17]

This anarchic situation, with each base making its own decisions, soon became unacceptable, and for several reasons. Some sailors and, of course, the Staff felt that it weakened the fleet's military potential. On 4 April the crews of the battleship *Grazhdanin* and the cruiser *Admiral Makarov*, then two of the most defensist ships, declared that 'the fleet has split into several parts' and called for a general 'Soviet of Deputies of the Baltic Fleet'. In fact, Maksimov's staff had had a similar idea in March, and they had gone so far as to work out regulations for a 'Fleet Committee'. Progress was slow, however, and the initiative was taken by other sailors, who were more interested in democratisation than in military efficiency. On 14 April, at the urging of a delegate from Reval, the Helsingfors Sailors' Section set up an organising commission to work out plans for a fleet central committee. This commission consisted of 15 ratings from all the Baltic bases and was headed by P.O. 1st Cl. P. D. Chudakov.[18]

The first meeting of the new Central Committee of the Baltic Fleet

(Tsentrobalt or the C.C.B.F.) was held on 28 April aboard a small, rat-infested transport, the *Viola*, which was tied up in Helsingfors opposite the Mariia Palace. The representatives from Reval and Abo had not yet arrived, but a draft charter was approved. Although this moderated the proposal of the organising commission, it still granted the new body a considerable amount of power. As 'the supreme instance of fleet committees', Tsentrobalt's approval was needed for any order (*prikaz*) concerning 'the internal and administrative life of the fleet', and it was to carry out all pronouncements in this area which the 'All-Russian Soviet' might issue. While rejecting the prior supervision (*kontrol'*) of operations, the committee reserved the right to investigate operations *after* they had been carried out; to this end it could present questions to the fleet Staff and send commissions into the field. Other powers included that of publishing the Staff's resolutions (*postanovleniia*) and co-ordinating the resolutions of the various soviets and naval committees. The committee was to be connected to (*pri*) the Staff and was also to have links with the 'All-Russian Soviet'.[19]

The chairman of the committee from the second meeting was a Bolshevik from the transport *Shcha*, Storekeeper Pavel Efimovich Dybenko. Dybenko was to become the most prominent of the revolutionary *baltiitsy,* and within six months he would be in charge of the whole Russian Navy. Aged 27 in 1917, he was from a poor Ukrainian peasant family. He received a few years of secondary education, but worked as a docker until called up for the Baltic Fleet in 1912. Before the war Dybenko visited Britain, France, and Norway aboard the new battleship *Imp. Pavel I.* He remained aboard the *Pavel* in the first year of the war, but at the end of 1915 he was transferred first to the Naval Infantry and then to the *Shcha*. Tall, handsome, jovial, well-read, and articulate, Dybenko possessed a charismatic personality which impressed most people he met, from the White General Krasnov to the veteran S.D. Aleksandra Kollontai (45 and a Bolshevik C.C. member), with whom he had a long affair. Most Soviet sources maintain that Dybenko became a Bolshevik in 1912, but possibly he was just an informal Social Democrat. Khovrin recalled that in 1915 he was too argumentative with the officers and something of a 'putschist'; as a result the *Pavel* S.D. cell was wary of giving him too much responsibility. In any event, Dybenko was sufficiently well-known to be elected by his shipmates to the Helsingfors Soviet, and he was sufficiently experienced as a Social Democrat to be one of 13 men elected on 21 March to the Helsingfors (mixed) S.D. 'Group Committee'.[20]

To Admiral Maksimov Tsentrobalt was a double-edged sword. On the one hand, it could help him run the fleet at a difficult time. The committee's resolution of 3 May made clear its attitude to duty, even if in this case the resolution referred to the duty of the officers:

the duty of every honest citizen who sincerely loves his motherland enjoins us at the present moment, not considering our personal situation, to disregard unwarranted self-interest, to add all our strength and knowledge in whatever field for the good of the motherland.

All refusals to execute service responsibilities without justifiable cause and without the approval of the C.C.B.F. will be considered a betrayal of free Russia and the C.C.B.F. will take all steps for its suppression.

The committee also accepted the Declaration of Servicemen's Rights.[21] As a result, relations with the Staff were fairly good; the Staff had a representative (not a delegate) aboard the *Viola*, and it published the fleet committee's first 28 announcements.

The other edge of the sword was also visible. Tsentrobalt claimed a major role in the 'internal and administrative life of the fleet', which included personnel affairs, internal organisation, pay and supply. On 11 May Maksimov and Onipko visited the *Viola* to express their dissatisfaction; the Staff particularly resented the provision in the charter about the committee's right to approve all orders concerning the internal and administrative life of the fleet. Tsentrobalt did not give way, and its only concession was the creation of a 'co-ordinating commission' between the Staff and itself. Meanwhile, the committee already showed signs of preparing to go beyond even the powers given to it in the charter. It felt able, for example, to discuss the choice of base for the new 3rd Submarine Flotilla and also to request that all minesweepers be given destroyer escort.[22]

Four weeks after the founding of Tsentrobalt, the 1st Congress of the Baltic Fleet (25 May – 15 June) opened, in the Helsingfors Girls Gymnasium. It was to be an important indicator of the fleet's mood at the end of the 'honeymoon' period. The moderates were present in strength; the Reval contingent had arrived with a strong mandate: 'Full confidence to the Provisional Government and at the first order of the Navy Minister we will go forward, not being stopped by any sacrifices'. A member of this group was the congress's first chairman, Paymaster Leonid Rubanin; he was from the defensist *Admiral Makarov*. Although Rubanin lost his post due to an electoral irregularity, his replacement was another moderate, Commander Il'ia Lodyzhensky, the elected captain of the *Andrei Pervozvanny* and chairman of the 2nd Battleship Brigade committee. Fedor Raskol'nikov, who was present towards the end of the congress, observed that Lodyzhensky and Commander Lev Murav'ev (the Staff representative) generally dominated the proceedings.[23]

The definitive Tsentrobalt charter was the most important item on the agenda. Two alternative proposals were debated, one worked out by a Tsentrobalt commission and the other by Onipko and the Staff, and the commission's proposal was accepted. It went considerably beyond the draft charter of 28 April. Power in the fleet was divided between two authorities: (1) Tsentrobalt, which 'fulfils all functions of the fleet, excluding the purely operational sphere and the technical sphere related to it (*vypolniaet vse funktsii flota, iskliuchaia chisto operativnuiu i sviazannuiu s nei tekhnicheskuiu chast'*)'; and (2) the C.-in-C., who was in charge of the operational-technical sphere. Rather than just approving orders concerning 'internal and administrative life', the committee was now to approve *all* orders outside the operational-technical sphere. Furthermore Tsentrobalt could now issue its own resolutions (*postanovleniia*), which had the force of orders (*prikazy*). The charter was moderated only in that the committee now executed all orders of the 'existing central state power' rather than just those of all 'All-Russian Soviet'.[24]

The rejected proposal of Onipko and the Staff demonstrated the gulf between officially-sponsored reform and popular demands. The spirit was not popular sovereignty but the control of popular sovereignty and the smoothing of relations between officers and men. The fleet central committee was to be an intermediate body, co-ordinating the activities of lower committees and following the instructions and directives of a superior committee, the Naval Section of the Petrograd Soviet. Tsentrobalt's jurisdiction was to include 'all questions concerning the internal and political life of the fleet', but this was defined as eliminating disagreements among personnel, translating the demands of the crews into reality, supervision of unit *artely* and of supply warehouses, and supervision of the technical-maintenance sphere (*khoziaistvenno-tekhnicheskaia chast'*). The committee's resolutions were only transmitted to the fleet when approved by the C.-in-C. and in the form of his orders or circulars; if the C.-in-C. disagreed with a resolution he could appeal to the Navy Minister. By implication the C.-in-C. also shared jurisdiction over 'internal and political life', because he could issue orders in this area; these orders had to be approved by the central committee, but in the event of disagreement the Minister was to decide. Two other points were of broader political importance: first, the committee was a provisional institution pending the Constituent Assembly, and second, the committee was to fulfil pronouncements of the Provisional Government (such an obligation had not been mentioned in the Tsentrobalt proposal).[25]

The government did not like Tsentrobalt's new charter, which went considerably beyond the Declaration of Servicemen's Rights. (And the congress had actually rejected the Declaration.) It also went beyond the Lebedev Commission's 'Definition' of 22 May. Vladimir Lebedev apparently threatened the congress with dissolution should the Tsentrobalt version of the charter be approved. The charter was passed regardless, and Lebedev was removed from his honorary place on the presidium; Khovrin later claimed that it was precisely Lebedev's tactlessness which goaded the moderates into supporting the charter. The congress sent a delegation to Petrograd to get Kerensky's approval, but this was not forthcoming. It had previously been resolved that the charter would have to be approved by the 'Central State power', but on 8 June the congress voted by 103 to 60 to approve the charter pending an all-navy conference.[26]

The charter left unclear the relations between Tsentrobalt and the C.-in-C. The new Commander-in-Chief, Rear-Admiral Verderevsky, said that he could not command without a clear definition of his authorities, and there was an attempt to do this towards the end of the congress. Commander Murav'ev and Dybenko read opposing plans for 'Regulations on the Administration of the Baltic Fleet'. The Staff plan provided for contact between the sections of the Staff and the comparable commissions of Tsentrobalt (e.g. the Assignments Section and the Assignments Commission), but with the latter having only a supervisory function. This plan was defeated, but Dybenko's proposal for a 'coalition Staff' of 3 officers and 58 sailors was also rejected. This important question was left unresolved, but in practice a system similar to that proposed by the Staff was used.[27]

The troublesome question of ship committees was discussed also at the congress. Again there was a Tsentrobalt proposal and a Staff proposal, and the former was successful. There were three areas of responsibility:

1. The ship committee was 'the organ of the internal self-government of the personnel and of the administrative (*rasporiaditel'naia*) sphere, excluding the navigational [sphere] and the operational sphere and the technical sphere related ro it'. There was a detailed list of its responsibilities, including supervision of work, regulation of leave, and political education.

2. To the commanders went 'the command of [their] sphere in military, navigational, and technical aspects'. They also handled military training and signals.

3. Commanders and committee together dealt with refit work, promotion, and changes in manning.

The committee was to be made up on the basis of 9 committeemen for the first 150 in the crew and one for each additional 100; it was to be re-elected every three months.[28] The regulations were surprisingly moderate and did not significantly differ from the regulations that the Lebedev Commission had issued a week before.

One final aspect of 'revolution from below' needs to be mentioned, and that is the body that 'crowned the edifice' of naval committees, the Central Committee of the All-Russian War Fleet, or *Tsentroflot*. The Petrograd Soviet on 16 May approved the formation of a 'Naval Section', with three functions: the organisation of the navy on a democratic basis, the preservation of combat-readiness, and the co-ordination of the various fleet central committees.[29] On 1 July this body was re-named Tsentroflot. It was, during its brief existence, a relatively conservative organisation; it was far from the grass roots, close to the moderate Central Executive

Committee, and most delegates came from fleets and flotillas less radical than the Baltic Fleet.

ADMIRAL VERDEREVSKY

The characteristics of the officer corps were indelible. The sailors' magazine *Moriak* published the verdict of the 1906 *Pamiat' Azova* trial – which has resulted in 18 executions – with the following note: 'Here . . . is the composition of the "court", several of whom already, praise Allah, have been promoted to admirals and wear, of course, red bows on their chests'.[30] It was surprising, then, that nothing was said at the Baltic congress about the selection (as opposed to the duties) of officers.

At the beginning of June, however, the issue of elected commanders suddenly became a central one, and the cause was the abrupt dismissal of the 'elected' C.-in-C., Admiral Maksimov. Despite his seniority and following among the lower deck, Maksimov was unpopular with the High Command and the Baltic Staff. This was partly because of his personality which, according to Timirev, was completely unsuitable for a senior post; he was self-important, impatient, and obstinate, and his promotion in 1915 to Chief of Mine Defence had been an 'honorary retirement'. More important, his brother officers in 1917 saw him as a demagogue. Commander Cromie, the British submarine commander, mentioned Maksimov, whom he called a 'popularity Jack', in several letters: 'All the officers are furious, as yesterday the C.-in-C. ordered them to remove their shoulder straps'; 'the present C.-in-C. is getting out of his depth fast'; 'Maximoff . . . is playing to the gallery, and has been requested to resign by the officers of the Fleet, but refuses. . . .' Disquiet was felt at higher levels as well. As early as 22 March Admiral Rusin had reported to General Alekseev, the Supreme C.-in-C., that Maksimov had neither prestige among the officers nor respect from the men, and he proposed possible replacements. 'I am glad,' replied Alekseev. 'I had no faith in Admiral Maksimov and saw in his activities a surrender to the terror of the mutineers.' The government and Stavka delayed action until June, however. By then the situation in the fleet was even more worrying: Tsentrobalt had emerged, and the Kronstadt sailors caused a national scandal in mid-May (see below). There was also a 'new broom' at the Stavka; Brusilov replaced Alekseev on 22 May, and the new Supreme C.-in-C. decided that Maksimov could no longer be endured. Kerensky wired Commissar-General Onipko and asked him to offer the post of C.-in-C. to either Vice-Admiral Bakhirev (Chief of Mine Defence) or Rear-Admiral Verderevsky (Maksimov's chief of staff). Bakhirev – the senior surviving admiral – refused on the grounds that his volatile character was not suited to the new situation. Verderevsky likewise expressed reservations, but he agreed to take on the job. On 1 June Maksimov was appointed Chief of

Naval Staff at the Stavka, and the next day Verderevsky was made Baltic C.-in-C. Maksimov was in fact being 'kicked upstairs' to reduce protests from the lower deck; he was to have only a nominal role at the Stavka, and he was removed in September.[31]

Dmitry Nikolaevich Verderevsky, aged 44, was one of the most able officers in the navy. A member of the 'Essen School', he had been hand-picked by the admiral before the war for the best command in the fleet, the new destroyer *Novik*. For most of the war he was captain of the cruiser *Bogatyr'*, and at the end of 1916 he was made commander of the Submarine Division. The young rear-admiral was able to make the transition from the old regime to the new, even though the revolution went against his convictions. He had been successful in preventing trouble at Reval during the February Revolution, and his Submarine Division had begun offensive operations on 6 May. When Verderevsky was made Baltic chief of staff in late April Cromie reported, 'I should not be surprised to see him C.-in-C. soon, and I shall feel much relieved when he is'; later Cromie wrote that he regarded Verderevsky as 'our one hope of a strong man in the Staff'. He was also popular among the lower deck, particularly at Reval. The Baltic congress approved the appointment and sent Verderevsky the following resolution: 'The Congress . . . greets its new C.-in-C. and asks [you] to believe that under your leadership the fleet will fulfil its fighting duty to the beloved motherland'. And after the sudden end of Verderevsky's Baltic career even the Bolshevik *Volna* could describe him as 'a fully worthy man and even a liberally-minded citizen'.[32]

All the same, the replacement of Maksimov by Verderevsky was not universally popular at the time. Some Helsingfors sailors resented the end of 'elected' command and the arrival of an 'outsider' from Reval. On 2 June the crew of the *Petropavlovsk* hoisted Maksimov's vice-admiral's flag and sent a delegation to the *Krechet* to demand the lowering of Verderevsky's flag. Later the same day, however, a plenary meeting of the crews of five battleships and three cruisers resolved: 'Temporarily to execute the orders of Rear-Admiral Verderevsky, who occupies the post of fleet C.-in-C.' But significantly this was coupled with a protest against that clause in the 'Declaration of Servicemen's Rights' which forbade elections. The Helsingfors Soviet approved Verderevsky, but it made the important point of principle that 'unilateral assignment by the minister without the preliminary agreement of the majority of crews . . . is in future impermissible'.[33]

Almost immediately, the new C.-in-C. encountered problems. He demanded the assignment of commanders from above, while Tsentrobalt and the committees became increasingly insistent that the crews should have the right to elect commanders or at least to approve new appointments. Verderevsky refused to allow the election of Captain Sergei Zarubaev as commander of the 1st Battleship Brigade, and he threatened to resign if this officer was elected rather than appointed. A similar question arose over Verderevsky's replacement in the Submarine Division.

The C.-in-C. appealed to Tsentrobalt, which attempted to find out the opinion of the fleet. On 16 June the Helsingfors Sailors' Section, 'recognising the principle of electivity to all responsible posts as the only correct means, which alone can bring about the realisation of the idea of popular sovereignty', declared that all committees were to begin the realisation of this principle. A meeting of ship committees at Kronstadt also endorsed the principle of elective command. More surprisingly, the vote of a meeting of ship committees in Reval was also overwhelmingly in favour of electivity; 108 voted for and no one opposed though 8 abstained (there was some question about what electivity meant, however, and most ships were for the expulsion of unwanted commanders rather than for 'pure' electivity). Indeed, opposition to electivity was quite limited; only at Moon Sound and in isolated organisations such as the 3rd Submarine Flotilla and the Reval Naval Officers Union was the principle rejected. On 1 July there was a report to the fleet central committee on this subject; it was decided to refer the question to the Naval Section of the Petrograd Soviet and meanwhile – through a special commission – to vet all officer appointments.[34]

Verderevsky also had difficulties in 'his' sphere – 'operations and related technical matters'. The 2nd Cruiser Brigade refused to leave Helsingfors for the Finnish Skerries in mid-June, despite appeals by the C.-in-C. and Tsentrobalt; the crews believed that such a move would divide the revolutionary forces. The *Slava* would not go to Moon Sound, claiming that it was the turn of the *Respublika* and the *Andrei Pervozvanny*. On 23 June Tsentrobalt declared that since this was a purely operational question, the *Slava* should obey the orders of the C.-in-C.[35] The ships finally moved, but only after some delay.

This first period of democratisation showed that the government and even the naval command were prepared to make major concessions. This was partly because, as Kerensky put it, the official democratisation of the services was nothing more than the registration of the conquests of the servicemen. In addition, many officers saw committees as the only bodies capable of preventing anarchy, as a necessary evil. But there was also, especially among defensist socialists, like Kerensky and Lebedev and those further left, a principled belief that democratised armed forces would have higher morale and would be a check to any possible counter-revolution by the generals. Kerensky stated the theory of the new 'conscious' discipline in a speech to the Helsingfors E.C. on 10 May: 'I want and, as the War and Navy Minister, demand the creation in the navy of discipline . . . on the basis not of compulsion or of force but [on the basis] of mutual confidence and the agreement of each to do his duty in his place'.[36]

Could the authorities have better controlled or channelled the desire for naval democracy? The answer is probably no. Certainly the government was not served by very astute men; Zalezhsky believed that 'a series of tactless actions by Piter' alienated the basically moderate Baltic congress and the replacement of Admiral Maksimov was delayed. But there was also a fundamental inconsistency between what the authorities could concede and what the lower deck demanded. If one adds the heritage of distrust, the inherent conservatism of the officer corps, and the revolutionary confusion of that spring, then the crisis in the fleet seems well nigh inevitable. The eventual breakdown at Reval and in the Black Sea indicates that even under good conditions there was little hope for stability. Later on in the year the journal *Svobodnyi flot* offered a 75r. prize for the best answer to the question 'How is it possible to establish and strengthen mutual confidence among all ranks of the fleet?'[37] But given the situation there could be no effective answer.

How does one explain the pressure of the lower deck? On the whole it stemmed from the grievances already outlined, from the general revolutionary excitement of 1917, and from the lack of any serious distraction. The demand for committee control, better conditions, etc., cannot be blamed on exogenous factors. Émigré officers stress the disruptive effect of government and soviet legislation, but it should be clear from this and the first chapter that government reform usually came in the wake of major shifts from below, that it did not anticipate such pressure.[38]

Another outside factor might be the Bolsheviks, but their influence can be exaggerated. The word 'Bolshevik' was often simply a synonym for someone who opposed the authorities; Admiral Razvozov reported that 'there are ships, different from the others by their bad mood, which may be characterised by the current term as "Bolshevik"'[39] The 'real' Bolsheviks certainly agreed with the need to eliminate the power of the potentially counter-revolutionary officer corps; Lenin was railing against the 'Cavaignacs' and 'Bonapartes' before July or Kornilov, but Bolshevik activity only accelerated the collapse. (Where it possibly was important is that it won supporters for the Bolsheviks, but this is bringing us back to the political struggle.) Dybenko maintained in 1934 that Tsentrobalt was the creation of the local party organisation and especially of the civilians Antipov and Antonov-Ovseenko. But there is no such claim in the earlier (1923) version of his memoirs, and we know that Dybenko himself was away agitating at the South-Western Front when the Tsentrobalt organising commission was formed; moreover this commission contained only one known Bolshevik. One is inclined to take more seriously Antonov-Ovseenko's claim to the party centre that 'we control [the ship committees] with invisible influence'. But in his memoirs this author stressed the difficulties the party had in asserting its control. Indeed, by his own account Antonov-Ovseenko showed that the Bolsheviks had to restrain the most radical sailors. He maintained that their Helsingfors Committee played down the Maksimov affair as 'it was inopportune to sharpen the conflict' – presumably in light of the Kronstadt events; 'the Bolshevik faction in Tsentrobalt received orders: limit yourselves to protest and accept Verdervsky'.[40]

There were important differences between the political struggle described in Chapter 2 and the struggle for control in the navy described here. Men who accepted the need for a defensive war, or for a coalition, would still want their own professional privileges and rights increased. At the fleet congress Lodyzhensky declared that 'on a ship . . . the captain with the officer-specialists . . . are a kind of Provisional Government, and the committee is a supervisory organ like the Soviet of deputies'; Dybenko's plans, he argued, were tantamount to saying 'Down with the staff, all power to the Central Committee'.[41] The fact that Lodyzhensky should assume that the congress still opposed the idea of 'All Power to the Soviets', that he should use this kind of logic, shows the split that still existed in May and June between political and service demands. Within a short time, however, the political demands of the sailors would catch up with their service demands and become, like them, very radical.

4 The Government Challenged: May–July 1917

The united meeting . . ., considering the question of the crisis of power . . . demands immediately of the All-Russian Executive Committee of the Soviets of Workers', Soldiers' and Peasants' Deputies that it take full power in its hands.

Tsentrobalt and Ship Committees, Helsingfors, 4 July 1917

The Russian Provisional Government enjoyed general popularity only briefly. The ministers of the government formed on the morrow of the February Revolution were nearly all members of the centre parties; the sole exception was Aleksandr Kerensky. The coalition of 5 May brought in five more moderate socialists, but the balance of power still lay with the so-called 'ten minister-capitalists', whose number included the Minister-President and the Foreign Minister. The government seemed incapable of pushing the revolution forward. The war continued, and by late June Russia was more ensnared in it that ever before. The economy was in a terrible state. Little progress was being made towards land reform. The imperial family was under house arrest in the palace at Tsarskoe Selo, and retired tsarist officials were receiving state pensions.

Before May the Provisional Government could regard the Baltic Fleet as one of its more anarchic 'instruments' – one which the February Revolution had caused to malfunction in its role of defending the fatherland – but not a danger to the government itself. The events of May, June, and July made it apparent that the fleet contained deadly enemies of the government, who were capable of threatening its very existence. This chapter will show how that threat emerged.

THE KRONSTADT REPUBLIC

Despite the butchery of the February Revolution, Kronstadt at first raised no challenge to the government. The first session of the local soviet was dominated by moderate socialists; towards the end of April it approved the

Liberty [War] Loan – thus giving tacit support to the war – and at the beginning of May it rejected the idea of an all-socialist government, on the grounds that 'the removal of the progressive layers of the bourgeoisie from the Provisional Government undermines the country's ability to oppose economic and military ruin'. Miliukov's famous pro-war note to the Allies caused a scandal in Kronstadt, as elsewhere, but the final decision of the soviet was simply to follow the Petrograd Soviet; it rejected a Bolshevik proposal to support 'the revolutionary acts of the Petrograd Soviet . . . including the transfer of power to the people'.[1]

Then, on 5 May, a new session of the soviet began. Eight days later the opening shot of Kronstadt's duel with a government was fired, when the E.C. declared itself the sole power in the town and announced its intention to take the place of the government's commissar, V. N. Pepeliaev. This line was endorsed by the soviet as a whole on the 16th: 'The sole power in the town of Kronstadt is the Soviet of Workers' and Soldiers' Deputies which in all questions of state order will enter into direct relations with the Soviet of Workers' and Soldiers' Deputies of Petrograd' (the more moderate E.C. resolution had specified the Provisional Government).[2] This amounted to non-recognition of the central government. Shortly afterwards Pepeliaev resigned.

The affair had no great practical significance, but the resolution was a direct challenge to the authority of the central government; Kronstadt was so close to the capital that its 'independence' made the new government look impotent and ridiculous. The press did not help matters by printing allegations that the 'Kronstadt Republic' had seceded from Russia (one rumour had it that the reasons the Kronstadters wanted Nikolai Romanov imprisoned there was so that they could make him king of an independent Kronstadt!). The Provisional Government and the moderate soviet organisations in the capital condemned what the Petrograd Soviet called 'a defection from the revolutionary democracy'. The congress of peasants' soviets voted overwhelmingly to threaten to cut off food supplies. Delegations of pro-government socialists visited the island. In the end the affair fizzled out, with Kronstadt making contradictory resolutions but accepting the principle of a *locally-elected* civil representative (i.e. commissar) of the Provisional Government.[3]

Who was to blame for the confrontation? The Bolsheviks? It is true that Trotsky had addressed the Kronstadt Soviet on 14 May. He called for all power to the soviets and described the coalition ministry as 'the politics of lies'; more important, he approved the E.C. resolution, saying, 'What is good for you is good for any town. You are ahead and the rest have fallen behind'. But Trotsky later denied any responsibility and, in any event, he was not yet officially a Bolshevik. (And on the 27th he returned to call for compromise on the ground that the mainlanders might cut off food supplies.) Only one of the local Bolshevik leaders (M. D. Lebedev) had actively endorsed the 16 May resolution. But there is no sign that the

Kronstadt Committee tried to block it. On 18 May a member of the C.C. made a special trip to the island to summon Raskol'nikov and Roshal' to Lenin; the party leader admonished them for a breach of party discipline and issued instructions that Raskol'nikov was to call him every day. Lenin certainly felt that the resolution had been a tactical mistake, and he told the Petersburg Committee that 'the incident at Kronstadt was undoubtedly harmful for the party. That is why control is necessary'.[4]

But the sin of the local Bolsheviks was one of omission rather than commission; no one accused them of instigating the resolutions of 13 and 16 May, they simply failed to block them. It was the Kronstadt S.R.s under Seaman 1st Cl. Brushvit who put forward the 16 May resolution; the local Mensheviks, pointing out the responsibility of the S.R.s for the affair, criticised the 'primitive political thought' of the peasantry. The Bolsheviks laid the blame on the votes of the non-partisan 'swamp'. The fact is that the idea of replacing Pepeliaev was a popular one. It was regarded as the regularisation of a *de facto* situation; the soviet had declared itself the sole power in early March, and the commissar had been inactive. The Kronstadters could not see what the fuss was all about; one Kronstadt delegate said that he felt the Petrograd Soviet was making 'an elephant out of a fly'.[5]

The effect of this affair was as important as its cause. It hardened the hostility of Kronstadt to the Provisional Government, which was felt to have acted in a high-handed fashion. And Kronstadt became more conscious of its nation-wide reputation: as one decree put it, 'We Kronstadters will remain at our posts on the left flank of the great army of the Russian revolution'.[6]

Despite the set-back – indeed partly because of it – the following five weeks were a time of rising tension. On 9 June the Bolshevik leadership (the C.C., the Petersburg Committee, and the Military Organisation) called for Kronstadt to participate in a demonstration on the following day. A mass meeting was held in Anchor Square where Orlov, Flerovsky and other Bolsheviks urged the sailors to take part. Many of the sailors needed little prompting, and their slogans went beyond those approved by the Bolshevik leadership; some of them intended to use the demonstration to overthrow the government. But the congress of soviets, which had just begun, forbade the demonstration, and at the last moment the Bolshevik central leadership gave in. A new mass meeting was held on the 10th at which representatives of the various parties, including the Bolsheviks and the Anarchist-Communists, now tried to restrain the crowd. Flerovsky later recalled that it took 'inhuman strength' to hold it back; only his idea to send a delegation to Petrograd prevented a mass departure.[7]

The Bolsheviks now found themselves falling behind the most radical of the *kronshtadtsy*. On the 11th the Kronstadt Committee appealed for calm; 'Victory will only be possible,' it stated, 'when we can act in an organised manner together with the whole revolutionary democracy'. Il'in-Zhenevsky, temporarily editor of *Golos pravdy*, recalled the impatience of many sailors with the Bolshevik leadership during this period. The congress of soviets and the Petrograd Soviet arranged their own demonstration for 18 June. Despite the pro-government and defensist attitude of the organisers, a number of Kronstadt sailors took part – carrying the slogans intended for the week before; at the request of the Kronstadt Soviet they went unarmed. Some of the sailors were roughly handled by counter-demonstrators, and they vowed that *next* time they would take arms for self-defence. Another incident took place on the following day. Anarchists who had occupied the Durnovo Villa in Petrograd were forcibly ejected by government forces; one anarchist was killed and a Kronstadt sailor named Anatoly Zhelezniakov was arrested (with some justification, as he had threatened government troops with a hand grenade). The following day the Kronstadt Soviet condemned the government's action and called for the punishment of the officials responsible. Once again there was talk of sending a mass demonstration, but in the end only a small delegation went.[8]

The Kronstadters did not yet know that the government was already committed to an action which the radicals among them would find even more unacceptable. On 18 June the Russian Army began a major offensive. On the 23rd the Kronstadt Soviet passed with an overwhelming majority a resolution condemning the offensive as being inspired by Entente and Russian imperialists and a stab in the back of the German revolution. For the first time the soviet resolved in favour of the slogan 'All Power to the Soviets'. There was renewed agitation for a demonstration in Petrograd, but a tri-party delegation of Roshal', Brushvit, and the Anarchist-Communist Khaim Iarchuk was sent to the capital to clarify the situation and so restrain the masses from a foolhardy action.[9]

To some extent the government brought the danger on itself by doing practically nothing about Kronstadt during these months. Pepeliaev had reported that 'the whole mechanism of administration is destroyed'; the government, he later complained, did little to help him, and brief visits by Kerensky, Kornilov, and others had only a temporary effect. After the 'Kronstadt Republic' affair the training ships finally put to sea and a revived commission of inquiry began to investigate the cases of the imprisoned officers, but this did not amount to much. A special commission found later that naval training had proceeded slowly in the months before July – despite the steps taken in May. Even some sailors complained of the indiscipline; the 1st and 2nd Companies of the 1st Depot were accused of being full of 'drunkenness and debauchery', and in the end the Kronstadt Soviet dissolved them.[10]

Strong action *was* considered. Tereshchenko, the Foreign Minister, informed the British Ambassador at the end of May that it had been decided to seal off the island with Cossack troops until the 6,000 sailors 'who have caused all the trouble' were handed over; these defeated sailors were to be put to work on the Murmansk railway. Kerensky later testified that there had been a plan to dismantle the fortress in June or July at the latest 'for purely military and strategical reasons'. In the end, however, the only official step was an order of the Chief of Naval Staff at the Stavka (Admiral Rusin) which reorganised the Kronstadt command structure by creating a 'Chief of All Naval Forces of Kronstadt, of Training Detachments, and Schools'.[11] The order stated that the post – which in fact had existed for some time – should be held by a vice-admiral, but no such officer was appointed. The incumbent stayed on, Sr Lieutenant Lamanov, a revolutionary-minded officer whose only distinction was to have been the first Baltic commander to lose his ship in the World War.

THE JULY DAYS AND KRONSTADT

The situation in the fleet was already tense when a major political crisis erupted. On Sunday, 2 July, the Kadet ministers resigned over the question of Ukrainian autonomy. On the evening of the following day some of the more ill-disciplined troops in the capital began to riot. Among the leading spirits were the men of the 1st Machine-Gun Regiment, who did not want to be sent to the front.

The catalyst for the intervention of Kronstadt was the arrival from Petrograd on Monday afternoon of three delegates with news of an insurrection planned by the machine-gunners. The three were coolly received by the E.C., and they left to appeal directly to the masses. Within the hour a huge meeting of as many as 8,000 – 10,000 men was taking place in Anchor Square. The meeting resolved for an 'action' (*vystuplenie*), but for an action delayed until the next day. That night a second smaller meeting took place, this time involving part of the E.C. and delegates summoned from the units. This meeting, in the name of the whole E.C., unanimously called on the masses to assemble with arms at 6 a.m. and 'in strict order to set out for Petrograd where, together with the forces of the Petrograd garrison, an armed demonstration will be held under the slogan "All Power to the Soviets of Workers' and Soldiers' Deputies"'.[12]

In the end, from 5,000 to 10,000 Kronstadters set out – in a flotilla of requisitioned tugs and barges, many decked out with red flags and banners. On arrival – in the rain – the demonstrators disembarked on both sides of the Neva, below the Nikolai Bridge. They marched to the Ksheshinskaia Mansion and then across the river to the Nevsky Prospekt – *en route* to the Tauride Palace, the seat of the C.E.C. Just off the Nevsky there was some shooting, and the march became disorganised. The disorderly procession arrived at the palace at about 3 p.m., and it was in an ugly mood. Almost immediately there was an incident involving Viktor

Chernov, leader of the S.R.s and Minister of Agriculture. Part of the crowd had tried to break in to arrest the S.R. Minister of Justice, P. N. Pereverzev, who was regarded as responsible for the Durnovo Villa affair, and Chernov came out to protect his party comrade and calm what had become an angry mob. In fact, he was dragged into the crowd, and only the efforts of Trotsky obtained his release. The mood was so bad that Iarchuk remembered that he 'expected [the sailors] might destroy the whole Tauride Palace, not just arrest Chernov'.[13]

At this point, with their leaders not allowed in to address the C.E.C., the demonstrators stalled. Many returned home that Tuesday night, and others went to find a place to sleep in the Petrograd barracks. On Wednesday morning loyalist forces sacked the offices of *Pravda*, and the rebels went over to the defensive. The Bolshevik C.C. ordered the remaining Kronstadters to stay in their barracks. Raskol'nikov arrived at the Ksheshinskaia Mansion and was made 'commandant' by the M.O. His force of 500 men was the sole active force left.

The end in Petrograd came on Thursday morning. The rebels, confronted by a superior force of armoured cars, officer cadets, and loyal regiments, had withdrawn to the Peter-Paul Fortress. Il'in-Zhenevsky, Iarchuk, and a sailor then went out and, with the help of Joseph Stalin, negotiated the surrender of the remaining 300 sailors and 200 machine-gunners. General Polovtsev, the Petrograd Commandant, took the surrender himself; he recalled, 'I made a few jokes expressing my regrets for not having been able to visit Kronstadt and my delight at seeing at last the brave army of the Kronstadt Republic'.[14]

How important were the Kronstadt sailors in the July Days? The 1st Machine-Gun Regiment was the motive force on Monday, and the Tauride Palace was surrounded by a large crowd on Monday night, long before the Kronstadters appeared. Masses of workers were involved between 3 and 5 July, and the government was later to demand the disbandment of six regiments of soldiers who had particularly disgraced themselves. On the other hand the Kronstadters clearly were important. One moderate Kronstadt S.R. said in the soviet that he 'got the impression that in Petrograd we were in a small group, that we acted alone, that it was shameful that Kronstadt alone did this'. And the diarist Sukhanov, who was on the spot, went so far as to claim that the Kronstadters 'were undoubtedly the main force not only in the technical but also – one might say – in the political sense'.[15] Bearing in mind that a variety of demonstrators were involved, it would probably be true to say that the Kronstadters, especially the sailors, were the most identifiable group, that they were the spearhead of the demonstrations on the 4th, and that they were among the last to give up.

Kerensky declared on 7 July that German spies and 'instigators' had pushed Kronstadt into counter-revolutionary action. A government judicial sub-committee found eight Kronstadters (six Bolsheviks and two anarchists) responsible for building up, from March, local hostility to the Provisional Government and for trying to organise, 'with the goal of overturning the Provisional Government', an 'armed action'. Moreover in mid-July Raskol'nikov and Roshal' were accused, with others, 'of having entered . . . by a preliminary agreement between themselves and other persons, and for the purpose of aiding the enemy countries at war with Russia – with said countries into an agreement to assist in the disorganisation of the Russian army and the rear'.[16] The charge that the Kronstadters or their leaders were the conscious agents of Germany can be dismissed, like the fraudulent documents which later appeared. Likewise there is no point in denying that the Bolsheviks did everything possible to stir up opposition to the government. There remain however two questions raised by the charges which demand an answer: (1) Who was responsible for the Kronstadters moving to the capital? (2) Was this movement a planned attempt to overthrow the Provisional Government?

The central organs of the R.S.D.W.P.(b) were at best lukewarm in their support for armed action. It seems clear that neither the C.C. nor the Petersburg Committee initiated the Kronstadt demonstration. At about the time of the Anchor Square meeting on Monday L. B. Kamenev of the C.C. telephoned Raskol'nikov to inform him that the machine-gunners were acting on their own, and that Kronstadt should be held back. Later on, during the rump E.C. meeting, G. E. Zinoviev did give telephone permission for an 'action' (after talking the matter over with his comrades in the C.C.) – but so did the S.R. leaders who were consulted; all had been told that there was no alternative, that the Kronstadters would act regardless. On Monday night the Bolshevik C.C., Petersburg Committee, and other organs released a proclamation calling for 'a *peaceful* and *organised* demonstration' as a means of bringing to the attention of the C.E.C. 'the will of the revolutionary population of Petrograd' that it should take power. There is no sign that the main Bolshevik leaders were really enthusiastic about what was happening in the streets. On Tuesday, Lenin, Sverdlov, and Lunacharsky addressed the Kronstadt procession from the balcony of the Ksheshinskaia Mansion; some witnesses maintained that Lenin spoke of his pleasure that the slogan 'All Power to the Soviets' would now be realised, but Lenin himself claimed only to have expressed the pious hope that the slogan would be a success – and to have called for restraint at the present moment. A Menshevik worker told the Kronstadt Soviet that 'on a private visit to Zinoviev, Kamenev, and Trotsky [on 4 or 5 July] we found that they did not occupy the position that Kronstadt did; they urged us to follow the decree of the Soviet of Workers' and Soldiers' Deputies'. It was also these three who persuaded Raskol'nikov to surrender his men without arms.[17]

The situation as regards one major party organ is less clear. Members of the Bolshevik Military Organisation were certainly agitating for a demonstration; and one of the three delegates to Kronstadt on Monday was an M.O. member. Also, Artemy Liubovich, a Kronstadt soldier and an experienced Bolshevik, telephoned from Petrograd on Monday evening and, in the name of the M.O., requested troops or demonstrators.[18] So it appears that there was a division among the Bolsheviks in the capital and that some party organs bore part of the responsibility for the July Days.

What about the responsibility of the Kronstadt Bolsheviks? At the Anchor Square meeting on Monday afternoon Raskol'nikov and Roshal' at least called for common sense, i.e. deferring action until the next day; the Bolshevik sailor Fedor Gromov and a Bolshevik soldier, however, demanded *immediate* action. And the anarchist Iarchuk wrote in his memoirs that Roshal' was all in favour of the principle of armed uprising; the more cautious Raskol'nikov said, 'And what if the party decides not to act?'; Roshal' replied, 'That's not important, we'll force them [to act] from here'. This account is supported by that of the Bolshevik sailor Kolbin, who felt that Roshal' was actually whipping up the crowd on Monday. Raskol'nikov also sympathised with the idea of action, but he later recalled that he was held back by a sense of party discipline.[19]

The local party's role in later developments was even more conspicuous. The rump-E.C. meeting on the night of 3–4 July was chaired by the Bolshevik Bregman, and two-thirds of the organising committee it elected were Bolsheviks. (The E.C. moderates later testified that they tried to summon the whole soviet as the meeting was unrepresentative, but that those present rejected this due to lack of time.) Raskol'nikov told the meeting that Flerovsky had reported from Petrograd that the Workers' Section of Petrograd Soviet was supporting the demonstration and that his C.C. had informed him that an armed 'action' was taking place. The demonstrations themselves began with a speech by Raskol'nikov at the embarkation point. He later maintained that at this point he warned against provocation; others asserted that he advocated energetic support for the slogan 'All Power to the Soviets'.[20]

It would be difficult, however, to accuse Raskol'nikov and his comrades of leading an armed rebellion. They allowed the march to be detoured to the Ksheshinskaia Mansion, far from the citadels of the Provisional Government. Sukhanov believed that Raskol'nikov had instructions to take power in favourable circumstances, but this is belied by the young Bolshevik's inactivity at the Tauride Palace. On Wednesday Raskol'nikov did ask Kronstadt and the Naval Firing Range to send artillery and Helsingfors to send a gunboat or a destroyer, and he recalled in his memoirs that only one powerful ship would have been required to overturn the government; but the most logical need for reinforcements was not for continuing revolution but for self-defence. It should also be noted that the other Kronstadt Bolsheviks opposed sending more forces to Petrograd, until they received Raskol'nikov's note.[21]

Sukhanov described the wandering leaderless Kronstadters on the morrow of the 4th as 'the spineless, uncomprehending, blind fragments of an unsuccessful experiment, left to the mercy of fate'.[22] But the experience of the Kronstadters hardly bears out Sukhanov's general conclusion that the July Days were an abortive Bolshevik coup. The fact that no attempt was made to assault either the Provisional Government or the C.E.C. suggests strongly that the party leadership went along with the idea of an armed demonstration only because of pressure from below and that they never intended it as more than a reconnaissance in force. There is moreover no evidence that any of the Kronstadt Bolsheviks ever openly called for an armed uprising. Some were guilty of opportunism, but others were simply trying to maintain their credibility with the masses.

The Kronstadt Mensheviks did dissociate themselves from the movement, but other parties were not guiltless. The S.R.s' *Oblast'* (Regional) Committee in Petrograd approved the demonstration on Monday night, with the aim – like that of the Bolshevik C.C. – of making the movement more ordered. It is true that unlike its Bolshevik counterpart the S.R. C.C. did on Tuesday morning denounce all demonstrations, but the S.R. leaders in Kronstadt did nothing to dissociate themselves effectively from the 'action', at least until the Bolsheviks refused the remove their C.C. banner from the front of the procession. And Mariia Spiridonova, the prominent Left S.R., was involved early in the day in attempting to organise the demonstration.[23]

The anarchists bore even greater responsibility. They had increased their agitation in Kronstadt for several days prior to 3 July, and they were involved in the very opening of disturbances in Petrograd on Monday. Iarchuk was as prominent in the leadership of the Kronstadt demonstration as Raskol'nikov, and he and Iosif Gurvich (alias Venik) were among the eight Kronstadters accused by the Provisional Government. According to Iarchuk the Anarcho-Syndicalist-Communist organisation believed that an armed demonstration would turn into an uprising and bring the government down.[24]

But the real 'culprits', in my opinion, were the Kronstadt masses. Practically every source agreed that the Kronstadters did not have to be whipped up or manipulated; many of them were ready to act, 'spontaneously', on Monday afternoon. They were genuinely fed up with the 'ten minister-capitalists', their war, and their offensive. They assumed it would not take much to convince the C.E.C. to take power. And so, with or without the intervention of the parties, the move on Petrograd had wide popular support in Kronstadt; as the Left S.R. Brushvit put it, *all* were guilty.[25]

THE JULY DAYS IN THE ACTIVE FLEET

Unlike Kronstadt, the Active Fleet first became involved in Petrograd politics only during the July crisis. Helsingfors had been relatively loyal in the early months. After the March massacre the local E.C. declared, 'We all love Russia, we all have faith in the Provisional Government, and we want to carry the war to a victorious conclusion'. It approved the Petrograd Soviet's peace resolution of 14 March, with the proviso that its constituents would in the meantime fight the enemy, both internal and external. On 26 March it resolved support for the Provisional Government, as long as it acted in agreement with the Petrograd Soviet. In April the Helsingfors Soviet repeated these sentiments and also accepted the Liberty Loan.[26]

Many ratings, as may have been guessed from Chapter 2, shared this view. Probably the most well-known resolution came from the dreadnought *Sevastopol'*, on 4 May. The resolution began: 'We recognise that the way out of our situation is to continue the war. We have no right to conclude peace under present conditions'; it also called for an offensive, supported the Liberty Loan, opposed fraternisation, stressed the need for a coalition, demanded the unity of all parties, and declared that those who opposed the war and the government were enemies of the people. The *Sevastopol'* resolution was supported by a number of other ships – mostly from the forward positions. The *Andrei Pervozvanny* remarked on the need to 'destroy our strong and stubborn enemy Germany', and not only supported the Liberty Loan but also called on the workers to produce more; later the ship approved the coalition. The *Rossiia* called for an offensive and for increased discipline.[27]

A hint of the potential radicalism of Helsingfors appeared during the crisis over the Miliukov note, when the soviet unanimously passed an extraordinary resolution that 'with all of its armed strength it will support all revolutionary actions of the Petrograd Soviet . . ., being ready at the first order to overthrow the Provisional Government'. The formation of the coalition at the beginning of May, however, was enough to satisfy the Helsingfors Soviet; it now expressed confidence in the 'new Revolutionary Government' which it would support 'with all available means'.[28]

On 9 June the Bolshevik central organs telegraphed the Helsingfors Committee asking it 'without fail to send most impressive possible delegation to take part in demonstration in Petrograd on 10 June at 2 p.m. against impending counter-revolution'. This was an important precedent; for the first time the Petrograd Bolsheviks called for help from the Finnish capital. But the demonstration, as we know, was cancelled, and Antonov-Ovseenko later reproached the C.C. for not informing him until midday on the 10th. The moderate-sponsored demonstration of 18 June was accepted more warmly in Helsingfors than in Kronstadt, and the Helsingfors Committee strongly endorsed it. As many as 50,000 people took part in the march and demonstration in Senate Square. But this was no clear victory for the Bolsheviks. On the 24th the soviet approved by a vote of 217 to 64

(32 abstentions) a resolution supporting the offensive and promising aid to the front; this resolution was put forward by the S.R.s and followed a similar statement by the Petrograd Soviet.[29]

It was clear however that the offensive was not universally popular. On the 21st a meeting of 12,000 people in Senate Square 'unanimously' opposed the offensive, called for the withdrawal of the 'capitalist' ministers from the government, and urged all power to the soviets. The strongest reaction came from the fleet. The *Petropavlovsk* issued on 21 June a five-point resolution: the ten 'minister-capitalists' were to be removed, Nikolai was to be imprisoned in Kronstadt, the old governing organs, the State Council and the State Duma, were to be abolished, and the secret treaties were to be published; if these terms were not met within 24 hours the dreadnought would sail to Petrograd and bombard the town! Two days later the Helsingfors Sailors' Section approved all the points of the resolution except the final ultimatum, and went on to demand power for the soviets. The *Slava* also objected to the offensive and called on the 'congress of soviets . . . to the stop it immediately'.[30] These resolutions were the real beginning of the July Days in the fleet, for what happened two weeks later was a logical continuation.

When rioting began in Petrograd on Monday, 3 July, the Naval General Staff began sending situation reports to Admiral Verderevsky. Word reached the lower deck through informal channels; rumours had been spreading as early as Monday evening, and two sailors who arrived from the capital the following morning provided Tsentrobalt with further information. An emergency meeting of Tsentrobalt and the ship committees began aboard the *Poliarnaia zvezda*. Some ships began to take action into their own hands: at 14.35 on Tuesday the *Respublika* committee radioed the Kronstadt Soviet: 'Urgent you report on recent events. Do you need help?' A similar request for information was sent to the Petrograd Soviet by the *Petropavlovsk*.[31]

The Provisional Government and the Navy Ministry were most alarmed at the threat of revolutionary action by the sailors from Finland; it was only 13 days since the *Petropavlovsk* ultimatum. In any event, panic reigned in the capital on Tuesday. Armed 'rioters', many from Kronstadt, had surrounded the Tauride Palace. At the N.G.S. confidential papers were being burned. Two considerations, the need to get 'loyalist' reinforcements and the need to prevent intervention from Helsingfors, led Vladimir Lebedev, the Right S.R. Director of the Navy Department, to take action. From a meeting with members of the government and the C.E.C. at the headquarters of the Petrograd Military District, he telephoned Captain Boris Dudorov, the 1st Assistant Navy Minister, and asked what steps could be taken to prevent the return of the demonstrators to Kronstadt. The two men worked out an order for Verderevsky to send four 'Novik'-type destroyers to Petrograd for a *demonstratsiia* (presumably a demonstration in the military sense of a show of force) or, if need be, for 'action against the arriving Kronstadters'; this was approved by Lebedev's meeting. Dudorov had despatched the signal when the Director rang back, asking what could be done if the *Petropavlovsk* or *Respublika* should attempt to come to the aid of the demonstrators. It was agreed that submarines could be stationed off Gogland Island to prevent this; the measure was also approved by Lebedev's meeting. A second signal was sent, ordering Verderevsky to take steps that no ship should go to Kronstadt without his consent; he was not to stop 'even at sinking such a ship with a submarine' and was to send submarines to suitable positions.[32] The assumption must have been that the relatively patriotic new destroyers and submarines, manned by battle-hardened specialists, would be loyal to the Provisional Government and would obey their C.-in-C.

At Helsingfors, the revolutionary developments which had been one of the causes of Dudorov's signals led to a perversion of his intentions. The number of signals being received by the *Krechet* had attracted the attention of Tsentrobalt, and the committee decided, as an emergency measure, to assign commissars to the Hughes teletype apparatus aboard the flagship. The job was entrusted to a special 'Secret Section' of three, including the Bolshevik Khovrin. When Dudorov's signals arrived (at 19.15 and 19.30) and were decoded, Khovrin and another sailor were present. Naturally, the two signals caused consternation: here was the 1st Assistant to the Navy Minister ordering one part of the fleet to fight another part. Furthermore, the distinction between political and military orders seemed to have broken down, since the N.G.S. had sent this political message as an operational order (apparently due to a technical mistake). Moreover in the heat of the moment the first signal had been both incorrectly encoded and decoded; an introductory phrase indicating (incorrectly) that the order had the approval of the Provisional Government and the C.E.C. was omitted, and the mutilated text made it unclear what the destroyers were meant to do.[33]

Verderevsky realised the dangerous implications of the messages, and at 20.50 sent a reply to Petrograd: 'I cannot execute your order; if you insist, tell me to whom I am to hand over the fleet'. Then the C.-in-C. attempted to persuade Khovrin and his comrade to keep the two signals secret, and they consulted the fleet central committee. The 'ardent Dybenko', Khovrin recalled, insisted that the messages be read ('what curses in his vocabulary he didn't use against the Assistant Navy Minister and the Provisional Government'). So Verderevsky bravely decided to go over to the *Poliarnaia zvezda* himself. There he gave the essence of the messages in his own words and also read his reply. He urged restraint and then, attempting to prove that as an officer he was not involved in politics, left for his dacha.[34]

Opinion in Russian Helsingfors had meanwhile taken a sharp turn to the left. In addition to the *Poliarnaia zvezda* meeting of Tsentrobalt and the ship committees, the Helsingfors democratic organisations – the E.C., Tsentrobalt, the Regional Committee, and the committees of the S.R.s, Left S.R.s, Mensheviks, and Bolsheviks – had sent delegates to a meeting in the Mariia Palace. This meeting resolved that, considering the crisis in Petrograd, the transfer of power to the C.E.C. was urgent. While calling for restraint and the avoidance of 'unorganised actions', it called on the population 'to be ready to stand in support of the revolutionary democracy in its struggle for power'.[35]

A similar line was taken aboard the *Poliarnaia zvezda*:

> The united meeting of ship committees and the Central Committee of the Baltic Fleet . . ., having considered the question of the crisis of power, finds that the experience of the administration of the old coalition ministry, consisting of the revolutionary democracy and of the bourgeoisie, has clearly shown that their policies are leading towards counter-revolutionary goals and to the complete economic ruin of the country, [and] it demands that the All-Russian Executive Committee . . . immediately take full power in its hands.
>
> The united meeting . . . announces that only power emanating from the revolution will be in line with the voice of the toiling people and will be recognised by all.

The resolution concluded by stating:

> To revolutionary Petrograd in the person of the workers and soldiers who have risen (*vosstavshie*) in defence of the people's interests we express sincere comradely greetings in the people's struggle to which we, the revolutionary Baltic Fleet, will always accord active support.

As an immediate step a delegation was to be sent to the capital aboard the destroyer *Orfei*; its mission was to get exact information about the situation and to bring Dudorov back for trial 'for counter-revolutionary activities and slander'. Simultaneously, the meeting removed Commissar-General Onipko from his post on the grounds of dereliction of duty.[36]

The *Orfei* left at 3.45 on Wednesday morning with a delegation headed by Khovrin and Clerk 1st Cl. A. S. Loos. No further word was received in Helsingfors – in fact, this delegation was arrested in the capital by loyal troops. Meanwhile, on Wednesday Tsentrobalt called on the fleet not to obey Dudorov's orders, and a second sailors' meeting resolved that only orders from the soviets would be recognised; 'There can be no return to the past. We find that any delay is like death. Each minute without power is a blow to the revolution'.[37] A second delegation, including Dybenko, was sent to Petrograd with the new resolution on Wednesday night aboard the destroyer *Gromiashchy*; this second group shared the fate of the *Orfei* delegation.

On Friday, 7 July, Kerensky lashed out against the fleet for its misdeeds of the past three weeks. He declared that, at a time when the army was committed to battle with the enemy, 'Kronstadt and several ships, led by the *Respublika* and the *Petropavlovsk* stabbed their comrades in the back' by passing resolutions against the offensive, by calling for non-obedience to the Provisional Government, and by trying to put pressure on the C.E.C. When the government summoned ships 'for quick and decisive influence over the Kronstadters participating in the criminal disorders, the enemies of the people and the revolution, acting through the Central Committee of the Baltic Fleet, by means of a dishonest explanation of these measures, provoked trouble (*smuta*) among the ships' companies'; the 'traitors' provoked the dismissal of Onipko, an order for the arrest of Dudorov, and the presentation of demands to the C.E.C. 'The treasonable and criminal activities of a number of individuals' forced the government to order the immediate arrest of their leaders, including the delegation sent to Petrograd. Kerensky then went on, ordering: (1) Tsentrobalt to be dissolved; (2) the sailors 'to eject from their midst suspicious people who called for no obedience to the Provisional Government and who are agitating against the offensive'; and (3) the men of Kronstadt, and the *Petropavlovsk, Respublika,* and *Slava* ('whose names have been stained by counter-revolutionary actions and resolutions') to arrest the 'instigators', sending them to Petrograd within 24 hours; they were also to declare their subordination to the Provisional Government. Four days later, on the basis of this order, Dudorov ordered the Baltic C.-in-C. to arrest eight Bolsheviks and three S.R.s and to close four Bolshevik newspapers.[38]

On 11 July a naval investigator, Colonel Shubin, presented findings against 15 members of Tsentrobalt, including Dybenko and Khovrin. They were accused of causing the orders of the government to be disobeyed by blocking the despatch of four destroyers, of releasing in a distorted form a secret telegram, and of inciting the *Poliarnaia zvezda* meeting to order the dismissal of Onipko and the arrest of Dudorov; with these actions 'they provoked an overt uprising (*vosstanie*) against the Provisional Government among the crews of the ships at Helsingfors and perpetrated state treason, opposing the sending of armed forces at the demand of the Provisional Government and of the All-Russian Soviet . . . and they introduced disorganisation among the men of the fleet, thus weakening the strength of the Active Fleet'.[39]

Who *was* responsible for these remarkable events in Helsingfors? Turning first to the June resolutions, it seems clear that the instigators were not the Bolsheviks. Khovrin laid the blame for the *Petropavlovsk* resolution (of 21 June) on 'anarchist' agitation. The only prominent socialist involved seems to have been the Left S.R. Prosh Prosh'ian; he was later accused of having provoked the *Slava* resolution and was apparently involved in the *Petropavlovsk* affair.[40] On the other hand the resolution – less its ultimatum – was consistent with the Bolshevik line; the party, along with the Left S.R.s, could properly be accused of long-term responsibility in that they agitated against the government.

Did the Bolsheviks mastermind the resolutions and actions in Helsingfors of 4 and 5 July? Antonov-Ovseenko, who was in overall charge of the party in the Finnish capital, recalled that he had instructions from the C.C. to be cautious, and his first reaction on hearing the news from Petrograd was to state that he felt action premature. Nevertheless, Antonov-Ovseenko also maintained that even at this time – presumably late June – there existed a contingency plan to move heavy ships to Petrograd and Kronstadt, because the Bolsheviks 'recognised that an explosion was unavoidable' (he also claimed that the sailors' leaders, including Dybenko, were reluctant to act in so radical a fashion). Some junior Helsingfors Bolsheviks, like those at Kronstadt and Petrograd, did welcome action. A 21-year-old student named Boris Zhemchuzhin was the editor of *Volna*. When news of the Petrograd disturbances arrived by telephone at the offices of the newspaper he cried out in delight, 'There's an uprising in Piter! The waiting is over! Our lads are leading it . . .!'[41] This sort of reaction was probably typical of many rank-and-file party members; was this not, after all, what Bolshevism was all about?

Nevertheless, the only concrete charge that the government could make in the aftermath of the July Days was against Pavel Dybenko, and this was for misinformation rather than for direct incitement to rebellion. The Main Naval Procurator concluded that at the *Poliarnaia zvezda* meeting on Monday 'Dybenko read a telegram, ostensibly received by him, which said that all power had been transferred to the All-Russian Soviet'; moreover, he did not say that the two Dudorov telegrams had the approval of the Provisional Government and the C.E.C. (this was not his fault, as we have seen). Thus the 'meeting . . ., under the influence of alarming and unconfirmed rumours of events in Petrograd, received the first information from sources which, in the circumstances, were supposed to be reliable (Dybenko and the presence of Verderevsky)'. Fifty of the *Orfei* delegates were freed, in part because it was felt they had been misled.[42]

The real cause of the precipitate resolutions and actions of Helsingfors was the confusing situation on 3 and 4 July, following the beginning of the government crisis. It is not clear to which telegram Dybenko was referring at the meeting on Monday, but its contents might have involved the resignation of the Kadet ministers on the previous day. In any event, there was no sign that the government was still functioning, and many rumours were abroad (one rumour had it that Kerensky was dead). Antonov-Ovseenko recalled that 'they definitely began to say that the power of the provisional government had been overturned' (it is interesting to speculate whom he meant by 'they'). Khovrin stated that 'hot-heads' had claimed that a rising had begun. This misunderstanding explains the radical resolutions passed by the democratic organisations of Helsingfors; two

Reval cruisers were later to claim that their delegates had not opposed the Tsentrobalt resolutions as they had been misled by 'false information' regarding the Provisional Government';[43] the same could be said about many other delegates. The whole affair showed that the majority would still accept the cautious leadership of the C.E.C., but the passing of the resolutions, whatever the circumstances, was proof that they had little confidence in the Provisional Government.

In May, June, and July 1917 the Baltic Fleet became a major political force, and a force hostile to the Provisional Government. One reason for this was that the weakening of the local authorities in the February Revolution and the continuing process of democratisation put more and more power in the hands of the sailors and their committees. Politicisation combined with democratisation led to the 'Kronstadt Repbulic' and the July Days.

The Bolsheviks appreciated the political potential of the fleet, and they certainly played an organising role in the abortive 10 June demonstration and in the July 'action'. But Lenin's party was still in no position to use the sailors as puppets. Mass enthusiasm for radical action was such that the Bolsheviks were often following the movement rather than inspiring it. Bolshevik propaganda urged on the masses, but the main reason for popular action was the policies of the Provisional Government. The Bolsheviks encouraged hostility to the government, they did not create it.

So much for the *causes* of naval political activity; the *effects* were equally interesting. At one level the radicals had been unsuccessful. But the movement did not suffer in the long term. 'The young Kronstadt leaders did in this first action [i.e. the July Days] over-reach themselves', wrote Trotsky, 'But how can you make a revolution without the help of people who over-reach themselves?' The experience was instructive. The realisation that mass enthusiasm was not enough, that the C.E.C. was not prepared to take power, constituted what Flerovsky called a 'political lesson';[44] the same illusions would not be entertained in future.

5 Ebb and Flow: July – September 1917

And do not think that we are weak; this government is not that of Nikolai II.

V. I. Lebedev to Tsentrobalt, 27 July 1917

REACTION

The Provisional Government was sent reeling by the July Days. Prince L'vov resigned as Minister-President on 7 July and handed power to Kerensky. The new 'Government of the Salvation of the Revolution' announced its programme of 8 July, stressing an intention to work for peace, to convene the Constituent Assembly on schedule (17 September), to impose state control over the economy, and to carry out real land reform. Unfortunately, prolonged negotiations were required before the governing coalition could be reconstructed – on 24 July. This second coalition was similar in composition to the one formed on 5 May, but the forces of the right were to play a more important role, and the programme of 8 July was forgotten. Meanwhile the problems of revolutionary Russia remained unsolved, and the economic crisis worsened. In early August the Constituent Assembly, to which issues were constantly deferred, was itself put back two months – to 28 November.

All this contributed to a further decline of the government's popularity, at least after the shock of the July Days had worn off. Another negative influence were the very steps which the government took to restore its authority. Bolshevik newspapers were closed; Lenin and other leaders were forced to go into hiding; prominent Bolsheviks, including Trotsky, were imprisoned. 'Strong' measures were taken in the armed forces as well – a result not only of the Petrograd demonstrations but also of the collapse in early July of the 'Kerensky Offensive'. Units which has taken part in the 'armed rebellion' were disbanded. All leave was cancelled, meetings of front-line forces were forbidden, military censorship was increased, and the death penalty was restored. Far from consolidating the government's position, these measures were increasingly interpreted as showing its counter-revolutionary nature.

A key test for the government in this period was whether it could, as Kerensky put it, 'liquidate the Kronstadt scandal'. There *was* some initial success when a few local Bolshevik leaders were persuaded to turn themselves in and their newspaper, *Golos pravdy*, was closed, but that was the extent of the 'repression'. Captain N. D. Tyrkov, former commander of the patriotic *Admiral Makarov*, was made Commandant, and he arrived on 14 July with 'reliable' troops from the front. All he did, however, was search for Lenin aboard the training ship *Zaria svobody* and hold a mass meeting; the former was fruitless and the latter counter-productive. When Director Lebedev arrived on the 17th he agreed to remove Tyrkov, evidently because the man was too inflexible for Kronstadt. (Lebedev himself had a 'rather sour' meeting with the garrison.) Major L. K. Artamanov, who had led the detachment from the front, became the new Commandant. An S.R. named Kolosov was assigned to be military commissar, but he left after a month. Little else was achieved. The movement of surplus 6-in. guns from the forts was blocked, as was a transfer of two companies from the 1st Depot; Lebedev sadly announced that only 72 sailors out of 173 had 'stood to the defence of the motherland'.[1] The only real success was the release of the remaining officer prisoners.

Once again, proposals to deal with Kronstadt never got beyond the planning stage. Brusilov, while Supreme C.-in-C., believed that 'the most decisive measures must be taken for the liquidation of Kronstadt'. Once the struggle with Bolshevism had begun the 'nest of Bolshevism', that is, Kronstadt, had to be destroyed; the island should either submit or be shelled, and in the latter case, if the harbour was not damaged, there would be no 'unhealthy effects'. Admiral Maksimov worked out a plan for demilitarising the fortress, removing the army garrison, disbanding the 1st Depot, and transferring the naval training detachments to the forward bases; this was approved by Kerensky on 8 August and embodied in an order issued by the Stavka on the 23rd.[2] But then came General Kornilov's attempt to take power, and the whole plan was forgotten.

The political measures which the government directed against Kronstadt had little effect. The Bolshevik press was not even checked, as *Proletarskoe delo* (Proletarian Cause) appeared on the day after the closure of its predecessor; several of Lenin's post-July articles were first published in this 'new' paper. One success for the government was that it kept Raskol'nikov and Roshal' out of circulation until October, but the Bolsheviks quickly established a 'third generation' leadership on the island. The key man was Ivan Flerovsky, a 29-year-old professional revolutionary of worker origin; he was assisted by a senior comrade, Liudmila Stal', transferred from the Petersburg Committee. The Bolsheviks received a third of the vote in the Town Duma elections, coming only slightly behind the victorious S.R.s in the general returns and well ahead of them in the naval returns. The party also gained some ground in the soviet elections held on early August; the chairman of the E.C. was now the Bolshevik Lazar' Bregman, a 23-year-old military doctor.

The Kronstadt Soviet did on 28 July recognise the 'Government of Salvation' but only on condition that it kept to the 8 July programme. The unrepentant sailors met in mid-July to instruct their Tsentrobalt delegates to demand the wide democratisation of the navy and all power to the soviets – 'Russia, having overthrown tsarism *must also overthrow capitalism*'.[3]

In the period of a month and a half when the government was in a relatively strong position, it failed to settle the Kronstadt question, and the combination of threat and inactivity was the worst possible policy. In the autumn the government was left with a hostile fortress at the gates to the capital.

A second major problem was the Active Fleet. There, the central committee and several major units had directly challenged the government. Control seemed to be slipping out of the hands of the C.-in-C. Could the government and the officer corps reassert their authority?

Admiral Verderevsky was the first victim of the 'strong' measures. Not only had he disobeyed Dudorov's orders on 4 July and allowed his men to learn of them, he had gone so far as to request the dismissal of Dudorov (this was the only way to get the commissars out of the signals compartment of the *Krechet*). Verderevsky was summoned to Petrograd and arrested. When Director Lebedev hurried off on an agitational tour of the Baltic he immediately realised that cashiering Verderevsky had been folly. From Reval he despatched a signal to Kerensky proposing Verderevsky's 'rehabilitation' if it could be shown that the July episode had been based on a misunderstanding. Verderevsky, reported Lebedev, was too valuable a man to lose; 'literally everyone loves him, both officers and sailors'.[4] But it was too late.

Captain Aleksandr Vladimirovich Razvozov, the commander of the Destroyer Division, was appointed C.-in-C. on 7 July. Lebedev presented him to a mass meeting in Reval declaring, 'Captain, I order you to raise an admiral's flag'. The Director was surprised to hear a roar of applause and realised too late that what he *should* have asked Razvozov to raise was a 'Fleet C.-in-C.'s flag'. He had inadvertently committed himself to a promotion, and there followed another hurried telegram to Kerensky apologising for the mistake and requesting Razvozov's promotion to Rear-Admiral! Razvozov was only 38, and in 1916 he had been 182nd in the list of 207 captains; despite this, and despite his comic promotion, he proved to be the most durable of the revolutionary C.-in-C.s. Pilkin, commander of the 1st Cruiser Brigade, regarded him as probably the best officer in the fleet, and Commander Graf felt that 'no one could have been better suited to the role of Fleet C.-in-C. in such demanding times'. According to Captain Timirev, he was the last senior appointment satisfactory to officers and 'comrades' alike, and even Dybenko remembered him as 'one of the most talented admirals'.[5]

There remained Kerensky's ultimatum of 7 July to be fulfilled: Tsentrobalt was to be dissolved, agitators were to be expelled from the fleet, and the most revolutionary units were to declare their subordination to the government. Captain Zelenoi, Verderevsky's chief of staff, had balked at publishing the ultimatum for fear of the reaction of the lower deck. He need not have worried, because the bubble of rebellion in the Active Fleet had burst. Admiral Razvozov dissolved the second session of Tsentrobalt (elected in late June, it met only once, on 10 July). The new chairman, Lieutenant R. R. Grundman, meekly accepted the dissolution, and it was also approved by a plenary meeting of the Helsingfors Soviet with the E.C., the Regional Committee, and the army and navy unit committees.[6]

Finding the 'instigators' and ejecting 'suspicious persons' proved more difficult. Some 100 'suspicious' persons fell right into the lap of the government in the form of the delegations on the *Orfei* and the *Gromiashchy*, but it was decided that most had simply been misled. A 'hard core' of 15 were held longer, but they were treated leniently. Nikolai Khovrin was held in the Kresty prison, interrogated (by some of the same men who had questioned him in 1916), and had his trial set for May 1918; he was however let out on parole at the end of July.[7] Others were released at the same time, and after a fleet ultimatum in early August all the remaining prisoners except Dybenko were freed. And Dybenko, the head 'instigator', was released on 4 September.

Meanwhile at Helsingfors the climate of opinion had shifted abruptly, and the moderates temporarily dominated the soviet. (Or, as Antonov-Ovseenko sourly put it: 'All the counter-revolutionary reptiles crawled out of their holes'.) On 6 July the Bolsheviks withdrew their representatives from the soviet-sponsored Information Bureau, evidently because it was taking the charges against Lenin at face value. A delegation including N. D. Sokolov, N. D. Avksent'ev, and I. I. Bunakov, was sent out by the C.E.C. to win over the Finnish capital. On 9 July, the soviet, the Regional Committee, and various unit committees passed a resolution suggested by Sokolov, which recognised 'as criminal the conduct of groups and persons who acted from 3 to 5 July in the streets of Petrograd with weapons in hand, in the face of the direct prohibition of the All-Russian Congress [*sic*]'; all revolutionary forces were to rally around the soviets and the government that they supported.[8]

The C.E.C. delegation was able to extract apologies from the most revolutionary ships. The *Petropavlovsk* passed a resolution expressing confidence in the government, requesting that a commission of inquiry be set up 'to detect all those guilty of creating the shameful events of 3 and 4 July', and apologising for the June anti-offensive resolution; the *Respublika* and *Slava* joined this resolution. The sincerity of these apologies was, however, doubtful. The government set up a commission of inquiry headed by a naval judge, but the commission made little progress as neither the *Petropavlovsk* nor the *Slava* allowed it to come aboard to take testimony.[9]

Rather more short-term success was had against the political 'instigators'. At a plenary meeting on the 12th the Bolsheviks were not allowed to speak; as Antonov-Ovseenko remembered, 'our announcement was drowned by the howls and stamping boots of the soldiers'. The meeting resolved by a vote of 339 to 1 (41 abstentions) 'To accord unconditional support to the government' and to apologise to Onipko, the dismissed Commissar-General. On the 14th there was another mass meeting, this time dominated by the C.E.C. delegation; Antonov-Ovseenko and Prosh'ian were heartily jeered and could hardly be heard. The final assault on the left came on 16th July with a series of arrests, carried out with the approval of the Helsingfors moderates. Antonov-Ovseenko, Stark, and several other Bolsheviks were imprisoned, and *Volna* was closed down. The leaders of the Menshevik-Internationalists and the Left S.R.s were also arrested, and *Sotsialist-revoliutsioner* was suppressed. To bolster the government's authority further the 3rd (Ekaterinodar) Regiment of Kuban Cossacks arrived in Helsingfors in mid-July.[10]

Mixed success had been achieved in fulfilling Kerensky's ultimatum of 7 July. What were the long-term prospects for stabilising the situation in the Active Fleet? After dissolving the second session of Tsentrobalt Razvozov replaced the committee's charter with a temporary one based on the ship committee regulations which the Lebedev commission had issued on 22 May; these were less vague than the old charter, and gave more power to the officers. (On the 19th he also repealed Tsentrobalt's ship committee regulations in favour of Lebedev's.) In a speech to the new session of Tsentrobalt on 25 July Razvozov outlined what he expected: the committee was urged 'to interfere less in the political side of things, to support the central organs in Petrograd, and not to slow down their work with independent acts'. Director Lebedev visited an early meeting of the committee. 'After all, the fleet exists not for the sailors, but for the people,' he said, 'it is necessary to remember and to know just what popular sovereignty is'.[11]

The surprising thing is that the third session tamely followed Razvozov, and for a few months Tsentrobalt was – relatively speaking – quite a conservative organisation. It elected a Menshevik as its chairman, P.O. 1st Cl. Sergei Magnitsky from the cruiser *Bogatyr*'. Magnitsky's view was simple: 'The central committee is not a meeting but an institution'. Tsentrobalt, he felt, would only function properly if it confined itself to service questions; its political role should be to follow the central democratic organs and to discourage the masses from incautious acts. The third session frequently referred questions to Tsentroflot in Petrograd, and at the same time it tried to get the local committees to take responsibility for minor issues. Any initiative by the crews outside the organised committees was rigorously opposed. In early August Tsentrobalt asked 'the comrades to undertake no individual statements [*vystupleniia*] without the knowledge of the Central Committee'. Magnitsky announced that as long as he was chairman 'not one delegation will be allowed into a general meeting of the Central Committee'.[12]

Tsentrobalt not only accepted that it would not deal with political questions, it also resolved to keep to its own sphere in naval affairs. The unique responsibility of the C.-in-C. for operational questions was readily accepted. The committee refused to intervene when Razvozov disbanded the Abo (Turku) Air Station for 'mutinous' activities; 'Whether some military unit or another is needed is a question related to the operational sphere, and therefore, in accordance with its charter, Tsentrobalt will not consider it'.[13]

Why was the third session so different from the first? There was, of course, the experience of the July Days when the C.E.C. had refused to take power and the Baltic Fleet found itself isolated and condemned. The elections for the new session had taken place at a time when revolutionary fervour was at a low ebb, and the new delegates perpetuated this mood. One delegate, for example, condemned the issuing of ultimata.

> What will this lead to? To disaster, of course. The majority of the Russian democracy will at long last decide to be rid of us, as a sick member of its organism, i.e. simply, to destroy [us] in order not to contaminate the whole organism.

The government had arrested the most radical leaders of the first session, and the committee was a small organisation over which individuals – like Dybenko or Magnitsky – could have strong influence. Meanwhile Razvozov had acted to reduce the pressure that the left might put on the committee. He exiled the radical battleships to remote harbours, and he forbade civilians to board ships without special credentials.[14]

This symbiotic relationship between a compliant Tsentrobalt and the Baltic Staff was, however, doomed to failure, although it only gradually became clear that this was the case. Tsentrobalt accepted indignities like Razvozov's refusal to let it fly its own flag (two white anchors and the initials Ts.K.B.F. on a red field) and the transfer of its headquarters, the *Poliarnaia zvezda*, back to Petrograd. But resistance began to build up over the lack of a proper charter; even Magnitsky recognised this as 'an extreme necessity, like air'. A radical ginger group, led by Khovrin, complained on 18 August of the 'unproductive work of the C.C.B.F. and the decline, with each passing day, of its authority among its electors'. The cause was 'the lack of a charter and the impossibility of establishing the rights and activities of the Central Committee and of the fleet Commander-in-Chief', and the solution they demanded was either the readoption of the old charter or an immediate congress. Magnitsky however carried the day, and by a vote of 32 to 9 the demands of the Khovrin group were rejected. Later in the month Magnitsky explained his objections to a congress:

> Comrades, a congress cannot be convened right now, not because [this] would harm the technical combat-readiness of the fleet (although this is partly the case), but because [it would harm] morale. The elections and the work of the congress would, understandably, distract the attention of the comrades in the forward positions from the critical business now before us – the repelling of the external enemy.[15]

But this line was unlikely to be successful in the middle of a political revolution and at a point when the war was becoming increasingly unpopular.

Many issues caused dissatisfaction among the rank and file. Some stemmed from the government's attempts to restore order following the July Days. Tsentrobalt had been restricted, and several delegates were still in prison. The Bolshevik press was being persecuted. The death penalty was an important cause, as was the ending of leave. Razvozov's dissolution of the air station at Abo was an important local issue. In addition there were the familiar service complaints about food, wages, and shore service for the older men; the national economic crisis was making many of these more acute.

If the arguments of the radicals were still falling on deaf ears in Tsentrobalt, they had great success in another important fleet committee, the Sailors' Section of the Helsingfors Soviet. It had been untouched by the July Days, and its electors were among the most radical in the fleet. The voice of the Section was amplified because it often met together with the local ship committees; this also made it more responsive to changes in public opinion. One of its first steps, on 18 July, even before Tsentrobalt was reconvened, was to protest against changes that Razvozov had made in the medical attestation commission: 'The Navy Ministry is not entitled to reduce our rights which were won by the revolution, and therefore no orders which repeal announcements of the All-Fleet Congress of the Baltic Sea and of the Central Committee of the Baltic Fleet will be followed'. Even more important was the Section's call for the continuation of leaves, for the liberation of the remaining July prisoners, and for an end to the death penalty. On 7 August, meeting together with the ship committees, it issued an ultimatum demanding the release of the Tsentrobalt delegation, the clearing of Verderevsky, and his return to the fleet as C.-in-C.; 'We announce to all who are listening that if these demands are not met we will not recognise any orders of the present Commander-in-Chief'. Razvozov was forced to make a trip to Petrograd, where he secured the release of all the Helsingfors July prisoners except Dybenko. Tsentrobalt for its part refused by a large majority to support the ultimatum, and in response the Helsingfors Sailors' Section demanded the recall of the moderates there. Tsentroflot condemned the Section for going beyond its rightful sphere, but the Section resolved that it could consider any question it wanted. Unlike Tsentrobalt the Section was overtly political. It defended the Bolshevik newspaper *Priboi* ('the voice of revolutionary democracy') and supported Dybenko ('a worthy, honest, and steadfast freedom-fighter . . . the spokesman of the whole mass of the Baltic Fleet').[16]

Repression made little impact on the Bolsheviks' organisation in Helsingfors. The R.S.D.W.P.(b) opened a new newspaper, *Priboi* (Surf), after a pause of 12 days (although it could not be printed on the original press), and the arrested leadership was replaced. In early August the C.C. sent one of its members, Ivan Tenisovich Smilga. Smilga was only 25, but a hardened Bolshevik. His father had been killed by a tsarist punitive expedition in the Baltic provinces in 1906; Smilga himself had been a Social Democrat for ten years – five of which he had spent in administrative exile.[17] He quickly became the most important Bolshevik in Finland.

The shift in the political mood of the fleet was also apparent, despite the passivity of Tsentrobalt. Zalezhsky was able to report to the 6th Bolshevik Party Congress (26 July – 3 August) that 'the most firm part of the organisation is the sailors'. The *Gangut, Sevastopol', Andrei Pervozvanny, Riurik, Rossiia, Diana*, and *Gromoboi* were now all sympathetic to the party, while only the *Petropavlovsk* and *Respublika* had been so before the July Days. In his view the crisis had helped rather than hindered the party:

> Before the events of 3 July the sailors did not come to us very willingly, as they regarded us as opportunists, but the events of 3 – 5 July taught the sailors a great deal, it showed them that mood alone is not enough to achieve desired ends.[18]

In late July the Helsingfors Soviet voted by a large majority in favour of the C.E.C.'s call to support the Provisional Government, but public opinion was gradually moving to the left. The radical part of the population began to express itself again. On 6 August a meeting of 15,000, chaired by the anarchist sailor Eizhen Berg, passed a resolution 'unanimously': 'The country and the resolution are in the greatest danger as a result both of the complete military defeat and in view of the counter-revolutionary intrigues on the part of the bourgeoisie and on the part of the government "of the salvation of the revolution"'. The only way out was the transfer of all power to the 'democratic organs'. The Helsingfors Soviet was gradually won over to this position. On 26 August (i.e. *before* the Kornilov affair) it acknowledged the great danger from counter-revolution, the Germans, and the supply, transport, and production crises, all of which 'the sham saviours of Russia could not stop'; since 'only a Revolutionary organ is able to save the country and the revolution from destruction', the soviet demanded 'the immediate calling of the second congress of soviets'. The situation was well summarised by the local Mensheviks: after the great 'anti-Leninism' of July, 'by 15 August the political barometer again indicated Bolshevik weather'.[19]

Throughout the spring and summer of 1917 the tumult in Petrograd, Kronstadt, and Helsingfors produced only a faint echo in Reval. As one *Baian* sailor told a visiting delegation: 'No, we won't go along with Kronstadt, to the devil with them'. The Reval Soviet had been pro-government, supporting the coalition and the Liberty Loan and condemning the planned 10 June demonstration as 'a riot against the will of the majority'. When news of the July demonstrations arrived there was no movement to support them. The soviet accepted an S.R. resolution of 6 July that the C.E.C. should take power if it wanted to, but it condemned both Kadets and street demonstrators; 'the realisation by force of the slogan "All Power to the Soviets" is an encroachment on that power'. Dudorov's orders for the arrest of the Bolshevik leader Ia. Anvel't and the closure of the party's newspapers, *Kiir* and *Utro pravdy*, were carried out with the approval of the local E.C. Anvel't was released after a few days, but the new Russian-language party newspaper, *Zvezda*, appeared only after an interval of three weeks.[20]

The town of Reval was conservative, and the Reval sailors were the most conservative in the fleet; Khovrin recalled that 'the submariners and the destroyer division . . . were ardent chauvinists'. Unlike their comrades at Helsingfors and Kronstadt the *revel'tsy* had taken an oath of loyalty to the government. In late March their sailors' general meeting supported the government and in mid-May a similar meeting agreed to the idea of an offensive. Many welcomed the offensive when it came, and naval volunteers flocked to the Reval 'Battalion of Death', which left for the front on 22 June. The July Days reinforced this attitude, as was shown on 8 July by a general meeting of sailors:

The meeting condemns the irresponsible minority, which is demanding by mutiny to impose its will on the majority of the Russian democracy and [it] announces that the ships, squadrons, and shore personnel of Reval are fully at the disposal of the [Central] Executive Committees . . . and of the Provisional Government.

The *Admiral Makarov* and *Bogatyr'* branded the July events as criminal and counter-revolutionary, and the destroyer *Turkmenets Stavropol'sky* demanded the strictest investigation of the rioting sailors who, 'having very little in common with the vast majority of the Baltic Fleet, acted just as though they had received strict directions from the German staff'.[21]

Despite the patriotic sentiments of much of the garrison, the Bolshevik Party gradually gathered strength in Reval, especially among the mass of industrial workers. When elections were held for the Town Duma and the soviet in mid-August it emerged as the largest socialist faction. In July and August the Reval sailors began to follow their worker-comrades and move left. A significant meeting of ship committees took place on 25 July, when representatives of the four dreadnoughts – then exiled to the south shore – met with those of the *Riurik, Admiral Makarov, Oleg, Bogatyr'*, and 45 smaller units. The meeting condemned the disbanding of the Abo Air Station and the introduction of the death penalty, and it called for the final dissolution of the State Council and the State Duma, 'the cliques of the living dead'. Other mass meetings began to criticise the government. The forces' newspaper, *Svobodnoe slovo soldata i matrosa* (Free Word of the Soldier and Sailor), dropped its strongly anti-Bolshevik line. When the military authorities on 8 August arrested several committeemen from the 469th (Arzamas) Regiment there was a great scandal, and the crew of the *Riurik* threatened to release the prisoners themselves. The general situation in Reval led to a report at the mid-August conference of the Bolshevik North-Baltic Organisation that 'Kerensky's most recent steps have brought the fleet significantly closer to us'.[22]

KORNILOV

At the end of August there took place an event of the greatest political importance, the mutiny of General Kornilov, the Supreme C.-in-C. On 24 August Kornilov put General Krymov in command of a new 'Detached Petrograd Army' (including the Baltic Fleet, Kronstadt, and the 42nd Corps in Finland). Krymov was instructed to occupy and disarm the capital and to dissolve the Petrograd Soviet; ostensibly this was to be a response to Bolshevik demonstrations expected on 27 August, the half-anniversary of the February Revolution.[23]

The conspirators devoted considerable attention to Kronstadt. Krymov was ordered to 'detach one brigade with artillery to Oranienbaum and demand from the Kronstadt garrison the disarming of the fortress and transfer to the mainland'. He was to form field courts in the Baltic Fleet and to use part of the 1st Ussuri Cossack Division to arrest and disarm the Kronstadt sailors after they had been moved to the mainland. Another part of Kornilov's plan was the sinking of stone-laden barges in the Sea Canal to prevent any intervention by the Kronstadters.[24]

Kornilov began to move his forces on Sunday, 27 August, after an exchange of telegrams with the Minister-President. Kerensky then ordered the general's dismissal, and civil war threatened.

For once the Minister-President had the support of the soviets – and of the fleet. Kerensky was protected in the Winter Palace by a detachment from the *Avrora*; other sailors were assigned to defend the Smolny Institute, home of the Petrograd Soviet and the C.E.C. Some 600 sailors from the two Petrograd depots occupied the Astoria Hotel, where many officers were billeted.[25]

Another possible source of support against Kornilov was the 'rebel' island of Kronstadt. On Monday, 28 August, the Kronstadt Soviet imposed supervision on all communications and formed an emergency organisation, the 'Military-Technical Commission'. The next day, at the request of the C.E.C., Kronstadt sent 3,000 men to Petrograd (Boris Savinkov, appointed Governor-General of the capital, ordered the return of 2,000 of the men so that 'Petrograd did not fall into the hands of the Bolsheviks'). The training ships were summoned from Biorko Sound, and a Red Guard was created. All this bore out Trotsky's prediction of late May: 'When a counter-revolutionary general tries to throw a noose around the neck of the revolution, the Kadets will soap the rope, and the Kronstadt sailors will come to fight and die with us.' Fortunately however neither fighting nor dying was required. Kornilov's putsch broke up; his men hesitated, and the railwaymen blocked the tracks. The only sailors who came face to face with the insurgents were from the 2nd Depot; they had served alongside Kornilov's 'Savage' Division at the front and, at the suggestion of Tsentroflot, they were sent out to agitate among their old comrades.[26]

The affair had a dramatic effect in the Active Fleet as well. Surprising as it seems, Kornilov actually counted on the battle fleet to destroy Helsingfors with shellfire should there be a Finnish rising. In reality the opposite happened, and it was the local cossacks who were threatened with naval bombardment if they attempted to entrain for Petrograd.[27]

When Tsentrobalt met to discuss the crisis on Monday morning, 28 August, there was a representative from Tsentroflot present. At his suggestion the committee assigned commissars to the C.-in-C. and to the most important ships; this was a most important precedent for future naval democracy. Tsentroflot provoked another important step by requesting that four destroyers be sent to the capital to protect it against Kornilov; Tsentrobalt readily agreed. Meanwhile representatives from Tsentrobalt joined with those from other democratic organisations to form a special 'Revolutionary Committee'.[28]

The most obvious danger of this coup by army officers was that it would rekindle civil war in the fleet. Some naval officers no doubt secretly sympathised with the Supreme C.-in-C; Captain Timirev of the *Baian* described – in retrospect – Kornilov's action as the last energetic attempt on the part of reasonable 'state-minded' individuals to take power from the Bolshevism and anarchy which were leading the country to ruin. Admiral Razvozov on the other hand took a clear position by publishing Kerensky's dismissal of Kornilov. According to the diary of the staff officer Rengarten, both the C.-in-C. and his chief of staff, Cherkassky, were sincerely on Kerensky's side. Nevertheless, on the initiative of a representative from the Peasant C.E.C., Tsentrobalt asked ships' companies to make officers sign a loyalty oath. Razvozov signed the oath, and most officers followed his example. On the *Petropavlovsk* however four officers, Lieutenant Tizenko and Sub-Lieutenants Kandyb, Kondrat'ev, and Mikhailov, refused to sign. On the orders of the ship committee they were taken ashore and shot dead.[29]

Because of the threatening strategic situation the fleet flagship, with Razvozov and Onipko abroad, remained at Reval. At Tsentrobalt's request the C.-in-C. sent two Reval-based destroyers, the *Raziashchy* and *Boevoi*, to Petrograd to support the government, but he did this grudgingly (the committee had requested four ships). As elsewhere, a revolutionary executive was created, the 'United Executive Committee', including the Reval E.C., the Estonian E.C., the Local Naval Committee, and the army committees. This new organ announced that no orders were to be executed without the approval of the unit committees.[30]

The Kornilov affair upset the delicate balance in the Baltic Fleet – although things were shaky enough without Kornilov. It served as a dress rehearsal for the October Revolution. Especially important were the revolutionary executives, containing, as the anarchist Iarchuk put it, 'the most energetic people'.[31] The Kronstadt Military-Technical Commission, the Helsingfors Revolutionary Committee, and the Reval United Executive Committee were the prototypes for the organs which would seize power in October. The control of communications, the assignment of commissars, the creation of Red Guard units, and the despatching of 3,000 men from Kronstadt and two destroyers from Reval also prefigured the coming revolution.

Furthermore nothing could have been better calculated to break the last remaining bonds of trust between the officers and their men. What the Bolsheviks had been saying for so long now appeared to be true; the officers were actively on the side of the counter-revolution. The murder of the *Petropavlovsk* officers and the dismissal of others were just the most obvious signs of an important change. Timirev, captain of one of the more conservative ships, the *Baian*, recalled that the Kornilov affair marked a real turning point:

> The failure of the Kornilov action had a very serious effect on the position of the officers in general, and on the naval [officers] in particular. The crew, knowing the former popularity of Kornilov among the officers, not without foundation considered all officers to be secret sympathisers with Kornilov – 'Kornilovites' as they called them; from this began the general slandering of all officers.

The soviet authorities no longer supported the officer corps and began to issue their own orders.

> The crew soon worked out who had the real power, and they began to have confidence only in those orders which came from or had been sanctioned by the Soviet or by various Central Committees.[32]

The revealed danger from the right had deep political effect. When the Kronstadt Soviet elected four delegates to the C.E.C. on 29 August its 'Instruction', written by the Bolshevik Flerovsky, called for 'the complete liquidation of the bourgeois counter-revolution and the transfer of power in the country to the revolutionary workers, peasants, and soldiers'. The first meeting of the Revolutionary Committee in Helsingfors resolved that 'all power must be transferred to the revolutionary democracy in the person of its central organs, both in Petrograd and in the provinces'. As the local Mensheviks put it, 'When the Kornilov bomb went off, revolutionary Helsingfors rushed without hesitation right into the arms of the Bolsheviks'. In Reval the United Executive Committee passed a Bolshevik resolution which called for a new congress of soviets; the Kadets were to be expelled from the government and the old policy of 'compromise and irresponsibility' was to be abandoned.[33]

Even the ostensibly apolitical Tsentrobalt was shaken. On 28 August it plucked up sufficient courage at last to raise its own flag. And two days later it voted for a new all-Russian congress of soviets, for a socialist government, and for 'taking the most decisive steps against the traitors to the motherland and the revolution'. No less important for the fate of the fleet, it resolved at last to call all-naval and Baltic Fleet congresses.[34]

The idea of counter-revolution was now fixed in the minds of the Baltic sailors. The next time that they were told the 'enemies of the revolution' were moving, they would act on reflex.

RESURGENCE

In September the government's position deteriorated further. On 30 August Kerensky made himself Supreme C.-in-C., and two days later he became head of a five-man Directory including himself, a Menshevik, an industrialist, a general – and the recently-arrested Admiral Verderevsky as Navy Minister! On the same day Russia was declared a republic. The C.E.C. – inspired Democratic Conference, held in mid-September, offered the possibility of broadening the base of the regime, but neither the conference nor its offspring, the Council of the Republic, had any real effect on the situation. A proper cabinet was not created until 25 September; it was like the first two coalitions and promised no further advance for the revolution.

The left consolidated its hold on the fleet in September. This process was more dramatic in Finland than at Kronstadt (where the Bolsheviks had been dominant at least since the end of July). On 6 September, the committees of six battleships, six cruisers, and eight other units resolved that Kerensky's republic was not enough and that only a *democratic* republic with all its rights would suffice. The fleet, it was announced, would raise red flags on the 8th and would not lower them until a democratic republic had been declared. Even Tsentrobalt joined the resolution. After four days most ships were persuaded to lower the red flags – in honour of the Democratic Conference – but those at Gange and Lapvik did not.[35]

Tsentrobalt, shaken by the July events, now slid firmly into the camp of the left. On 6 September Magnitsky was replaced as chairman by the Bolshevik Fedor Averichkin, a sailor from the *Krechet*. When three radicals were elected to the Democratic Conference it was the turn of the moderates to protest; but now they could only summon a minority group of twenty-five. The radical demand for the recall of moderate delegates was beginning to take effect as well, and Magnitsky was among those recalled. The final sign that Tsentrobalt was back on radical form came on 19 September. On the previous day the government had dissolved Tsentroflot due to a difference of opinion; Tsentroflot backed down and the government rescinded its order, but in the meantime, a joint meeting of Tsentrobalt and the ship committees intervened. In the chair was none other than Pavel Dybenko, released from prison on 4 September on 5,000 rubles bail. The meeting, by a nearly unanimous vote, declared the dissolution illegal and impermissible. Until the order was withdrawn the fleet would refuse to obey the government's orders. The resolution was the most extreme action of Tsentrobalt since the July Days.[36] (Because the government did not persevere the resolution had no practical effect.)

Meanwhile the R.S.D.W.P.(b) was extending its control in Finland beyond Tsentrobalt. The party dominated the 3rd Finnish Regional Congress (9–12 September), and on the fourteenth Ivan Smilga was elected chairman of the new session of the Regional Committee. Six days later the committee announced that, until truly democratic power was established, strict control was needed, and henceforth its approval was required for all orders; 'power in Finland has in fact passed to the democracy', it resolved. The party completed the hat trick on the same day, when Aron Sheinman was elected chairman of the Helsingfors Soviet. As the Mensheviks put it a few days afterwards, '"Russian" Finland has lived since 20 September under a Bolshevik dictatorship'.[37] The party was now poised for decisive action.

Razvozov's diary shows that he was acutely aware of how his position was slipping:

9 September. The [red] flags . . . are all still flying. There is no authority. An illegal Reg[ional] congress (without the consent of the commanders). . . . They demand the return of Koval'sky, Chief of the Southern Region Signals Service. All this, together with information about the personal danger to many members of the Staff, makes the continuation of [my] command completely impossible. I think that the prestige of command demands the replacement of me.and the chief of staff [Prince Cherkassky] with other people. I suggest that [Rear-Admiral V. K.] Pilkin could unite the fleet better than I. They have written a report on the state of the fleet, and today I think I will go to Petrograd to make a personal report to Verderevsky. Will ask him to relieve me from duty. Feel that I'm exhausted and can do nothing more.

10 Sept[ember]. Petrograd. Arrived in Petrograd by train. Drove directly to Verderevsky with Rengarten, Demchinsky, and A. P. Zelenoi [three officers from the Staff]. Told him everything about the situation in the fleet. Said that the C.C.B.F has already lost its footing and that a congress is necessary. The congress will definitely be Bolshevik. The crews are already demanding the right of supervision over the operational sphere. There is a complete lack of confidence in everything. . . .

The Baltic Staff had felt that Verderevsky's appointment as minister and the Democratic Conference created the possibility for change, and they suggested a new command team, possibly Pilkin and Lodyzhensky. Razvozov did agree to resign, but within hours he learned that the German fleet was at sea and decided that he had to stay on; he was to leave only in early December. In any event things had already progressed too far for a mere change of commanders to have much effect. The Staff no longer felt that anything could be done with the existing fleet. Rengarten, Chief of the Operations Section, worked out a project to man a reduced fleet with volunteers.[38] But this was in the future. For the present the officers could only hope to carry out a holding action until winter, the Constituent Assembly, or something else improved the situation. The initiative lay with the crews.

One clear sign that the fleet had become radical again was Tsentrobalt's decision on 16 September to hold a fleet congress at the end of the month. (The committee had on 30 August agreed in principle to a new congress, but nothing happened until Kronstadt and the Helsingfors Sailors' Section threatened to call their own congress.) This 2nd Congress of Representatives of the Baltic Fleet, held in the Mariia Palace in Helsingfors from 25 September to 5 October, was an event of great importance. In the discussion of both political and service issues the views of the left were dominant – as Razvozov had predicted. The first congress

(25 May – 15 June) had been influenced by popular officers like Lodyzhensky, and among the 232 delegates there had been only 23 Bolsheviks and 21 sympathisers. At the second congress Dybenko was chairman, the anarchist Zhelezniakov was secretary, and among the 120 delegates, as Antonov-Ovseenko told the party C.C., there was 'no sniff of the defensists'. Much of the preparatory work had been done by the radicals; Dybenko worked out the new charter, the Left S.R. Blokhin was in charge of policy on the supervision of commanders and communications, and the Left S.R. Izmailov compiled the new ship committee rules.[39]

From the first the congress took an interest in political questions. It appealed to the forces to support its demands for an end to the coalition, a democratic peace, land to the land committees, and workers' supervision of industrial production. In another statement the congress declared that the Council of the Republic was designed for collaboration with the bourgeoisie and could not deal with the threat of a new Kornilov; the soviets were the only viable governing body. While appealing to the C.E.C. to call a new congress of soviets, the fleet congress threatened to ask the Petrograd Soviet to do so on its own initiative.[40]

The congress approved a new charter, which was generally an elaboration of the old one. The C.-in-C. was once again given responsibility for operations. Tsentrobalt's orders however no longer had to agree with the orders of 'the existing state power'. The C.-in-C. was to be left in charge of the general training programme, but Tsentrobalt looked after 'the training of sincerely revolutionary, technically-trained sailors for command staff [duties]'. The charter was innovative in that it created machinery for co-operation between the Staff and Tsentrobalt in five areas: assignments and promotions; supply (*intendantskaia sfera*); judicial affairs; refitting work; and medicine. There would be seven Tsentrobalt Sections (*sektsii*), each of which was to co-operate with the corresponding Section (*otdelenie*) of the fleet Staff. Both the chairman of the Tsentrobalt Section and the officers of the Staff Section were to report to the chief of staff or to the C.-in-C.; in the event of disagreement, a question was referred first to the C.-in-C. – or chief of staff – and to a plenum of Tsentrobalt; finally, the disagreement could be appealed to Tsentroflot and the Navy Minister. It was significant that this time the congress did not bother to send the charter anywhere for confirmation.[41]

The decisive changes in the delicate relationship between Staff and Tsentrobalt came *after* the passing of the charter. The congress accepted Blokhin's proposals on commissars. These contradicted the idea – contained in the charter – that operational orders were the sole domain of the officers. Under Blokhin's scheme, ship commissars were to decode, along with the duty officers, *all* incoming messages, and they were to consider, with the commanders, *all* secret messages. Political orders were to be referred to Tsentrobalt or, in an emergency, to the unit committee. In addition, Tsentrobalt was to elect one commissar to supervise the fleet Staff. Not only would he sign all outgoing orders, he would also be present at 'strategic meetings'. Verderevsky wired Razvozov that he objected: 'The congress had no right to make such an announcement, and I categorically demand its withdrawal.' Another innovation not mentioned in the charter was a Military Section (*Voennyi otdel*); in December this organ was to assume the powers of the C.-in-C. Finally, the congress approved Khovrin's proposals on elective command; 'From now on,' it resolved, 'in the Baltic Fleet [the right of] the election of commanders belongs to the crews'.[42] These three proposals – the commissars, the Military Section, and elective command – were not put into effect right away, but they amounted potentially to a naval revolution.

The fleet congress marks a convenient transition point. At the beginning of October the first preparations began, both in Petrograd and in the Baltic Fleet, for an armed uprising.

The preceding three months had seen the resurgence of radicalism. The government's counter-attack had failed. In the long run the efforts of the 'hard men' around Kerensky had allowed the radicals to pose as martyrs to the counter-revolution. The fact that the measures taken were so half-hearted meant that the Left got the best of both worlds. The Kornilov affair was the next important step; it finished off the reputation of the government and the officer corps. Antonov-Ovseenko was arrested at the beginning of this period and returned to Helsingfors towards the end of it. On 6 September he sent the party C.C. his impressions:

Another indication of the great change is that the most reactionary-minded ships are inviting me to lecture. I gave one (for two hours) to 4,000 sailors from the ships *Oleg, Bogatyr', Admiral Makarov, Riurik*, etc. (of these the first 3 would not long ago have been ready to tear a Bolshevik to pieces and now they listen almost reverently); on the *Poltava* (a dreadnought), where they haven't allowed any Bolshevik lecturers aboard during the revolution, I also gave a lecture and [the crew listened] with great and favourable attention.[43]

6 Naval Operations

Comrades, we tell the world that the revolutionary Baltic Fleet, defending Free Russia, will perish but will never retreat before the fleet of the German emperor.

Tsentrobalt, August 1917

It is now necessary to make a sharp turn, from the Mariia Palace and Anchor Square to the open grey Baltic. Like its political potential, the military effectiveness of the Baltic Fleet was very important. General Alekseev made the following report in March:

The Petrograd direction was considered completely secure, even if we should have to retreat somewhat is some sector, since, being masters of the Baltic Sea, we were not afraid of the loss of some space on land.

Events of recent days have sharply changed the picture and the strategic situation. The Baltic Fleet is not, at the present moment, battle-ready and it is difficult to say whether its full battle-readiness will be restored by the beginning of navigation in the Baltic Sea.

The danger was that,

Operating on land and acting simultaneously on the Baltic Sea, carrying out landings in Finland and on the south coast of the Gulf of Finland, the Teutons will be able to force us to abandon the approaches to Petrograd and in June could, with luck, take the capital.[1]

The Baltic Fleet was a vital part of the Russian defences. How well did it perform in 1917, and what underlay success or failure?

PREPARATIONS

What was the value of the Baltic Fleet as a combat force before the February Revolution?

Nearly the whole fleet was lost in the war with Japan, and Russia was slow to make this up and slow to copy the new types of ship appearing in the West. Germany's new dreadnought battleships and battle cruisers, her new light cruisers and destroyers, were all faster and better armed than the surviving Russian ships, which could now neither fight nor run away. It was not until June 1909 that the first four Russian *drednouty* (the 'Sevastopol's') were laid down as part of the 'Small Programme'. Then nothing happened until June 1912, seven years after Tsu-shima, when the 'Enlarged Shipbuilding Programme' of 4 battle cruisers, 4 light cruisers, 36 large destroyers, and 12 submarines was approved.

Naval construction, when resumed, was ill-conceived. The N.G.S. favoured a traditional battleship (*lineinyi*) fleet, but the big ships laid down were unsuited for use in the shallow Baltic near the bases of the enemy's light forces. During the war, those battleships which had been completed had to be kept in port for their own protection. The army had suggested the quick construction of a defensive fleet of destroyers and submarines (*minnyi flot*), but this did not suit the autocracy's great-power pretensions.[2] With the benefit of hindsight it can be said that the army was right; strong destroyer and submarine forces would have made the German offensive operations of 1915, 1917, and 1918 much more difficult.

The backward Russian shipbuilding industry could not complete the belated pre-war programmes. Some orders were placed with shipyards which did not yet exist, and other yards had to be evacuated during the war. It proved impossible to complete the battle cruisers or the light cruisers. Just 15 of 36 'Noviks' were commissioned before October 1917, and only 11 of 18 projected 'Bars' class submarines. German superiority increased with each passing year. At the outbreak of war Germany had 19 modern capital ships and the Russians none; by 1917 the balance was 24 to 4. Similar disparities existed for all types of vessels.[3]

Inferior *matériel*, combined with caution at the Stavka, led to a defensive strategy. The battle fleet was to be committeed only if the enemy attacked the Forward and Central Mine-Artillery Positions in the Gulf of Finland. Despite this, the fleet performed creditably in the first 32 months of the war: the Germans lost more ships, and their naval operations did not capture any Russian territory.[4] The main reason for this was that the German 'Baltic Force' consisted of half a dozen cruisers under the command of the Kaiser's brother; only on a few occasions were heavy ships from the High Seas Fleet sent east. The Germans regarded the Baltic as a theatre of secondary importance and were not prepared to commit precious troops to a major landing there. They feared losses due to mines, Russian light forces, and British submarines. There was also the attitude of neutral Sweden to consider. Another reason for the success of the Russians, however, was the quality of their navy. Minelaying raids, initiated in 1914 by Admiral fon-Essen and executed by the best cruisers and destroyers, carried the war to the enemy's coasts and inflicted serious losses. British and Russian submarines later contributed to German attrition. It is true that after 1915 the Russians had less success (as a result of the loss of Kurliand, increasing German counter-measures, and the replacement of fon-Essen by the lacklustre Kanin), but the balance of losses and the early success of offensive operations testified to a high level of competence, at least in some ships.

REVOLUTIONARIES AT WAR

The Stavka's directive of 30 March 1917 assigned to Admiral Maksimov a limited task: 'the quickest possible restoration of the battle-readiness of the fleet'.[5] How 'battle-ready' was the Baltic Fleet in the first six months of the revolution?

Economic disruption affected *matériel*. In April many shipbuilding contracts were cancelled for lack of funds, and the work which continued was delayed by shortages, labour unrest, and the evacuation of the Reval shipyards. Only a small proportion of the 4 light cruisers, 15 'Noviks', 6 'Bars' class submarines, 65 minesweepers, and 93 motor launches scheduled for completion in 1917 were actually finished. And by September coal stocks were only half what they had been the previous year (consumption however was also down). Sufficient fuel oil, mines, torpedoes, and shells were available, but the provisions situation was becoming very difficult.[6]

'Battle-readiness' was also a question of leadership, and the naval high command was badly shaken by the revolution. Only late in the year did an authoritative professional – Verderevsky – head the Navy Ministry. The Naval General Staff lacked authority (ironically, it regained it after October). There was a vacuum at the Stavka, with the general instability there and especially after the resignations of Admirals Rusin and Maksimov, the heads of the Naval Staff; Maksimov's successor was a relatively junior officer. But this situation was mitigated by the fact that few decisions needed to be made at this level; the only sensible policy, given the situation, was one of passive defence. In the Baltic the C.-in-C. and his Staff were less experienced than their predecessors, but they were not unqualified. Their orders were sometimes disobeyed, but Tsentrobalt did not contest their control over operations. The C.-in-C. and Tsentrobalt both wanted naval 'defence of the motherland', and neither called for an offensive strategy.

The leadership problems at unit level were summed up by a Commander Kallistov at the Moscow State Conference. He reported three major 'illnesses' of the navy: 'the humiliating rightless position of the officers, who feel themselves to be the last people in the state'; low productivity among some officers, sailors, and dockyard workers; and the loss of the warrant officers and extended-enlistees, who had handled the most complex machinery. It was also true that retirements, dismissals, elections – and murders – had led to a shortage of officers. The Baltic Fleet had been nearly 600 officers short at the beginning of the year, 200 more were lost due to the February Revolution, and a further 100 had left by 1 August. The losses were partly made up, but only by new and very junior officers; the unbalanced total was only about 90 per cent of the establishment of 4,900.[7]

The crews, through their committees and through more informal means, now had a great deal of control over their own activities. As early as 8 March the men of the 6th Destroyer Flotilla were refusing to fit vital A.A. guns to their ships. Cromie reported from Reval in April that 'only one or two [Russian] crews do any sort of drills these days, they prefer unlimited leave and the pictures'; in October he wrote that Razvozov 'can't make these swine work, and their officers are not much help'. An observer sympathetic to the revolution, the American journalist Albert Rhys Williams, reported that now 'the polishing of sailors' wits upon democracy and internationalism had higher rating than polishing the brass and mahogany'[8] But Williams was thinking more of the age of sail, and in a modern ship or shore installation complicated armament and propulsion equipment demanded a high level of maintenance. In battle and active operations teamwork and skill were important in maintaining accurate navigation in difficult conditions, the highest possible speed, rapid accurate gunnery, and efficient damage control; this teamwork and skill could only be developed by practice and drill.

After the October Revolution Admiral Bakhirev wrote, 'From the technical point of view . . . the whole Russian fleet in 1917 was in a significantly worse state than in previous years, thanks to the poorly completed refits and the near absence of constant correct supervision of equipment by the command staff'. It would seem however that the battle-readiness of certain types of unit was more affected than that of others. The preparedness of isolated shore units suffered particularly. The men here lived through enervating periods of inactivity, and there was no central source of discipline. When Lebedev visited one battery in the Aland Islands he found no sentries on duty and part of the garrison asleep.[9]

Equally serious was the situation in the submarines, which required high levels of maintenance and operating skill; here a minor slip could lead to disaster. Four boats were lost in 1917 before the October Revolution, and others were paid off for technical reasons; in addition to eight British boats only eleven 'Bars' class were operational. At the end of October the acting head of the Submarine Division showed Cromie 'an official letter where he acknowledged that the Russian submarines were in such a state that the C.O.s' one idea when going to sea was to get safely back with the unpractised and undisciplined crews'. At first, the fighting spirit of the division had been sustained, and the 1st Flotilla actually petitioned Maksimov for orders to begin offensive patrols. Four boats sortied on 6 May, but these and later patrols were mostly unsuccessful. German shipping was well convoyed, and it kept behind defensive minefields or inside neutral waters. Moreover a proportion of the few available boats was held back to defend the Forward Position. So the only success of the Baltic Fleet's offensive operations was the sinking of a small merchantman – inside Swedish territorial waters.[10]

The Minesweeper Division, popularly known as the 'Suicides Club', was short of minesweepers, and many of the existing ships were so old that they constantly broke down; during 1917 on average only a third of the destroyer-minesweepers and half the other minesweepers were serviceable. On the eve of the Battle of Moon Sound only one of thirteen minesweepers there was operational. Other units demanding skilled maintenance – like the Aviation Division – or utilising old equipment – like the Patrol Boat Division – were similarly affected.[11]

An exaggerated fear of U-boats and a defensive strategy kept the battleships and some cruisers in port, except for one or two gunnery exercises. The crews of these big ships were especially affected by the revolution. The *Slava* delayed going to Moon Sound, and it took some convincing to get the 2nd Cruiser Brigade to move from Helsingfors to Abo. Nevertheless, despite the fears of the officers, the technical efficiency of the big ships was relatively little affected.[12] During the Moon Sound battle the *Slava* and the *Grazhdanin* fought quite well, the *Andrei* and *Respublika* were at readiness at Lapvik, and the four dreadnoughts were ready near Helsingfors. In general, the battleship men might have checked any operational orders with Tsentrobalt, their gunnery and damage control might have proved – when put to the test – to be of low standard, but the battleship brigades were operational. That they did not see action was more the product of the strategic situation than the revolution.

The 1st Cruiser Brigade and the Destroyer Division were both operational and active, and it is generally accepted that they were less affected by revolutionary disruption. Captain Ruzhek's Minelayer Detachment effectively completed the passive defences. More mines (13,418) were laid than in any previous year.[13]

Doubts about the fleet's battle-readiness seem to have been felt at two different times. In March there was a simple reaction to mutiny, as expressed in Nepenin's signal that the 'Baltic Fleet does not now exist as a fighting force'. It soon became clear however, as routine naval activity resumed, that the fleet was still operational. General Klembovsky's tour of inspection in April was encouraging, and Kedrov, the Assistant Navy Minister, reported at about the same time that 'in general the defence of the Baltic Sea this year . . . is stronger than before and it cannot be described as unreliable'. Cherkassky, the Baltic chief of staff, testified as late as the end of July that the fleet was ready to complete both offensive and defensive tasks; some training had actually been better than in 1916. A second stage came after the political crises of July and August. The fleet, having survived the February Revolution, seemed to be getting out of control. Kerensky announced that the fleet should now 'prove that it is worthy' of the revolution – 'one must stop playing, wittingly or unwittingly, into the hands of the enemy'. Cherkassky, relatively confident in July, told Rengarten in early September that the fleet no longer existed.[14]

Tsentrobalt on the other hand boasted even after the fall of Riga on 21 August that the sailors would never retreat. The fleet, it declared, 'has always executed and will always execute the military orders of the command staff'.[15]

The Germans were slow to show whose assessment was correct. At first they suspended offensive naval activity as part of a campaign to coax Russia to the peace table. Operations, even when resumed, were confined to U-boat minelaying in the Gulf of Bothnia and around the entrance to the Gulf of Finland. Up to the end of September Russian losses (excluding submarines) were no worse than in previous years: 3 destroyers, 2 mine vessels, and 4 auxiliaries, mostly sunk by mines or air bombing.[16] The final test was to be the Battle of Moon Sound.

THE BATTLE OF MOON SOUND

During the First World War the islands of Ezel', Moon, and Dago occupied an important strategic position. At the southern tip of the archipelago, at Tserel' on the Svorbe peninsula, heavy batteries commanded the Irben Strait – the main entry into the Gulf of Riga. The battery at Cape Takhona, the northern extremity of Dago, was one anchor of the Forward Position. Moon Sound, between the islands and the mainland, provided a safe channel between the Gulf of Riga and the Gulf of Finland. Enemy control of the archipelago would turn the Russian Army's right flank and provide a base for enemy naval operations in the Gulf of Finland.

On 5 September 1917 (o.s.) the German High Command approved an attack on Ezel' and Moon. The planned operation had limited goals; Dago was initially not an objective (only by taking Dago could the Forward Position be outflanked), and there was no plan for trapping the Russian fleet in Moon Sound. After some delay due to the weather the operation, codenamed 'Albion', began. In the fog and drizzle of Friday morning, 29 September, the German armada arrived off Ezel'. The German commander was Vice-Admiral Schmidt; his Task Force included a battle cruiser and 10 dreadnoughts. German troops were landed at Taggalakht Bay on the north-west coast; by Saturday evening the Svorbe Peninsula had been cut off, and Arensburg (the main town) and the approches to the Ezel' – Moon causeway had been captured. On Monday the Germans captured most of the Ezel' garrison, overran the Tserel' batteries, and landed on Moon and Dago; by Thursday they had control of Moon and by Saturday, the 7th, of Dago. Throughout this 'battle', Russian land forces offered only weak, uncoordinated, and half-hearted opposition. (Among the few reliable units were the naval volunteers; the Ezel'-Moon causeway was stubbornly held by a landing party from the *Slava, Grazhdanin, Baian,* and *Admiral Makarov* and then by the 600 sailors of the Reval Battalion of Death.) The commander of the army garrison and the navy coastal batteries, Rear-Admiral D. A. Sveshnikov, was a military incompetent who seriously dislocated the defence.[17]

The officer entrusted with the naval defence of the islands was Vice-Admiral Mikhail Koronatovich Bakhirev, who had been appointed the 'C.-in-C., Gulf of Riga Naval Forces' on 20 July. 'Koronat' Bakhirev was of Don Cossack descent, his slit eyes and high cheekbones showed his Tatar ancestry. It was said that imperial disapproval of his drinking and association with ladies *de petite vertu* had blocked Bakhirev's promotion to high command; he sometimes shocked revolutionary puritanism as well by arriving drunk aboard his flagship. He was an uncompromising monarchist who on 2 March had been the only one of Nepenin's subordinates to reject the Provisional Commitee. (He was to be shot by the *Cheka* during the Civil War for plotting against Soviet power.) For all his 'faults' Bakhirev was a first-class naval commander, an officer described by Graf as 'a seaman to the core'. He had received flag rank for a cruiser action in December 1914 and subsequently commanded the 1st Cruiser Brigade, the 1st Battleship Brigade, and the Baltic Sea Mine Defence. By mid-summer 1917 he was, at 49, the most senior officer in the Active Fleet. Admiral Bakhirev was greatly respected by officers and men alike.[18]

But even the authority of a Bakhirev was limited, for in Moon Sound, as elsewhere, discipline was slipping. A week before 'Albion' the 'Novik' *Pobeditel'* raced past the Destroyer Division flagship, rocking it in its wake. When reprimanded, the *Pobeditel'* signalled: 'The Fleet is informed that the commander of the Destroyer Division is seasick.' Infuriated, Bakhirev and Rear-Admiral Stark, the division commander, submitted their resignations to Razvozov.

> Despite my strong nerves [, explained Bakhirev,] the constant friction and the futile effort to maintain order hinder my devoting all my abilities to the defence of the gulf, they force me to waste my strength, and I am beginning to lose hope of success.

He suggested the appointment of a more popular commander, but the question had not been resolved when the Germans landed.[19]

Whatever other difficulties Bakhirev and Razvozov were labouring under, they were *not* surprised by 'Albion'; indeed, it was the knowledge of an imminent German operation that kept Razvozov from resigning in early September. The source of this information was British W/T intelligence, and on about 11 September the Baltic Staff learned definitely that the German IIIrd and IVth Battle Squadrons were coming east. More detailed information arrived in the following weeks; the precise time and location of the German landing were known on the 28th, and the German course was actually plotted in advance by the N.G.S.[20]

Bakhirev's ships fought in two areas, Kassarsky Bay and Moon Sound. Kassarsky Bay, between Dago and Ezel', connected Moon Sound with the Baltic. The Russians had made the inexcusable mistake of not blocking the western entrance, Soelo Sound (the channel was actually *deepened* in the spring; the only reason for leaving the sound open was to permit Russian destroyer attacks out into the Baltic, but these were never seriously considered). On the night of 30 September – 1 October the Russians lost their last chance when a blockship ran aground prematurely and – in the battle's worst insubordination – the crew of the minelayer *Pripiat'* refused to lay mines.[21] The German flotillas could still enter the bay, reinforce their troops, and force Bakhirev to commit his destroyers; had the sound been blocked, the Russians could have landed behind German lines, and all their destroyers could have been used in the south.

Thirteen German destroyers steamed through Soelo Sound at midday on Sunday, 1 October. A dreadnought and a cruiser provided artillery support from the open sea. Bakhirev sent in the gunboat *Khrabry* and the same 'reliable' 'Noviks' which Dudorov had summoned in the July Days, the 11th Flotilla. The 'Novik' *Grom* was disabled by a battleship shell and pummelled by the German destroyers. Two courageous attempts by the *Khrabry* to tow her to safety failed, and during the second attempt the 'Novik's' crew abandoned ship in panic. The *Grom* finally sank, but only after the Germans had boarded her and captured secret charts. Razvozov had ordered Rear-Admiral Stark to hold the bay at all cost, but the 11th Flotilla had to give way in the face of superior numbers. A council of war was held (including Razvozov, who had hurried to the scene in a destroyer). Stark rejected the idea of a general counter-attack with the available destroyers, on the grounds that he did not have enough ships and that he could not rely on his raw crews. The enemy was left in control of Kassarsky Bay. On Tuesday night there was some consideration of a Russian destroyer attack against a possible landing on Moon, but this came to nothing when the destroyer commanders refused to take part.[22]

Even more dramatic were events in the south. The anchor of the whole position was naval battery No. 43 at Tserel', four 12-inch guns which controlled the Irben Strait. According to Razvozov's orders the battery was to hold out even if all the rest of Ezel' were lost (a council of flag-officers decided to hold Tserel' and certain other key positions in the archipelago 'even if everything around them falls, they will be little Port Arthurs'). In late August the Tserel' sailors sent a resolution to Kerensky recognising their 'responsibility before the motherland' vowing 'to hold out until the

last shell', and requesting seven month's provisions – presumably to last
through a winter siege. Unfortunately their morale was badly shaken in
mid-September when a German bomber blew up a magazine; 74 men
were killed outright, and 47 were injured. In addition the battery had a
limited field of fire (frequently restricted by poor visibility) and – as the
explosion made appallingly clear – the guns and magazines were poorly
protected.[23]

German troops had sealed off the neck of the Svorbe peninsula by
Saturday evening, 29 September. German dreadnoughts had been
bombarding the batteries since Friday, their 12-inch shells sending columns
of smoke 175 feet into the air. The Russian batteries replied when they
could, but their shooting was inaccurate; the rangefinders were out of order
and the gunlayers rattled. Bakhirev steamed over from Moon Sound in the
Baian on Sunday afternoon but left again almost immediately (because of
the Kassarsky Bay action). This made the gunners feel deserted, so the
moral effect of the admiral's visit was negative. That night complete panic
spread, and the guns were abandoned. When the *Grazhdanin* arrived on
Monday the sea was full of boatloads of men fleeing from Tserel'. The old
battleship could do nothing except shell the batteries in the hope of
destroying them. Many survivors were picked up; the crew refused to talk
to such cowards. The Germans captured 120 officers, 4,000 men, and 49
guns. Battery No. 43 had not even been destroyed.[24]

The Irben Strait lay open. On Tuesday Vice-Admiral Behncke broke
through with the dreadnoughts *König* and *Kronprinz*; the following
morning he arrived off Moon Sound. Bakhirev for his part was determined
to fight, if only to sustain the morale of the army, and he steamed south to
meet the enemy. It was a very unequal action, since two new German
dreadnoughts with twenty 12-inch guns were engaged with two 12-inch
guns in the *Slava* (one of the *Slava*'s turrets had broken down, and both the
Grazhdanin and the *Baian* lacked sufficiently long-range guns). In the 27-
minute artillery 'duel' Behncke's ships were not hit at all; all three Russian
ships were damaged. The *Grazhdanin* was only slightly damaged, but the
Slava, which had been hit by seven shells, was burning, listing, and down
by the bows. She set off up the sound. With his remaining battleship
surrounded by shell splashes and, according to Timirev, 'considering the
absurdity of the idea of continuing the battle in the existing conditions',
Bakhirev ordered a withdrawal up Moon Sound. The *Baian* bravely
covered this, taking a 12-inch shell hit forward. The *Grazhdanin* and the
Baian made it through the dredged channel, but the shattered *Slava* had
taken in too much water. Her crew, who had performed well throughout
the engagement, now panicked and left the stricken ship. Russian
destroyers fired six torpedoes (only one of which went off) and the *Slava*
sank in shallow water.[25]

Bakhirev's main task now was to extricate his ships. On the evening after
the battleship action Admiral Schmidt had been so encouraged by the

rapid Russian naval withdrawal that he proposed a 'Northern Operation' in which four battleships would block the Russian retreat into the Gulf of Finland. For the first time, however, fate smiled on the Russians, and enemy minesweepers trying to clear a channel through the Forward Position were held up by bad weather. On Friday evening the operation was cancelled. Bakhirev had quickly learned of the German plan. With considerable *sang-froid* he decided that the Germans could not mount their operation quickly enough, and he put off evacuation from Thursday to Friday evening. Tension aboard the Russian ships must have been very great, as on Friday afternoon the C.-in-C. signalled: 'Today I expect breakthrough of the Forward Position to cut you off'. At sunset however the Russian fleet safely withdrew.[26] The battle of Moon Sound was over.

The Soviet historian A. S. Pukhov maintained that the battle was 'the first victory of the revolutionary Baltic Fleet'; much closer to the mark was the verdict of another Soviet authority, B. B. Zherve (commander of the Reval coastal batteries in 1917), that it was 'the only combined operation of the World War which was accompanied by such complete success for the attacking side'. The Soviet argument that the battle was at least partly a Russian success rests on the claim that it discouraged a further attack on Petrograd, but the opposite is true, since the Germans only extended their operation to Dago and the Forward Position when they saw the weakness of Russian resistance. The German army lost 54 men killed, the navy 156. The Germans captured 20,130 prisoners and 141 guns. German naval losses were a destroyer (mined), two old torpedo boats (one wrecked, one destroyed by a German mine), and two patrol boats (mined). Two dreadnoughts, two large destroyers, a transport, and a depot ship were damaged by mines. (Pukhov claimed that 15 German destroyers were sunk and 14 damaged, and he dismissed the German account as 'fairy-tales'!) Russian naval losses were the *Slava*, the *Grom*, and a patrol boat.[27]

The Russian position in the Baltic had been irreparably damaged. German troops on Dago were now only 80 miles from Reval, 115 miles from Helsingfors, and 300 miles from Petrograd. The German navy held new forward bases at Kuivast' and Arensburg. The coastal flank of the Russian 12th Army was exposed, the Forward Position had been outflanked, and the entrance to the Gulf of Finland lay open.

In making conclusions three questions need to be answered. What was the effect of naval operations on democratisation and politicisation? How 'battle-ready' was the Baltic Fleet? Why was the fleet finally defeated?

The first question can be dealt with briefly. The fleet lay in port for the first seven months of the revolution. Active operations might have improved morale, raised the authority of the officers, and made the defensist policy of the government more acceptable. Cromie hoped for 'a couple of air raids' on Reval to 'shake things into order', and some destroyer captains actually requested that their ships be moved into the air-bombing zone.[28] Nevertheless, if the experience of the more active Black Sea Fleet is anything to go by, the effect of greater activity would have been limited. An additional point about naval operations is that the Moon Sound defeat must have further lowered the prestige of the Kerensky government in the eyes of the Baltic ratings, and it contributed to their willingness to help overthrow that government three weeks later.

The question of the fleet's military effectiveness is a difficult one. The argument of some Soviet historians that it was a fully effective force (led by the committees) is not acceptable. It would be equally wrong to go to the other extreme and argue that the fleet was a military nonentity whose morale had collapsed. In contrast to the army, the Baltic Fleet held together remarkably well. Seven months after the Helsingfors and Kronstadt massacres, and only three weeks before the October Revolution, part of it fought against high odds in Kassarsky Bay and Moon Sound. One explanation for the fleet's resilience lies in the nature of naval service. It is true that a ship requires a higher level of technical skill than an infantry regiment, and thus the 'battle-readiness' of soldiers might be expected to be less affected by revolution. But other factors must be considered. An infantry regiment could have its morale cracked by long stretches in the trenches under artillery fire; it could often be living in primitive front-line conditions and poorly supplied. A colonel might find it hard to get his men out of the trenches to attack, he might have trouble persuading them to move from rest areas back 'into the line', and, most important, he might be unable to keep them from breaking and running under attack. The Baltic Fleet was different. Baltic seamen (submariners excluded) were not in the front line, since even the Moon Sound ships suffered only from ineffective air attacks before 29 September. The will of individuals was irrelevant, because a warship carried all its crew together into battle. Half a regiment could decide not to leave the trenches or to flee; the whole ship's crew moved where the men on the bridge decided to take it. Discipline broke down only *in extremis*. A meeting of admirals in October concluded that 'the experience of the Moon Sound operation indicates that the improvement of the morale of the crews is actually sufficient to go out and do battle'.[29]

What, then, led to defeat at Moon Sound? Graf blamed it on the decline of *matériel* and morale brought on by the 'February plotters'. The old fleet could have held out; 'Only the onset of disintegration brought the defences of the gulf [of Riga] to such a sorry state that the enemy needed neither intelligence nor special heroism to take it'.[30] I would agree that 'disintegration' *was* a factor, but it was not everything.

Razvozov had to fight the enemy with limited forces because he accepted the spirit of the campaign directive that the main task of the fleet was to prevent the enemy from breaking through the Central Position, between Reval and Helsingfors. Although practically the entire Destroyer

Division was committed to Moon Sound, the best heavy ships were kept in reserve for the great battle of the positions. As one Soviet commentator, Petrov, noted, at no point was there any thought of a surface attack against the invasion fleet, even 'at the most decisive moments of the operation, during the landing'. Even the half-dozen destroyer flotillas in the battle zone were not used effectively. And so 'lack of help by the fleet' was cited by the senior local army commander late on 29 September as one of the reasons explaining the initial withdrawals. This restraint seems to have been entirely the decision of the Baltic Staff, for General Cheremisov, the Main C.-in-C., Northern Front, favoured an active policy. On the 29th he called for 'the most decisive action at sea against the enemy warships and transports', and he repeated this the next day. A week later, on 6 October, when Razvozov was contemplating an all-out defence of the Forward Position to save Bakhirev, Cheremisov fully approved this 'bold decision'. Razvozov's change of heart stemmed from a fear that the German 'Northern Operation' might cut off the Moon Sound forces, and on 5 October he had signalled Bakhirev, 'If necessary will support with all forces, 1st Battleship Brigade inclusive.' But this meant, as a Soviet critic later pointed out, that the C.-in-c. did not consider using the core of the fleet on the 29th – when he should have – but only later, to save the old ships of Bakhirev's force and *after* it was clear that the battle had been lost.[31]

The Baltic Staff showed serious faults in its direction of the battle. Razvozov made no systematic plans for a defence of the Moon Sound area. Bakhirev lacked a proper staff of his own. The result, as one Soviet historian put it, was that 'all action was taken convulsively, under the enemy's blows'. 'The present Staff,' reported Cromie, 'seem unable to appreciate or anticipate the situation and are always just too late.'[32]

The British submarines did make two unsuccessful attacks in the Gulf of Riga, but their Russian counterparts played no active part. There seem to have been three main reasons for this: the technical collapse of the Submarine Division (already discussed), the inadequacy of its commander, and poor staff work. The division commander, Rear-Admiral Vladislavlev, had previously been a battleship captain and had no experience with submarines. What was worse, he mysteriously disappeared during the battle. Razvozov, meanwhile, not only kept a number of boats back for a defence of the positions, but also failed to work out a plan for the effective use of those available, evidently because he was thinking only in terms of a battle for the positions. Commander Cromie, in charge of the British submarines, regarded this as 'folly'. During the battle Cromie was given no information and had to base his operations on what he could glean from local newspapers! Bakhirev had no idea of the position of the Russian submarines, and so bad was co-ordination that Bakhirev's ships nearly attacked a Russian submarine during the evacuation.[33]

However, neither the revolution nor faulty strategy were ultimately responsible. The basic cause was outlined in the first section of this chapter: the tsarist naval programme had been inadequate and unbalanced. 'If the fleet has been successful up to now,' Maksimov had reported in March, 'it is only because the Germans have sent weak forces against it.' Captain N. Klado, the best-known naval publicist, wrote shortly after the battle that 'no matter how steady the Ezel' garrison could have been and what miracles of foresight and courage our fleet could have shown, the fate of Moon Sound was decided just as soon as the Germans seriously decided to conquer it'.[34]

The naval situation was now hopeless. On 18 October a meeting of admirals concluded that 'the fate of Finland and the approaches to the capital depend primarily on the will of the enemy'.[35]

1 One of the few existing photographs of the Baltic Fleet as it appeared at the time of the March 1917 mutiny. The four dreadnoughts frozen into the North Harbour at Helsingfors. (Courtesy of the Finnish National Museum)

2 An extremely rare photograph of a meeting on the ice of Helsingfors Harbour on 4 March 1917, the day after the great mutiny. Note the St Andrew's naval flags. In the background is the battleship *Slava*

3 Kadet F. I. Rodichev speaks to Helsingfors sailors in March 1917. On his left is Vice-Admiral A. S. Maksimov (with beard). (Courtesy of the Finnish National Museum)

4 Executive Committee of Helsingfors Soviet, spring 1917. (Courtesy of the Finnish National Museum)

5 S. G. Roshal', a student and one of the Bolsheviks' leading agitators at Kronstadt

6 P. E. Dybenko, first chairman of Tsentrobalt. Picture taken in 1916

7 Anarchist sailor A. G. Zhelezniakov, who closed the Constituent Assembly

8 Rear-Admiral A. V. Razvozov, C.-in-C. of the Baltic Fleet, July–December 1917 and March 1918

9 Demonstration in Railway Station Square, Helsingfors, 18 June 1917. Banner in foreground reads 'All Power to the Soviets'; flag in the background reads 'Death ...' ('... to the Bourgeoisie'?). (Courtesy of the Finnish National Museum)

10 Crew of Kronstadt training ship *Okean* before setting out for July demonstration. Note S. R. slogan, 'Land and Liberty'

11 The dreadnought *Sevastopol'* at Reval early in the war. (Courtesy of the Finnish National Museum)

12 The battleship *Slava* after Moon Sound battle. (Courtesy of the Finnish National Museum)

13 *Pobeditel,* a typical 'Novik' type destroyer

14 The minelayer *Amur,* the revolutionary HQ in October. In the background Nikolai Bridge and St Isaac's Cathedral

15 Revolutionary sailors at Gatchina

16 The HQ ships in Helsingfors South Harbour, winter 1917-1918: centre, *Krechet,* right, *Poliarnaia Zvezda* and *Shtandart.* (Courtesy of the Finnish National Museum)

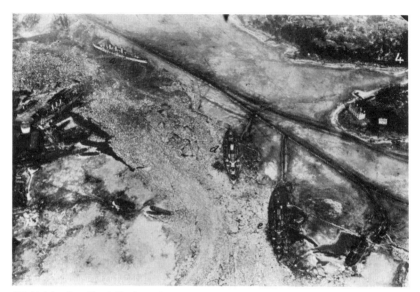

17 Helsingfors North Harbour from a German reconnaissance plane, 31 March 1918.
(a) *Oleg;* (d and e) *Respublika* and *Andrei Pervozvanny;* (k) *Pamiat'Azova* and
submarines

18 A ship of the 5th Destroyer Flotilla leaving Helsingfors during 'Ice Crossing',
10 April 1918. (Courtesy of the Finnish National Museum)

7 The October Revolution

> We inform the Exec. Comm. and the Military-Tech. commission that the landing has been carried out and firm contact with the Petrograd units has been established. We await a further offensive. We are now beginning a final operation in connection with the Winter Palace and the Staff.
>
> A delegation is presenting an ultimatum. If it is refused we will open fire.
>
> *P. I. Smirnov to the Kronstadt E.C., 6 p.m., 25 October 1917*

By October, political life in Russia was fast approaching a crisis. Tensions built up over eight months were about to be resolved. On 23 September the C.E.C. made 20 October the date for a new all-Russian congress of soviets (on 18 October the meeting was postponed until the 25th). All eyes were on the congress, which was bound to alter fundamentally the balance of power. What actually happened was even more dramatic, the 'Great October Socialist Revolution'.

What the sailors did during the Petrograd rising will be briefly summarised in the first section of this chapter. After that, I will look at three questions which seem to me to be of particular interest: Why did the sailors take part in the Bolshevik uprising? How well organised was their participation? And how much impact did they have on the successful outcome?

ATTACK

The Bolsheviks overthrew the Provisional Government on 25 October 1917. The first movement came over the week-end of 21–22 October when the Military-Revolutionary Committee of the Petrograd Soviet demanded control over the military units in the capital. Kerensky countered on Monday morning by calling loyal troops from the suburbs, ordering the removal of the M.R.C.'s commissars, and closing two Bolshevik newspapers. This in turn led the M.R.C. to announce on the following morning that the counter-revolution was about to strike.

Open revolt began during Tuesday night when rebel forces seized strategic points in the capital. Sailors from the 2nd and Guards Depots took part alongside soldiers and Red Guards. At 3 a.m. on Wednesday the cruiser *Avrora* anchored just downstream from the Nikolai Bridge; her crew supported men from the 2nd Depot who drove pro-government *junkers* (military cadets) from the bridge. It was news of the cruiser's arrival that first made Kerensky aware of imminent danger.[1]

Later that morning, at 10 o'clock, the M.R.C. declared the Provisional Government overthrown. Kerensky left for the front to get reinforcements. Rebel detachments secured most of the town. At midday sailors from the Guards Depot helped to take the Mariia Palace, where the Council of the Republic was meeting. Petrograd sailors also captured the Main Admiralty and the Post Office.[2] In the afternoon the M.R.C. decided to occupy the last strongholds of the government, in the area of the Winter Palace.

Early on Wednesday the Kronstadt E.C. had ordered detachments to Petrograd. The factory whistles blew at 5 a.m., and a large crowd began to gather in Anchor Square. The *Zaria svobody*, nicknamed 'the flat-iron of the Baltic Fleet', was towed out to cover the vital rail junction through which *junkers* from Oranienbaum and Petergof would have to pass if they went to Petrograd. To deal with these same *junkers* a detachment of 700 was landed at Oranienbaum. The main Kronstadt force, the 'Combined Detachment' left at midday for the centre of Petrograd. Its arrival was recorded by a naval cadet named Usarov, who was watching from the Naval Academy, near the Nikolai Bridge:

> At 1.13 p.m. the minelayer *Amur* arrived. Her deck and all her superstructure are strewn with sailors.
>
> At 1.27 p.m. a minesweeper [probably the *No. 14*] arrived, packed with soldiers. The steamers *Utro* and *Kotlin* arrived from Kronstadt overflowing with soldiers and sailors and deposited them on the pier.

Several other small ships arrived a little later, with more men. Some of the new arrivals were dispersed around the city on patrol; others were concentrated for the attack on the last redoubts of the government.[3]

During the afternoon the insurgents ordered the *Avrora* to prepare for action. The cruiser was not very effective, in the purely military sense, because the only shells on hand were blanks and because the gunsights had not yet been fitted. Despite this, at 6.50 p.m. the M.R.C. presented to the government the following ultimatum:

> The Winter Palace is surrounded by revolutionary forces. The guns of the Peter-Paul Fortress and of the *Avrora, Amur,* and other ships are aimed at the Winter Palace and the building of the Main Staff. In the name of the Military-Revolutionary Committee we order the members of the Provisional Government and forces loyal to it to capitulate.
>
> You are given 20 minutes to reply. Give the answer to our messenger. This ultimatum expires at 7.10 p.m., after which we will immediately open fire.

The ministers did not reply – and the ships did not open fire. Two hours of confrontation passed. Then, after 9 p.m., the *Avrora* fired a blank shell from her forward 6-inch gun. This served as a signal for a general fusillade. The besiegers, who by now included a large number of sailors, began to filter into the palace. At midnight an entrance on the south side was rushed, and about 2 a.m. Antonov-Ovseenko arrested the Provisional Government.[4] The Winter Palace had been taken. An hour later the 2nd Congress of Soviets resolved to take power into its own hands.

The appeals for help which the M.R.C. had made on the morning of the 24th were received in Helsingfors. A large meeting of all democratic organisations was held in the Mariia Palace that evening, and it resolved to support soviet power. 'After the close of the meeting,' noted the minutes, 'the walls of the former Throne Room shook with the mighty sound of the "Marseillaise"'. The Marseillaise was heard again as marching bands led detachments of sailors to the railway station. The first train left for Petrograd at 3 o'clock on Wednesday morning, and two others followed shortly afterwards. Other sailors boarded the destroyers *Samson*, *Zabiiaka*, *Metky*, and *Deiatel'ny*, which steamed out of the harbour at short intervals after 9 a.m.[5]

Although the men from Helsingfors arrived only after the Winter Palace had been taken, their presence was welcome. The success of the rising was not yet assured. In Petrograd a 'Committee for the Salvation of the Motherland and the Revolution' was formed by opponents of the new regime, and outside the city Kerensky was trying to rally forces loyal to the Provisional Government. Early on the 29th, 'Bloody Sunday', *junkers* acting in the name of the Committee of Salvation seized the telephone exchange and other important buildings. After considerable bloodshed the telephone exchange was recaptured by sailors on Sunday evening, while other ratings helped attack the *junker* schools.[6]

Meanwhile, danger threatened from the south. On Friday the 27th several hundred cossacks from General Krasnov's 3rd Cavalry Corps had ridden into Gatchina, 28 miles from Petrograd. The M.R.C. ordered sailors to Krasnoe Selo to block the way, but to no avail. On Saturday the cossacks advanced to Krasnoe, then took Tsarskoe Selo as well. Lenin personally got in touch with Tsentrobalt by teletype to demand ships and men, and he also sent Raskol'nikov to Kronstadt for reinforcements. The cruiser *Oleg* and the destroyer *Pobeditel'* arrived, in response to Lenin's teletype conversation, on Sunday afternoon. Early on Tuesday four destroyers began to move up the Neva to be ready to shell the Moscow-Petrograd railway. Naval heavy artillery proved unnecessary, but the sailors showed their value as revolutionary foot-soldiers. On 'Bloody Sunday' Krasnov's cossacks had remained inactive, in a huge sea of 'neutral' troops. During the week-end Dybenko and Antonov-Ovseenko arrived on the scene and rallied the rebel detachments. When the final attack of the cossacks came, on Monday, it was halted at the Pulkovo Heights. Then, as General Krasnov recalled, 'The sailors . . . went over to the offensive. With great skill they began to mass on both flanks; . . . . I ordered a withdrawal'.[7]

The rank-and-file cossacks decided to sue for peace, and the first counter-revolution collapsed. Here is how Krasnov described events:

On the morning of [Wednesday] 1 November the negotiators returned and with them came a crowd of sailors. Our cease-fire was accepted and signed by the sailors' representative, Dybenko, who visited us himself. This large handsome man . . . in a few minutes charmed not only the cossacks but even many officers.

Dybenko's sailors nearly captured Kerensky, but the former Minister-President fled, disguised – of all things – as a sailor. Finally, on the 3rd, Dybenko won over the last loyalist troops to arrive on the scene.[8]

MOTIVATION

Why did the sailors take part? One answer would be that they had two types of motive, 'defensive' and 'offensive'. The defensive motives came from the experience of the post-July reaction, from the Kornilov Mutiny, from a general distrust of Kerensky's Provisional Government. On 16 September the Helsingfors Soviet protested against the continued presence of counter-revolutionaries at the Stavka. Ten days later the Kronstadt Soviet declared the new coalition a 'union of obvious Kornilovites and "leaders of the democracy"' which had an 'irresponsible and criminal policy in relation to the Russian revolution' and was an 'undoubted organ of the bourgeois counter-revolution'. The second fleet congress made its view quite clear, by sending 'curses' to the 'traitor to the revolution, Bonaparte-Kerensky'. Tsentrobalt, in 'Instructions' of 19 October to its congress of soviets delegates, referred to the government as that 'of the criminal and bloodthirsty predator of the revolution Kerensky'; the 'Instructions' implied that the government planned to surrender Petrograd to the Germans in the hope of 'selling out the Baltic ships and with this liquidating the revolution'.[9]

On the eve of the congress of soviets these fears of counter-revolution assumed more substance. The Bolshevik-dominated M.R.C. carefully exploited Kerensky's steps of the 23rd. 'The enemies of the people went over to the offensive during the night,' it announced on the 24th; 'The Kornilovites at the Staff are trying to summon *junkers* and shock battalions from the outskirts.' 'They intend a treacherous blow against the Petrograd Soviet.' Trotsky, then Bolshevik chairman of the Petrograd Soviet, noted cynically the value of appearing to be on the defensive; Kerensky's 'pin-pricks' were just sufficient to convict the government of preparing a counter-revolutionary *coup d'état*.[10]

It was in response to the M.R.C. appeals for defensive help that the bases began to mobilise themselves. At Kronstadt the E.C. and a 'Military-Technical Commission' appointed commissars and took stock of available forces 'in case of action in defence of the revolution'. During the night the E.C. ordered the garrison to Petrograd 'for defence of the revolution and in support of the [Military-] Revolutionary committee'. The defensive aspect was also stressed by the Bolshevik leaders in Helsingfors. 'The plan of counter-revolution is finally being carried out,' reported Sheinman to the meeting of local democratic organisations on the evening of the 24th. Smilga reported that 'action by the Kornilovites must be expected at this very moment, before the opening of the IInd All-Russian Congress of Soviets, since this congress would be a strong, authoritative and – most important – leftist democratic organ against which the counter-revolutionaries would not be strong enough to fight'. The meeting was convinced. It resolved 'that the counter-revolution is taking the offensive on the eve of the All-Russian Congress of Soviets'.[11]

Once the congress had seized power on the 25th and until the threat from the south was liquidated on 1 November, the theme of defence was even more prominent – and also corresponded more to reality. Tsentrobalt put it in very dramatic terms: 'The sun of truth and of the people's triumph began to shine brightly when power went to the people. But dark clouds hang overhead, and they want to block the horizon of the great happiness – of fraternal love.' The Naval Revolutionary Committee, formed from sailor-delegates to the Soviet congress, declared on the 27th that 'Dark forces of reaction and counter-revolution, seeing that they have reached the last days of their rule, are gathering their criminal forces to smother the revolution and to restore slavery and the rule of the police'.[12]

In addition to their desire to defend the revolution against its enemies, real or imagined, the sailors were also motivated by the 'offensive' goal of establishing Soviet power through the congress of soviets – and destroying the hated Provisional Government. The government seemed incapable of satisfying popular aspirations, and there was also a sense of impending national disaster. By the end of August, for example, Russian non-combatants in Finland were refused rations and urged to leave; the first trainload of refugees left Helsingfors for Iaroslavl' on 12 October. Tsentrobalt's 'Instructions' stressed that Kerensky was 'leading the country to disaster'. One Helsingfors battleship put the message to Kerensky in the clearest terms: 'Get out, criminal, or we'll kill you'. (This provoked cheers in the Kronstadt Soviet.)[13]

Radical delegations were elected to the congress of soviets. The Kronstadt Soviet chose an S.R.-Maximalist, a Bolshevik, and an

Anarchist-Syndicalist (Rivkin, Flerovsky, and Iarchuk); the Helsingfors Soviet, two Left S.R.s and two Bolsheviks (Prosh'ian, Emel'ianov, Sheinman, and Pogodin); and the Reval Soviet, two Bolsheviks, an 'Internationalist', and two S.R.s (Anvel't, Smirnov, Pechnikov, Avsaragov, and Stepanov). Of the seventeen delegates elected by the Baltic Fleet there were twelve Bolsheviks, three Left S.R.s, one Anarchist-Communist, and one Right S.R.[14] The orientation of the fleet delegates was made clear by their 'Instructions':

> We order you, representatives of the Baltic, together with the representatives of the Black Sea and with the representatives of the toiling proletariat, which is expressing itself at the present congress, to take power in your hands, in the hands of the Soviets of workers', soldiers' and peasants' deputies.[15]

An important question was whether 'offensive' action should include the seizure of power *before* the congress of soviets. Rumours of impending Bolshevik action had been rife in the press since the second week of October. The Baltic S.R.s, at least, explicitly opposed such action. 'The temptation is very great, as it should be for every sincere revolutionary,' Prosh'ian told the Regional Committee on the 17th, '[But] We see nothing but destruction in unorganised action.' Although both the Helsingfors and Reval S.R. organisations said that they would support all decisions of the congress, both opposed separate action.[16]

The attitude of men who were not Bolsheviks was very important, considering that only in the Regional Committee and possibly in Tsentrobalt did the R.S.D.W.P.(b.) have an absolute majority; in the critically important Kronstadt Soviet they held only a third of the seats, and their position was similar in the other base soviets. Fortunately for the Bolsheviks, many S.R.s, Maximalists, Anarchists, and non-partisans were prepared to act with them, especially if such action could be seen as the defence or consolidation of Soviet power. The Kronstadt M.T.C., probably the most important organising body in the early stages of the uprising, included only seven Bolsheviks out of twenty-one members; there were also four each of the Anarchists, Left S.R.s, and S.R.-Maximalists, and even one Menshevik (and one unknown). The man whom the Kronstadt E.C. on 25 October chose to head the Combined Detachment was a Menshevik, the chief of militia, and one of his two lieutenants was a Left S.R.; only three of the eight detachment commissars (i.e. commanders) were Bolsheviks.[17] Among the handful of leaders on the *Amur*, the Anarchist Iarchuk and the Left S.R. Karl Kallis were very important.

The attitudes of the sailors were somewhat mixed in the early stages of the rising. Some units were still politically inert. Furthermore, the battle of Moon Sound, only three weeks before, had shown the seriousness of the

German naval threat. This, evidently, was the reason the Bolshevik planners could not count on massive support from the fleet. 'Even in Tsentrobalt,' recalled Antonov-Ovseenko, 'the most decisive of the Bolsheviks were forced to reckon with the 'revolutionary defensism'' of the masses and, in the name of preserving the battle-readiness of the fleet, they [the masses] agreed [only] reluctantly to send significant forces to help the rising in Piter.' The legendary *Avrora* took some time to convince. The ship's captain reported that the chairman of the ship committee (P.O. P.I. Kurkov) did not want to obey Dybenko's instructions to hold the ship in Petrograd over the 25th and 26th: 'The chairman of the ship committee insisted to Dybenko by Hughes machine on the necessity of the departure of the cruiser for engineering trials'. Khovrin did not think much of the crew: 'True, they were good lads there, but in revolutionary relations with us you might say that they were neither fish nor fowl.' The Guards Depot seems to have been generally against action. But if there were doubters there were also eager revolutionaries. Smilga wrote in 1919 that he had never seen such enthusiasm before or since as in Helsingfors on the night of 24–25 October; one sailor wept when he could not get aboard a train. Dybenko reported similar enthusiasm early on the 26th: 'The fleet is in an excited mood and spoiling for a fight on the barricades. It is necessary to hold [it] back'.[18]

Two points about the first phase of the revolution, before the congress, stand out. First, what was – properly speaking – an offensive action against the Provisional Government was widely held to be a defensive one; many sailors went to Petrograd to defend the capital against a new Kornilov. The other point is that the movement was always put in terms of *Soviet* power, even though it was the Bolsheviks who made the key decisions. The action, the sailors believed, was to defend the congress of soviets, and it was sponsored and organised by democratic organisations and not by parties. The attitude of the crew of the *Samson*, which arrived on the evening of the 25th, was probably typical. The anti-Bolshevik press later accused them of having been duped, but they hotly denied it. They had not been hypnotised by the Bolsheviks, they had not been sent by them; they had come on the orders of their elected democratic body, Tsentrobalt.[19]

Once the insurgents had overthrown Kerensky and declared Soviet power the situation became much more straightforward. Even the local leaders of the other radical parties actively supported the Bolsheviks in the struggle with 'counter-revolution'. 'I must say in honour of the Bolsheviks' said the Anarchist Iarchuk on the 29th, 'although perhaps they are in many ways incorrect and in future we will argue with them, that they proved that they were not joking and decided actively to fight when the moment arrived.' The Helsingfors Left S.R.s said almost the same thing on the 28th:

Let's concede that the Bolsheviks acted first, that they acted in an untimely way since they had the possibility to wait another day until the Congress of Soviets. That is a sin, that is a great sin. But we see that the business has ended successfully.

This Left S.R. support for the Bolshevik coup was linked with an attack on the C.C. of the P.S.R., which had supported the Committee of Salvation; 'You,' they told the C.C., 'are not Socialist-Revolutionaries. You are not even bad Socialist-Revolutionaries. You are reactionaries of the purest water.' (Iarchuk mocked the S.R. national leadership, saying that their slogan should now be 'In struggle, together with the *junkers*, cossacks, and women's shock battalion, will you attain your rights'!) There was no room for a middle path, as Sheinman told a plenary meeting on the 24th: 'He who is not with us is against us, he who is not for the Soviets is against them.' This polarisation was reflected in mass support. 'The whole Baltic Fleet is really spoiling for a fight,' reported Izmailov on the 30th, 'sailors from all the ships come to Tsentrobalt day and night and plead to be sent to Petrograd'.[20]

> We call on you, comrades, [appealed the Naval Revolutionary Committee on the 27th] ignoring the differences between socialist parties [and] groups, rejecting any ambition, to unite in the movement to defend the country and the revolution from the dangers which are threatening them. Know, comrades, that this great historical act, regardless of who first carried it out, was carried out only in the interests of the toiling masses, in the interests of the revolution.[21]

This kind of appeal was willingly accepted at first, but once the mirage of counter-revolution evaporated there arose doubts about the new governing Council of People's Commissars (*Sovnarkom*), which was headed by Lenin and composed entirely of Bolsheviks. This was especially true after negotiations began for the formation of a more broadly-based government, including either all socialist parties or at least those which accepted Soviet power. By the first days of November the movement for a left coalition was being supported by the powerful railwaymen's union and even by a number of Bolsheviks, who on 4 November resigned in protest from the C.C. and Sovnarkom.

Even the Kronstadt Soviet accepted (on the 29th) a resolution proposed by the S.R.-Maximalist Rivkin that power in the new government should be apportioned among those parties represented at the congress of soviets. It is true that four days later the soviet approved a Bolshevik resolution that there could only be a coalition with parties which accepted both the whole programme of the new government and the need for 'merciless struggle' with the counter-revolution, but this was still a call for a coalition.[22]

The attitude of Tsentrobalt was particularly interesting. The committee had called in advance for the congress to take power, and on the 29th it explicitly supported the new regime. On the 3rd a meeting of the C.C.B.F. with ship committees resolved that the experience of the past eight months had shown that 'not all socialist parties are able to carry out the programme of peace, bread, land and workers' control' and that power should go to 'those parties which have shown creativity and viability'. But there was some confusion on the night of the 6th, when the committee met to discuss the political situation. A rating just back from the capital urged 'the power not of parties but of people', and all speakers supported this populist line. Izmailov, the Left S.R. acting chairman, immediately got in touch with the N.R.C.: 'The Baltic Fleet announces openly that for eight months it tirelessly fought for power for the soviets and not for the leaders of parties, so that they could quarrel among themselves for twelve days'. He concluded with an ultimatum: 'If in a short time the power of the ministry has still not been organised and the socialist parties have not come to an agreement, the Baltic Fleet will go to Piter and determine who shall have power.'[23] Although this was evidently aimed against the inclusion of 'conciliators' in the government, it could be taken as an oblique attack on the government of one party.

There were other, more direct, signs of opposition to an all-Bolshevik government. 'The counter-revolution is celebrating, it is sharpening its dagger', declared an editorial in *Moriak*, a magazine put out by sailors in Helsingfors. 'It is time to end the babel. In the name of the innocently spilt blood there must be found a common language for all representatives of the toiling people; enough of blood and senseless misunderstanding, it is time to end all the horrors of civil war.' On the 9th the Helsingfors democratic organisations very nearly approved a Left S.R. resolution minimising personalities (Lenin and Trotsky?) and urging more power for the C.E.C., rather than for the all-Bolshevik Sovnarkom. From the left, the S.R.-Maximalist Zverin told the Kronstadt Soviet, 'We did not take power in order to give it to a party'; 'soviet power is not the power of this or that party'.[24]

But hostility to the Bolshevik-dominated government should not be exaggerated. The R.S.D.W.P.(b) was the most popular party in the Baltic on the eve of the revolution; of the 29 deputies sent to the congress of soviets from the main towns and the fleet, 17 were Bolsheviks. The Bolsheviks dominated Tsentrobalt and the local town soviets. They were the largest group among all the delegates to the congress, and they nearly had an absolute majority. Immediately upon taking power they passed a series of popular decrees, overthrowing the Kerensky government, declaring Soviet power, nationalising the land, and beginning peace negotiations. It was moreover not the fault of the Bolsheviks alone that no other party would share power with them; the right socialists refused to accept the revolutionary programme of the new regime and the other 'lefts' were still in an inchoate state. In the Baltic district the elections to the Constituent Assembly were a vote of confidence in the new all-Bolshevik government;

directly after the·uprising the party of Lenin and the Council of People's Commissars received 56 per cent of the naval vote.

ORGANISATION

Another interesting theme is preparation and organisation. How well planned was the fleet's part in the uprising?

The logical starting point is Lenin's letter of mid-September to the C.C. and the Petrograd and Moscow Committees; in this he wrote that the task of the party was now 'to put on the order of the day an armed uprising in Piter and Moscow . . ., the seizing of power, and the overthrow of the government'. But only on 10 October did the C.C. decide that the situation 'puts an armed uprising on the order of the day', and not for another six days did the C.C. call 'on all organisations and all workers and soldiers to make comprehensive and intensified preparations for an armed insurrection';[25] this was just eight days before the rising actually began.

Despite a lack of explicit directives from the top, the local bases had been getting ready for action for some weeks. In late September the Reval democratic organisations voted in favour of Soviet power; afterwards, the Bolshevik newspaper *Zvezda* assessed the situation as follows:

> The whole Northern region with the Baltic Fleet, including Finland, is a revolutionary ring around Petrograd; Moscow helps in the rear. This ring not only defends Petrograd against Kornilov or Kerensky, it can if necessary send help to Petrograd, as it has at its disposal military and transport means.

A conference of Bolshevik organisations in Finland on 28 September helped to tighten the ring further. An even more important co-ordinating meeting was the 'Congress of Soviets of the Northern Region', held in Petrograd from 11 to 13 October. The Bolsheviks had an absolute majority, and one of the meeting's stated purposes was to help the coming all-Russian congress take power. Lenin, on his own initiative, suggested to the Bolshevik delegates that the time was ripe for an insurrection, and if his advice was not heeded, the delegates were at least made aware that an uprising was on the cards.[26]

A key question is how much preparation took place in the two weeks before 25 October. According to Smilga the detailed planning for an uprising began with a 'revolutionary committee' set up by the northern regional congress; Antonov-Ovseenko, recalled Smilga, remained in Petrograd to work out plans with Trotsky, Lenin, and Sverdlov. Evidently the general outline of the plan was already known; 'Smilga', Trotsky wrote, 'returned from the Congress to Helsingfors to organise a special detachment of sailors, infantry and artillery to be sent to Petrograd at the first signal'.[27]

A considerable role was assigned to the fleet. 'Our plan,' Smilga later said,

> envisaged that if it was not possible immediately to occupy the whole town with the revolutionary workers and soldiers of Petrograd, then [it was necessary] without fail to take the islands [i.e. Vasil'evsky Island and the Petersburg Side] and the Vyborg Side where the Finland Station was. In this case the struggle would be decided with the help of forces from Finland and the fleet.

A similar plan was mentioned by Antonov-Ovseenko and Trotsky. Detailed preparations for the use of the fleet had evidently been completed by 17 October, because that night Lenin had a discussion on the subject with the leaders of the M.O. at his hide-out on the Vyborg Side. Lenin evidently hoped that the whole fleet would come to help the uprising, but Antonov-Ovseenko explained that this was impossible, because the channel was too narrow, because 'the heavy ships are rather afraid of the submarines and destroyers', and because 'the sailors don't want to leave the front bare'; all he could promise was two or three destroyers and a few hundred men. 'It's not much,' grumbled Lenin. The plan had still not been finalised on the eve of the uprising, for on the night of the 23rd Vladimir Nevsky of the M.R.C. and the M.O. met with Lenin, and the two decided that Nevsky should hurry to Vyborg and Helsingfors to work out a united plan of action with Dybenko and Smilga; Nevsky evidently carried out his assignment on the 24th. The result of all this planning was a coded message, 'Send Regulations' (*Vysylai ustav*); on receipt the Helsingfors Bolsheviks would send destroyers and several thousand men.[28]

Meanwhile ambiguous preparations were being made in Helsingfors. Dybenko proposed to Tsentrobalt on 17 October that each large ship should form a permanent 'fighting squad' , and this was accepted. Two days later the squads were put on alert. And on the 21st the Bolshevik leaders of the three main democratic organisations placed Finland on a war footing. Although this was ostensibly motivated by the activities of the Finnish nationalists and the fear of a German landing, it may have been connected with the Bolshevik plans. Tsentrobalt used the pretext of the German threat to get a thousand rifles from Petrograd.[29]

In Kronstadt the general preparations began about 10 October, when the local Military-Technical Commission was reorganised. On that day the Bolshevik leader Petr Smirnov told the Kronstadt Soviet that his 'faction considers that the Military-Technical Commission will play an important role in forthcoming events'. Indeed, the M.T.C. was busy collecting arms and assessing revolutionary resources; the local Army Committee complained on the 20th that unknown persons were going around the workshops telling people to prepare for action. 'Before the October revolution,' admitted *Golos pravdy* later, 'the military-technical commission . . . occupied itself exclusively with preparing Kronstadt for the revolutionary struggle'.[30]

The Kronstadt leadership was evidently brought into the detailed planning at a fairly early stage. The sailor A. G. Pronin was a Bolshevik assigned by the E.C. to the M.T.C. and, by his own account, one of the leaders of the rising. According to him, the first step came on Friday, 20 October, when Lazar' Bregman, the Bolshevik chairman of the E.C., returned from the capital with news of the C.C. decision of the 16th. Pronin and the Bolshevik soldier S. S. Grediushko were sent to Petrograd for more details. They found – after a long search – the secret offices of Iakov Sverdlov, who was the link between the M.R.C. and the Bolshevik C.C. Sverdlov told them to remain in readiness and not to act immediately. Beginning on the 21st the M.T.C. assigned commissars to the local commanders and to key institutions; two days later units were ordered to obey only orders that the commission had approved. Flerovsky took an unambiguous position in the soviet on Monday, the 23rd. 'The time for political discussions has passed,' he announced, 'we have now reached the stage of technical discussions'; the M.R.C. had let it be known that in an extreme case they might summon the Kronstadters to the capital; 'From the stage of resolutions, from the stage of words, we have moved to the stage of deeds'. He actually used the word 'uprising' (*vosstanie*) in connection with Kronstadt's coming struggle. That same day several thousand copies were printed of an announcement in which the Kronstadt garrison promised help to Petrograd in any armed struggle with the government, and on Tuesday evening Pronin took these leaflets to the Smolny.[31] But the timing of the action was still not clear.

In Reval, the soviet assigned a commissar to the Commandant on 19 October; three days later, with the Estonian E.C., it set up an M.R.C. For the next two and a half months this body would be the main executive power in Estonia; it was dominated by the Bolsheviks. On the evening of the 23rd control was applied to all communications, and so, as at Kronstadt, the seizure of power preceded the Petrograd uprising. But, in contrast to Helsingfors and Kronstadt, there were apparently no plans to send detachments to aid the revolutionary capital.[32]

The transition from planning to execution proved to be difficult. The navy's first concrete step came on Monday, the 23rd, when Tsentrobalt instructed the *Avrora* *not* to put to sea for engineering trials (it was also the first time that the committee had asserted its control over the fleet in such a way). The cruiser's captain reported this development to Razvozov: 'Dybenko insists that the cruiser remains in Petrograd on the 25th and 26th'. (This was probably not linked with a Bolshevik pre-congress coup, but the big ship was clearly in the minds of some party leaders; on the 24th

Kamenev spoke of the need to have a 'stronghold' on the *Avrora*, 'in the event of the destruction of the Smolny'.) Then came Kerensky's 'counter-revolutionary' steps. On Tuesday morning the M.R.C. sent an order calling all units to 'combat readiness'. Among the recipients were the *Avrora* and the Guards and 2nd Depots.[33]

But these steps, and even the order for the *Avrora* to move to the Nikolai Bridge, were probably only precautionary. Kerensky had, after all, taken action against the Bolsheviks, and the congress was due to meet on the 25th. There were as yet no signs that the Bolsheviks planned to seize power *before* the congress. Decisive offensive action against the government began only after midnight on Tuesday, when Lenin arrived at the Smolny. Only then did rebel detachments, including Petrograd sailors, begin to take important government installations.[34]

Kronstadt only learned of this development quite late, which supports the argument that there was no long-term plan specifying that the *coup* should begin in the small hours of the 25th. Flerovsky and Iarchuk, both delegates to the second congress, were present at an M.R.C. meeting on Tuesday evening, but they were told nothing definite. Trotsky took Flerovsky aside; 'Events are moving so fast,' he said, 'that each should be in his place.' Iarchuk confirmed this warning, although he attributed it to Antonov-Ovseenko rather than to Trotsky; Iarchuk also felt that the 'events' the Bolshevik leaders were concerned with were more the increased activities of the *junker* patrols than the birth-pangs of the proletarian revolution. It was apparently only later on, when Aleksei Pronin arrived with the leaflets, that Antonov-Ovseenko gave the vital orders; Pronin was told to go back and get the Kronstadters.[35]

The Kronstadt E.C. had put the garrison on alert, but it was only the return of Flerovsky and Iarchuk that precipitated more active preparations. Even then, all that had happened by 2 a.m. was that units had been put on alert and commissars assigned to a Combined Detachment. The only movement confirmed was for the *Zaria svobody* to be towed to the Sea Canal, and this was clearly a defensive step directed against the Oranienbaum *junkers*. The order from the M.R.C. for decisive action came only at 4 a.m., according to B. A. Breslav; probably this was connected with Pronin's return. The order had come so late that the Kronstadters could only participate in the later stages of the insurrection. Trotsky himself was critical of the performance: 'The Kronstadters were late – not, to be sure, through their own fault. They had been summoned too late.' The blame for this must largely lie with the last-minute order to act, but it should also be borne in mind, in defence of the Bolshevik planners, that telephone communications between the Smolny and Kronstadt had been cut and that they had to rely on couriers.[36]

In Helsingfors, as well, many people were eagerly waiting for news. 'If everyone [else] does nothing the fleet will act independently, alone'; that, according to Dybenko, had been the view of the radical sailors as far back as the fleet congress. But no order for action was received to supplement the appeals of the M.R.C. and, according to Dybenko, the Bolshevik chairman of the Helsingfors E.C., Aron Sheinman, was unwilling to act decisively on his own initiative. Until quite late on Tuesday evening all that had happened was that Tsentrobalt had ordered the *Samson* to Petrograd and assigned commissars.[37]

Real action came only at 9.40 p.m. with a further message from Tsentrobalt to the C.-in-C.: 'Immediately give orders to the destroyers *Zabiiaka*, *Strashny* and *Metky* to leave for Petrograd.' The pre-arranged coded message ('Send Regulations') had been sent to Smilga at the Regional Committee and Dybenko at Tsentrobalt. The sender was either Sverdlov or Antonov-Ovseenko – or both.[38] The interesting thing about the order was that it was apparently sent at about 9 o'clock, three hours before Lenin arrived at the Smolny. But this would not make it fit into an advance plan for action on the night of the 24th – 25th; rather it was a somewhat tardy call for Helsingfors sailors to be in Petrograd at the time of the congress of soviets. It is possible that Smilga had opposed action before the congress; on the 17th he had said that 'without the knowledge of the congress and before the congress there can be no uprising of any sort'.[39] In any event, the first destroyer did not leave for twelve hours (until dawn), and only two ships reached their destination on the 25th. The first train did not leave Helsingfors for six hours, and the sailors on board arrived in Petrograd early on the 26th; as Antonov-Ovseenko put it, 'they arrived after the end of the first act'.[40]

My general conclusion from the situation at Kronstadt and Helsingfors is that there was no detailed plan for fleet participation in an armed uprising planned to begin during the night of 24–25 October. Trotsky's memoirs support this:

> The arrival of the sailors in Petrograd had been dated in advance to coincide with the Congress of Soviets. To call the Baltic Sailors in earlier would have meant to take openly the road of insurrection. Out of this arose a difficulty which subsequently turned into a delay.

It might be added that the whole affair was hardly organised with military precision. The attack on the Winter Palace was highly disorganised, according to Khovrin, who was an eyewitness: 'Anyone who thinks that [the sailors] went in companies and crews is mistaken. Everyone was his own company commander'. Some of the sailors who arrived on Wednesday night actually decided to go home again almost immediately, and only by chance were stopped at the railway station.[41] But this does not mean that the armed insurrection in Petrograd was a wild gamble or that the Bolsheviks came out on top only due to good fortune.

In the Baltic, at least, the 'organisational' battle had been won by the beginning of October. Control of local military forces lay in the hands of the democratic organisations; this was the result of the democratisation and political crises which have been the theme of previous chapters. The radical fourth session of Tsentrobalt began on 16 October and made Dybenko chairman; the next day Dybenko told Razvozov that there would soon be an election for the post of C.-in-C. This cut the ground from under Razvozov in the crucial days of late October. He reported his position on the 28th:

> In spite of my protest, Tsentrobalt sent 4 destroyers to Petrograd and earlier countermanded my order to the cruiser *Avrora* . . . to rejoin the fleet. I had no chance to prevent this. Besides this, at the beginning of the present crisis Tsentrobalt informed me of the imminent introduction of elective command and of committee supervision of all orders, not even excluding operational [ones]. Once again my protests had no effect and supervision was in fact established, as I reported to you . . . on 25 October; then Tsentrobalt removed a member of my staff [Lt. Colonel A. N. Nordman]. . . . After these above-mentioned infringements of my rights I, in the name of national defence, considered it all the same my duty to continue to command the fleet, limiting myself to the operational-technical command of the forces entrusted to me.

(Tsentrobalt's orders to send the *Oleg* and *Pobeditel'* to Petrograd provoked Razvozov to offer his resignation, but he soon withdrew this.) The C.-in-C. and his Staff were completely powerless in political terms; when on the 25th an order slipped through from the Stavka ordering certain units to the aid of the Provisional Government the horrified Staff discussed the message and decided to do nothing.[42] The real power, the power to move powerful military and political weapons like Baltic warships and detachments, lay with the democratic organisations. There was never any doubt about this.

Most important, the men who controlled these democratic organisations were the Bolsheviks. Since 14 September they had controlled the Regional Committee and, (at least) since 16 October, Tsentrobalt. They were able to manipulate events, and to stress the importance of 'defence' against the Provisional Government. The minutes of a plenary meeting in Helsingfors on the afternoon of the 25th give a good example of the Bolsheviks' power:

> From the chair comrade Sheinman reports to the meeting that in recent days the leadership of all events has been the responsibility of the presidiums of three organisations – of the Executive Committee [chaired by the Bolshevik Sheinman], of the Regional Committee [chaired by the Bolshevik Smilga], and of Tsentrobalt [chaired by the Bolshevik Dybenko], and he asks the meeting either to approve the actions of these organisations and to give them in future the right to be the leaders, or to elect a special revolutionary committee.

After a short debate the meeting approved the work of the presidiums and asked them 'to continue to lead the political life of the Russian population of Finland'.[43] The Bolsheviks had the same kind of power at all the bases, and they used it on the 24th and 25th and in the following week. They had, as we have seen, the general support of the fleet. Given this situation the element of chance was limited, at least as far as the fleet was concerned. The organisation was far from perfect, but it was certainly equal to the tasks assigned it in October 1917.

ASSESSMENT

The final question concerns the relative contribution of the Baltic sailors to the success of the uprising.

The existence of a revolutionary fleet was one of the factors which led Lenin to propose an uprising in the first place. As early as 30 August he alluded to the value of forces from Kronstadt and Helsingfors, although this was in connection with operations against Kornilov. On 27 September, after he had decided on the necessity of armed uprising, Lenin wrote to Smilga suggesting that the party should concentrate on the forces in Finland – given that the Petrograd party organisation was doing nothing. On at least four occasions in the next nine days he wrote letters stressing the value of the fleet in an uprising.[44]

The experience of past crises was one reason why the fleet occupied a prominent place in Lenin's thinking. But it was also important that Lenin spent over a month in Helsingfors during August and September; he lived first in the Söörnäiste Rantatie (a few hundred yards from the North Harbour) and then in the suburb of Tëlë. He did not participate in the local Bolshevik organisation, and of the Russian comrades only a few knew of his presence, but he asked Smilga and Zhemchuzhin about the fleet and the garrison, and he read the local newspapers.[45]

A little later, in debates within the Bolshevik leadership, the fleet was mentioned by both the advocates and opponents of insurrection. The value of the sailors was discussed at meetings of the Petersburg Committee on 5 and 15 October and of the C.C. on the 16th.[46] The decision in favour of uprising was partly a reflection of confidence in the fleet.

The first stage of the revolution, from the point of view of the fleet, was the night of the 24th and the first part of the 25th. During this period there were about 9,700 sailors in Petrograd. Some 4,316 of these, from the 2nd and Guards Depots, were in barracks near the administrative centre of the town, where the 'action' was taking place.[47] Groups of men from these two units and from the *Avrora* helped to take government installations and bridges, but they probably did not have a decisive effect. The Guards Depot declared itself neutral, and so was similar to much of the army garrison.[48]

The latter part of the 25th was the critical time. The attack on the Winter Palace was delayed pending the arrival of the Kronstadters. The ships arriving from Kronstadt (with crews of 717) brought about 3,800 sailors, as well as 950 soldiers; 585 more came on the *Samson* and *Zabiiaka*.[49] These men, together with the Petrograd sailors, were not in numerical terms a very significant part of the potential revolutionary forces in the capital; there were 20,000 Red Guards (from a population of 390,000 factory workers), and an army garrison of 155,000 men.[50] But their importance was out of proportion to their relatively small numbers. They were definitely not 'neutral', and they had come to support Soviet power. The Baltic sailors, recalled Trotsky, were 'a fighting detachment combining proletarian resolution with strict military training'. Sukhanov also saw them as an important force: 'The most reliable [cadres] were the workers and their 'red guard'; then came the sailors; worst of all were the soldiers of the garrison.' The sailors, moreover, came in a compact group and landed close to the scene of action. They certainly played an important role in securing the administrative part of the town and taking the Winter Palace. And the moral effect of the pro-Soviet flotilla lying in the Neva that evening was considerable. In addition to the 6,700-ton *Avrora*, the 2,900-ton *Amur*, the training ship *Verny*, and the 'Noviks' *Samson* and *Zabiiaka*, there were five smaller naval vessels, the *Zarnitsa*, *Khoper*, *Iastreb*, and minesweepers *No. 14* and *No. 15*.[51]

The sailors from Finland arrived 'after the end of the first act' but in time to fight in Petrograd on the 29th and on the southern approaches. Warships and the railways brought several thousand more men from the morning of 26 October onwards.[52] The other forces were larger in number but still less effective. 'From the fighting . . . which I have seen with my own eyes', reported General Marushevsky, 'I have come to the conclusion that only sailors and armed workers were fighting in the streets here; the soldiers of the reserve regiments were apathetic and seem to have looked out for themselves and not especially to have desired active participation.' Sukhanov sketched out the unique value of the fleet in the battles against Kerensky and Krasnov.

Among the [Petrograd] garrison there were no halfway reliable volunteers. Out of an army of 200 thousand they scraped together *two or three companies*. Considerable reliance had to be placed on the worker-red-guards. But only their *morale* could be relied on. The military effectiveness of this army – which had never smelled powder, which had never seen a rifle until the last day or two, which had no understanding of military operations or discipline – was more than doubtful. To cap it all there were absolutely no officers.

Only the sailors could amount to a serious force. Kronstadt was able to send three or four thousand reliable fighters. And besides, as we know, 1,800 sailors arrived from Helsingfors. . . .

The M.R.C. protocol of 30 October showed that it was relying on the fleet to defend the south:

> *An announcement by a commissar from the front was heard*, from which it is evident that the commander-in-chief for the defence of Petrograd, Colonel Murav'ev, is not suitable for his assignment.
> *Resolved*: To inform the Naval Revolutionary Committee that the defence of Petrograd is not at the desired height, [and] to order it to take corresponding steps.[53]

General Krasnov's account shows that the sailors *were* an important stiffening force. When the cossacks charged near Pulkovo 'whole crowds of black figures ran off in disorder. But they were Red Guards. The sailors steadfastly remained in their places.' 'This unsuccessful attack,' noted the general, 'was very disadvantageous to us from the point of view of morale. It showed the steadfastness of the sailors. And the sailors were numerically 10 times greater than us. How was it possible to fight under such conditions?'[54]

At the meeting of the Petersburg Committee on 1 November both Lenin and Trotsky cited the fleet as an element of real strength which made it possible for the Bolsheviks to form a government without the moderate socialists; 'If you want a split,' thundered Lenin at the Bolshevik moderates, 'go ahead. If you get the majority, take power in the Central Executive Committee and carry on. But we will go to the sailors.'[55] So for over a month the fleet was one of the points used by Lenin to support his demands for radical action.

The question of the relative weight of the Baltic sailors in the forces that overthrew the Provisional Government is an important one, because it contributes to arguments about whether the October uprising was a 'proletarian revolution' or something else. As early as 29 October a Menshevik-Internationalist had the courage to get up in the Kronstadt Soviet and call the whole affair a *pronunciamento*. The Popular Socialist newspaper *Narodnoe slovo* implied the same thing by reporting on the 27th that the 'caliphs for the hour', the Bolsheviks, 'are in a hurry to leave and they are setting sail for Helsingfors'. The émigré historian S. P. Mel'gunov minimised the importance of the army garrison and the Red Guard and insisted that effective rebel operations only began in the afternoon of the 25th when the sailors arrived; 'the sailors were a real force which the young workers of the Red Guard could support'. After the *coup* 'the Kronstadt praetorians . . . remained the only real support the Bolsheviks had'. The American historian Stefan Possony took a similar line: 'the ultimately decisive factor [on the 25th] was the landing of 2,000 or 3,000 Kronstadt sailors and the demonstration by 7 warships'.[56]

My own opinion would be that the Baltic sailors had a major role in the events of 25 October to 1 November. Something like 10,000 sailors took an active part, and they were, man for man, more important than the average worker or soldier in Petrograd. They came *for the purpose* of establishing Soviet power, and they came in a concentrated group. Whether they were the *decisive* group is a virtually unanswerable question. I think however that the answer is no, if only because the pro-Kerensky forces were so feeble; the sailors would have been more necessary had resistance been greater.

8 Civil War: Politics after October

We announce for all to hear that the men of the Baltic will stop at nothing in order to slay the hydra of counter-revolution.

Tsentrobalt, November 1917

THE CENTRE

Even in Petrograd the new government needed firm support if it was not to drown in a wave of counter-revolution, anarchy, and crime. This support was provided by the sailors, together with Red Guards and pro-Bolshevik soldiers. Detachments of sailors were available when the Military-Revolutionary Committee wanted them. Sailors were called in to protect the Winter Palace and the Tauride Palace; the commandant of the Smolny was a sailor from the *Diana* named Pavel Mal'kov. On 20 November the Naval Revolutionary Committee issued instructions to another detachment of sailors to go to the Ministry of the Interior and arrest or dismiss those civil servants who refused to accept Soviet power. An example of the sailors' role in the preservation of public order was given in a report of the M.R.C.'s 'Commissar for the Struggle with Drunkenness and Gambling':

[On 27 November] the staff was set up in the premises occupied by the Helsingfors [*sic*] sailors (2nd Baltic Fleet Depot), from which orders for the destruction of liquor would be issued. Machine-gunners were summoned from Strel'na, and Helsingfors sailors were put on duty. Then the silver of Countess Bobrinskaia, 54 Galernaia [St], was removed to the State Bank; it had begun to be looted and was protected by the sailors. The liquor in this house had been destroyed earlier by the sailors before my assignment.

The navy had a high proportion of technically qualified staff, and these were pressed into service. The M.R.C. instructed the N.R.C. to 'send to . . . comrade Menzhinsky at the State Bank one hundred (100) sailors, preferably from the Guards'. Here, as elsewhere, naval clerks replaced

striking civil servants. Naval signals personnel helped to secure communications. The orders and decrees of Sovnarkom were broadcast by the
naval wireless station, the most powerful in Petrograd.[1]

The most important political event in Petrograd after October was the
brief meeting of the Constituent Assembly. The fleet's attitude was
somewhat confused. It had berated the Kerensky government for delaying
the Assembly. Tsentrobalt's 'Appeal' of 26 October listed the early
summoning of the Assembly as one of the main virtues of the new regime.
Even in December *Moriak* published an editorial stating that 'the
people . . . wait with trembling and awe the opening of the Constituent
Assembly, that great temple, from which will be heard the holy words of
the just law'. This was however probably already a minority view, because
the electoral returns disappointed the fleet. The main S.R. party had an
absolute majority in the Assembly, and only 30 per cent of delegates were
from those parties which by late November were partners in the
Sovnarkom, the Bolsheviks and Left S.R.s. In contrast, only 9 per cent of
the Baltic Fleet vote went to the Right S.R.s; 87 per cent went to the
Bolsheviks and Left S.R.s. (Lenin himself was a Baltic delegate; although
elected by several constituencies he chose to represent the Baltic Fleet.)
The Bolshevik Party opposed the Assembly, as a threat to their new
authority. They were supported by the Left S.R.s, whose delegate strength
in the Assembly did not reflect their actual strength in the country (they
had split from the mother party too late to have their own lists in most
electoral districts). The Left S.R. newspaper in Reval characterised the
Assembly as something 'in which all the opportunists, including the
Kadets, now see their liberation from the hated power of the Soviets'. So
the hostility of a large part of the fleet was understandable. The crew of the
Andrei Pervozvanny wrote a letter condemning the outcome of the elections
and demanding that the moderates – 'the vampire oppressors' – be
excluded.[2]

The Assembly was originally scheduled for 28 November and, at the
request of the Sovnarkom, Dybenko made contingency plans to concentrate sailors in the capital. As it turned out, however, too few delegates
appeared. The meeting was postponed until early January, when renewed
efforts were made to rally the fleet against it. The appeal which
Tsentrobalt issued on 4 January did not attack the Assembly *per se*, but
rather the intention of 'the Petrograd bourgeoisie' and 'the bankers and
stockbrokers of the whole world' to stage a coup, 'with the benevolent co-
operation of the lackeys of capital – the pseudo-socialists of the Dan-Liber-
Gots type'; 'having already made one attempt to sweep away Soviet
power, they want, come what may, to liquidate it once and for all on the
day of the opening of the Constituent Assembly and thus to fasten the noose
around the neck of the people'.[3]

The government had only 1,765 sailors on hand on 4 January, and
probably no more than 1,200 arrived later; the turn-out was much poorer

than in October, or even in July. Nevertheless, there were enough sailors, Red Guards, and soldiers available to contain the small pro-Assembly demonstrations. (Pavel Dybenko organised the defence of the Tauride Palace area; the leader of the combat organisation of the 'Union for the Defence of the Constituent Assembly' was Fedot Onipko, formerly Commissar-General of the Baltic Fleet. The worm had turned.)[4]

The most dramatic moment took place in the Tauride Palace, at the meeting of the Assembly itself. The head of the 'guard' was a handsome sailor, festooned with machine-gun belts. This was the Anarchist Anatoly Zhelezniakov, a 22-year-old rating from the minelayer *Narova*. His was a short and turbulent life: a feigned suicide in 1912 to get out of a school for medical orderlies; desertion from the navy in 1916; arrest at the Durnovo Villa in June 1917; escape from a 14-year prison sentence in August. He would even briefly be declared an outlaw by the Soviet government, but he died 'honourably' in the battle with Denikin in 1919. His detachment in the Tauride Palace was, evidently, an undisciplined one. They had even Lenin worried; according to Raskol'nikov, who was one of the leaders of the Bolshevik delegation, Lenin opposed a demonstrative walk-out with the following words:

> Don't you understand that if we return and after the declaration [of the Bolshevik delegation denouncing the Assembly] we leave the meeting hall, then the electrified sailor sentries will shoot down on the spot those who remain. In no circumstances must this happen.

But excesses were avoided. In the small hours of the 6th Zhelezniakov interrupted Viktor Chernov, the chairman, to announce that 'all present are to leave the hall of the building because the guard is tired'.[5] Surrounded by an intimidating group of sailors, the deputies gave in and closed the meeting. They were not allowed to reassemble later in the day. And that was the end of the Constituent Assembly.

The dissolution was approved by the fleet. Tsentrobalt's 'Appeal' of the 4th was echoed by its 'Instructions' of the 7th to delegates to the 3rd Congress of Soviets (10–18 January) (although the committee did call for a *parlament* to be formed 'from the members of the C.E.C. of the 3rd congress with a few (*s primes'iu*) members of the Constituent Assembly who honestly stand for Soviet power'). A plenary meeting of the Helsingfors democratic organisations approved the closing of the assembly, as did the Reval Soviet.[6]

The final major political task entrusted to the sailors in the old revolutionary centre came seven weeks later. The '1st Naval Shore Detachment of the People's Commissariat for Naval Affairs' was formed in Petrograd on 10 March. On the night of 11–12 March this detachment escorted the train which carried the Soviet government from Petrograd to Moscow – the new capital.[7] It was the end of an era.

THE PERIPHERY

Another struggle was taking place in the provinces. The Soviet government had inherited little of military value to enforce its rule there. It was left to Red Guards, sailors, and pro-Soviet soldiers to act as firemen for the government, preventing anti-Soviet sparks from becoming a general conflagration.

The first naval detachment was one commanded by Khovrin; it left Petrograd for Moscow on 2 November, but it arrived after the fighting there had ended. Another smaller detachment escorted Ensign N. V. Krylenko when he was sent to the Stavka to replace the Supreme C.-in-C., General Dukhonin. Krylenko lost control, and one of his sailors bayoneted the general.[8]

A larger detachment, led by Khovrin, Zhelezniakov, and Il'in-Zhenevsky, was formed around the sailors who went to Moscow. Khovrin's detachment set out along the railway line from Moscow to Kharkov, and near Belgorod it fought a series of battles with anti-Soviet troops trying to break through to the Don, the rallying point of counter-revolutionary forces. By the end of December Khovrin had only 109 men; commissars and organisers had to be left along the railway, and many men went home. The detachment became thoroughly demoralised; Antonov-Ovseenko later described how the sailors, engaging in looting and refusing to obey important battle orders, were finally disarmed by an armoured-car unit and led to the rear. Late in December the detachment was completely disbanded. 'We had, alas, neither understanding nor discipline,' admitted Khovrin.[9]

The '1st Northern Flying column' left Petrograd on 27 November to fight the Orenburg cossacks of Ataman Dutov; the column included soldiers, Red Guards, and 400 sailors, mostly from the *Petropavlovsk* and the *Andrei Pervozvanny*. The trip, to the border of European and Asiatic Russia, took seven weeks; on the way the column helped establish Soviet power in a number of towns. Orenburg itself was captured on 18 January 1918. The 'Extraordinary Commissar' in charge reported the particular value of the sailors: 'The sailors on the Dutov front were the crystallising agent. Around these 400 individuals . . . was formed all the remaining mass, and we saw as soon as the mass joined this basic core that our victory over Dutov was assured.'[10]

Another focus of the counter-revolution were the Don Cossacks of Ataman Kaledin. On 19 January a 600-man detachment led by the Left S.R. Karl Kallis left Kronstadt for the Don. The Kronstadters attacked Rostov-on-Don, Kaledin's main town, from the direction of Lugansk; other Red columns attacked from different directions, and on 22 February the town fell.[11]

The sailors also played a part in the confused fighting in Belorussia and the Ukraine. R. I. Berzin's '1st Minsk Revolutionary Detachment', set up in December, included in its '3rd Column' a 'Combined Naval Detachment' of 400 men. When Antonov-Ovseenko attempted to transfer the sailors he met with refusal. The commander of the naval unit reported, 'In view of the fact that the detachment of Baltic sailors is under the command . . . of comrade Berzin, who is unwilling to be left without sailors and who has ordered me to remain, I am unable to transfer my detachment in accordance with your orders.' The commander of the column, a naval sub-lieutenant named Iakovlev, explained that nearly all his troops were unreliable and 'all hopes [are placed] on the sailors; . . . the sailors are already badly overworked because everywhere they want sailors'. 'Only the firm word of the sailors . . .,' he added, 'sustains to some extent the other units.' These sailors were among the detachments which forced the nationalist Ukrainian Rada to give up Kiev on 26 January.[12]

These were just the largest and most important detachments. Smaller groups were sent to other places. A. L. Fraiman estimated that at least 3,000 ratings were sent in organised groups to the 'internal front' in the first months.[13]

Baltic sailors also fought in civil war battles nearer their bases. They helped to secure Soviet rule in Estonia during the October Revolution and afterwards. An Estonian nationalist assembly, the *Maapäev*, was closed with the aid of the Russian sailors. On 17 November the Reval M.R.C. expressed its gratitude to the fleet:

In Reval, the days of the recent revolution passed with an outward calm, but this calm was purchased at the great expense of intensive work . . . of the [1st] brigade of cruisers. The promptness in sending fighting units and the accuracy in fulfilling all assignments meant that in Reval and the districts [*uezdy*] various kinds of reactionary and provocative steps were easily anticipated and suppressed. . . .[14]

But fighting in Estonia was on a low level, even in the following months.

In Finland the situation was far more serious. The democratic organisations of the Russian minority (including the Regional Committee, Tsentrobalt, and the local soviets) tried to avoid involvement in Finnish domestic politics. But a series of shooting incidents involving Finnish nationalists led the Russians to declare a state of siege on 21 October. The October Revolution brought no immediate change, although Pavel Shishko, a Left S.R. sailor, was made Governor-General. The Finnish Senate (cabinet) was now controlled by the right. There was a general strike at the beginning of November, but the Finnish left made no attempt to take power. Two and a half months of uneasy peace followed, during which the Soviet government granted Finland independence. The democratic organisations of the Russian population ordered 'absolute non-intervention in Finnish affairs'.[15]

Civil war began on 14 January 1918. In Helsingfors the Red Finns overthrew the government; simultaneously the White Finns took over the northern part of the country. Ironically, the strength of the Whites was partly a reflection of the weakness of the Baltic Fleet. In May 1917 a U-boat had landed Finnish nationalist agents in the Aland Islands; another submarine took military supplies to the south coast in early November. More important, in October and November the German naval auxiliary *Equity* made two daring voyages into the Gulf of Bothnia with combat equipment.[16]

Smilga abandoned neutrality and called for 'merciless struggle with the White brigands'. Raskol'nikov and Dybenko spoke to a plenary meeting in Helsingfors on 19 January, and both promised aid to the Reds. But while the sailors made important contributions to the battles in central and southern Russia, they could do little in Finland. Demobilisation was well advanced, and Russian forces had to be concentrated against a German offensive in Estonia, which began three weeks after the Finnish civil war. Soviet Russia also did not want to give the appearance of intervening in the affairs of 'independent' Finland. In any event, on 23 February (10 February, o.s.) the Bolshevik C.C. accepted peace terms which included the evacuation of all Russian forces from Finland. An order was issued for sailors fighting with the Red Finns to retire from the navy.[17]

Only a few naval volunteers fought. They were of real help, as the Russian colonel commanding the Red forces recalled:

> The Baltic Fleet sent a detachment of sailor anarchists with 250 men who, appearing at Tammerfors [Tampere] with black flags, dispirited the Finnish bourgeoisie and raised the morale of the [Finnish] Red Guard and of the Russian volunteers.

In a fierce little battle north-west of Tammerfors on 31 January a naval detachment suffered heavy losses: 9 sailors killed, 29 wounded, and 9 missing.[18] But the Russian contribution was small. The turning point in the civil war came in early April when the Whites captured Tammerfors, the 'Red Verdun'. Most of the Finnish Red Guards were encircled. With the help of a German landing the Whites overran the whole country by the end of the month.

Finally, tens of thousands of individual sailors played an unrecorded part in the establishment of Soviet power in the countryside during the winter of 1917–18. Agitators had been going out on an organised and unorganised basis since the early months of 1917, but the October Revolution greatly increased their number and importance. Something like 40,000 Baltic sailors had gone home by mid-winter, bringing revolutionary enlightenment to the dark towns and villages. The following was perhaps typical:

> The 6th day of December, 1917. We, the [825] citizens of the village of Purdoshki, Purdoshki Township, Krasnoslobodsk District, Penza Province, all met on this day, where there was a discussion of how our common interests demanded in such difficult and troubled times a person who can be chairman of the Purdoshki Township Land Committee [, who can] take care of the needs of our village, of supplies, and of the establishment of order in the village, and therefore by general agreement we resolved:
>
> To elect as chairman of the Purdoshki Township Land Committee from among ourselves the artificer petty officer from the cruiser *Riurik*, one of the citizens of Purdoshki, Iakov Zakharov [*sic*] Alekeev, as a worthy and fair man, and to ask the ship committee of the cruiser *Riurik* for the release of Alekeev from military service to look after our common interests.

Ivan Kolbin, an instructor from Kronstadt and a Bolshevik, went home to Podol'sk, where he became first a member of the executive and party committees, then 'Commissar of Justice' for the town and district, chairman of the 'Council of People's Judges', chairman of the *Cheka*, and chief of staff of the local Red Army! Also worthy of note was Stoker 1st Cl. Pavel Khokhriakov, a 25-year-old rating from the *Zaria svobody*. He arrived in the Urals in September, where he was elected head of the Ekaterinburg Red Guard. In March he was sent to Tobol'sk to bring the former imperial family back to Ekaterinburg; as chairman of the Tobol'sk Soviet he prevented their escape, and ensured that they were escorted to Ekaterinburg – and death.[19]

At all levels the sailors made an important contribution. Evidence of the high esteem in which the Soviet government held them may be found in an order sent to the naval high command on 12 January by the People's Commissar for Military Affairs, Nikolai Podvoisky:

> In connection with the formation of detachments of the socialist army and of their imminent departure for the front it is essential that a squad of the comrade sailors be detailed to every group of volunteers (consisting of 1000 men) which is formed, with the aim of stiffening them [*spaika*].[20]

POLITICAL MOOD

In discussing the political mood of the Baltic sailors in the six months after the October Revolution, two inter-related factors must be borne in mind.

First, the composition of the fleet was considerably affected by the departure of a large number of revolutionary sailors. Second, the Bolsheviks as a governing party became 'responsible' for the condition of Russia and were thus open to attack.

The rapid contraction of the fleet began with the revolutionary detachments. They included the most revolutionary-minded ratings; with them went prominent sailor-Bolsheviks like Khovrin. The fairly thin layer of Bolshevik leaders in the fleet was further depleted when many of them, like Dybenko, left to staff Soviet naval headquarters in Petrograd. Then there was the effect of demobilisation. On 1 November Tsentrobalt decided to release the classes of 1905, 1906, and 1907 on 1 December, 15 December, and 1 January; these made up something like 10 per cent of the fleet, or between eight and nine thousand men. Another group of roughly similar size was lost when the classes of 1908 – 10 were demobilised in February. This was just the *official* demobilisation. The Kronstadt Naval Committee released *its* 1905 – 07 men on 15 November. On 20 December the staff officer in charge of personnel reported to Tsentrobalt that many units were already demobilising the classes of 1912 and 1913. Many others went off on unofficial leaves. On 18 December a Tsentrobalt delegate reported that crews were now at no more than 50 per cent of normal strength; on the 23rd it was reported that some ships were down to 30 per cent. One Soviet secondary source estimated the losses by 1 January 1918 as 40,000 ratings. The German invasion of February and the official release of all remaining conscripts on 5 March made the fleet even smaller. On 7 March the Left S.R. Brushvit, a sailor himself, bemoaned the situation in Kronstadt: 'The Kronstadt revolutionary masses have disappeared somewhere, in fact only the soviet remains'. 'Why,' he asked, 'did all the sailors here leave their ships, taking, as they say, even the kitchen sink . . .?'[21]

Revolutionary militancy seemed to be in decline among the sailors who remained. There was a growing reluctance to send revolutionary detachments despite – or because of – the fact that the new Soviet institutions, both at the centre and in the provinces, regarded the fleet as an inexhaustible supply of manpower. On 6 January, for example, the '1st Minsk Revolutionary Detachment' asked for 2,000 sailors to be sent to Gomel'; three weeks later came a request for another 2,000 to work in Siberian railway depots. Even Lenin on 15 January asked the navy to provide 2,000 more sailors for the struggle against the Rada. But Tsentrobalt had already given up sending men. On 9 December it refused a request from Podvoisky for 200 men to fight pogroms in Rybinsk. 'In no case must sailors be sent;' declared Artificer P.O. 2nd Cl. P. S. Sutyrin, a Left S.R., 'how many sailors have already been sent to all the ends of Russia, and no one has told us what happened to them.' The committee refused to send reinforcements to Khovrin in mid-December, despite a personal appeal by Raskol'nikov and others. Even Kronstadt delayed over a month before sending off a few hundred men against Kaledin.[22]

This was partly a practical judgement that if there was going to be a fleet at all some check would have to be put on the number of men leaving. But there was probably also a decline in enthusiasm, as Aleksei Baranov, from the central naval authorities, complained to a plenary meeting in Helsingfors:

Comrades, the whole Admiralty is now in our hands, but the spirit of the navy has fallen; we get the feeling that our comrades no longer trust Soviet power and [think] that it does not fulfil its responsibilities. But, comrades, . . . you, as members of committees, must instil a revolutionary spirit and explain to your comrades that they must give help in order to defeat the bourgeoisie.

At about the same time the Left S.R Kallis lamented the fact that the Kronstadt masses seemed to be losing interest in revolution. And this declining enthusiasm was caused in part by the changing composition of the fleet. 'The most passive and least steady element remained on the ships,' recalled Dybenko in his memoirs. 'They "creamed off" (*vyudili*) the best elements from among the sailors and soldiers for work in consolidating Soviet power in the provinces,' said an editorial in *Golos pravdy* on 25 January: 'The absence of the progressive sailors . . . is sharply felt.'[23]

Those that remained were often more interested in making a living than in making revolution. The *Riurik* for example sent a fifth of its crew to the internal front in the first two weeks after the October Revolution, and the remaining men began to grumble at the extra watches they had to stand. 'Let them take the naval infantry from Oranienbaum, let them use the fleet depots if they need bluejackets to fight saboteurs and speculators,' suggested Kvasov from the *Baian* at a meeting of the 1st Cruiser Brigade, 'but we must not give one sailor from the ships'. The brigade committee actually resolved in early November that no more men should be sent. Some sailors supported their own insular professional interests and had little sympathy for the rest of the population. In Kronstadt in mid-January the crews of three recently arrived ships, the *Grazhdanin*, the cruiser *Gromoboi*, and the gunboat *Khrabry*, demanded that the local soviet clear out of the former Officers Club, because it was naval property! If such attitudes were prevalent among the ratings who remained in November-January, they were even more common among those who stayed on after a volunteer fleet was officially set up at the end of January. The Helsingfors *Izvestiia* complained that the men who had signed on for short-term contracts were 'not the revolutionary element, but the worst, the laziest'. Their interest in politics was minimal. In late April Raskol'nikov attended the preliminary meetings of the third Baltic congress and reported that they had 'revealed the extraordinarily grey composition of the congress, the completely weak political development of the majority of its participants'.[24]

A side effect was a steady erosion of Bolshevik strength. The Kronstadt delegate to the 7th Party Congress (6–8 March 1918) reported that local party membership was only 3,500 and had not grown since the October Revolution. G. I. Boky, a member of the C.C., doubted whether even this assessment was correct; he felt that there could only be 500–1,000 left, mostly workers, since the sailors had been demobilised. Bolshevik delegate strength in the Kronstadt Soviet was at an all-time high after the elections of January 1918, but it plummeted from 46 per cent to 29 per cent after the March elections. The situation at Helsingfors and Reval was probably similar. The turmoil of February, March, and April further weakened the Bolshevik organisation. In the Destroyer Division, where an anti-Soviet mutiny took place in May, there was only one Bolshevik collective and only a few individual party members on other ships.[25]

Among the sailors who remained in the fleet all authority was being challenged. Common indiscipline, which had been a feature of life since the February Revolution, now became worse. In December the C.C. of the Coastal Front near Reval appealed to the sailors to be more orderly and cited cases of 'drunkenness, looting, shooting in the street, hooliganism in public places'. 'Our comrades are now dying on the barricades with the counter-revolutionary Kaledin,' declared one disgusted Tsentrobalt delegate, 'and we here are having a drunken orgy.' There were also numerous cases of what might be called 'revolutionary indiscipline' at the bases. At the end of January the Helsingfors democratic organisations sensed, more and more, 'cries of no confidence and hostility among the revolutionary soldiers and sailors towards their elected organs'. In mid-February 200 sailors from the fortress island of Vul'f arrived in Reval and, despite the protests of the local soviet, removed the local German 'barons' from the town prison and put them in the grain elevator. One eyewitness spoke of the situation in Helsingfors on the eve of the evacuation of the fleet: 'it was impossible to boast about the discipline among the remaining personnel, among whom there frequently appeared anarchist inclinations in an unnatural form'.[26]

It would be wrong, however, to blame the decline of discipline on demobilisation. The 'revolutionary' detachments which had been sent to the 'internal front' were just as bad. As an extreme case, Zhelezniakov's detachment developed into a drunken gang who engaged in robbery and extortion; things came to a head when it kidnapped three army officers and demanded a ransom. Two of the officers were killed, and when the survivor sought refuge in the Smolny the sailors' leader, Zhelezniakov's elder brother, threatened to attack the building. It was only with difficulty and after a personal order from Lenin that loyal forces disarmed them and drove them out of their barracks. On the night following the dissolution of the Constituent Assembly some sailors, apparently from the despatch vessel *Chaika*, murdered the former Provisional Government ministers Shingarev and Kokoshkin in their hospital beds. In mid-March a detachment just back to Kronstadt from the interior nearly massacred 16 White hostages; only the threat of the Kronstadt E.C. to resign stopped them.[27]

Discipline had in fact broken down everywhere. Russia in the winter of 1917–18 was a society in a state of near-anarchy. Enormous aspirations had been created, and enormous hardships were being suffered. All restraints were removed from a society which before February 1917 had been tightly restrained. No form of authority was respected.

This helps explain why Bolshevik popularity declined in the fleet. The Bolsheviks took responsibility when they took power. They had given the land to the peasants and made peace, but they could not provide food or employment. Nor could they grant the most extreme demands for democratisation and still be able to defend themselves against their enemies, both internal and external. They were now riding the tiger, just as Kerensky had been.

As a result there was a flow of support to parties even more extreme than the Bolsheviks, parties which challenged what little order remained. This was particularly evident at Kronstadt, which had long been 'on the left flank of the great army of the Russian revolution', and where there was no effective right-wing threat to tie the left together. Combined Anarchist and S.R.-Maximalist strength increased in the soviet there from $2\frac{1}{2}$ per cent in August 1917 to 24 per cent in late January 1918, and to 28 per cent in April. A 'Helsingfors Federation of Anarchist-Communists' emerged and hoisted the black flag over the former Officers Club; one of their leaders was a rating named Krylov from the *Respublika*. Anarchists had a strong influence in the fourth and fifth sessions of Tsentrobalt, which met in the winter of 1917–18; the most prominent was Seaman 2nd Cl. Petr Skurikhin, an Anarchist-Communist from the 2nd Depot.[28]

Despite all these problems, the Bolsheviks kept their hold on the fleet. The delegations elected to the 3rd Congress of Soviets (10–18 January), in the middle of this period, show their continuing strength. It is true that of the three-man delegation chosen by the Kronstadt Soviet the Bolshevik (F. Kh. Pervushin) had fewer votes than the Left S.R. or the S.R.-Maximalist, and that the Helsingfors Soviet elected two Left S.R.s and two Bolsheviks (all sailors). But the Reval Soviet chose four Bolsheviks and one S.R. and, more important, of the six delegates sent directly by Tsentrobalt four were Bolsheviks. (A further eleven delegates were elected by individual bases, but their party allegiance is unknown.)[29]

These voting figures help to explain why the Bolsheviks were able to control events. For one thing, there was no effective political challenge. The only effective 'right-wing' force, the 'orthodox' S.R.s had no support in the Baltic, where nearly everyone accepted Soviet power. The ultra-left, the Anarchists and S.R.-Maximalists, were important at Kronstadt and nowhere else in the Baltic. They lacked nation-wide organisations and effective political centres; their combined delegate strength made up only 3 per cent of the 3rd Congress of Soviets.

The only possible alternative party were the Left S.R.s, and they were pledged to a policy of alliance with the Bolsheviks. In November and December a number of Left S.R.s entered the government (Prosh Prosh'ian became commissar for post and telegraph). The alliance, even in the fleet, was sometimes stormy. At Helsingfors there was a contretemps over the editorial board of the local *Izvestiia*. At Kronstadt the problem of electing a new chairman for the soviet revealed differences and provoked a condemnation of the Left S.R.s in *Golos pravdy*: 'We Bolsheviks,' wrote Petr Smirnov, 'have always considered the Left S.R.s the spokesmen of the psychology and interests of the petty bourgeosie, whose characteristic is a wavering and vague political line.' But the alliance held together, at least until the peace of Brest-Litovsk; even then there was no effective challenge locally, because the Bolsheviks and Left S.R.s had so many common enemies. From November to March the Bolsheviks and Left S.R.s *together* controlled the fleet. Many of the most important posts were held by the latter party; Nikolai Izmailov was effective head of the fleet from December to March, and he was succeeded as Main Commissar by Evgenny Blokhin.[30]

The Bolsheviks also prevailed, because they kept control of the 'commanding heights'. Lazar' Bregman was chairman of the Kronstadt Soviet even after Bolshevik support began to decline, Sheinman led the Helsingfors Soviet and Smilga the Finnish Regional Committee; the Bolsheviks Kingissepp and Anvel't led the 'E.C. of Soviets of the Estliand Region' and the Reval Soviet until February – when they left aboard the last ship. And more important, the Bolsheviks kept control of the 'centre', a strategic position which enabled them, when necessary, to appoint 'from above' and to over-ride the demands of the ultra-democratic left.

9 The Red Fleet: Organisation after October

What was the people's blood shed for if not for elected commanders?
Seaman 2nd Cl. Petr Skurikhin in Tsentrobalt, 18 February 1918

NAVAL REVOLUTION

The new rulers of Russia understood that to control something as complex as the navy it was essential – at least in the short term – to make use of some experienced senior officers. The first choice was none other than Kerensky's last Navy Minister, Admiral Verderevsky, who was regarded as a liberal. The admiral had been arrested at the Winter Palace, but on 27 October he was released from prison and returned to his duties. Verderevsky probably co-operated because he thought, like many others, that Soviet power would be very short-lived, but he resigned on 4 November rather than accept the Soviet-appointed Captain Ivanov as Assistant Minister.[1]

Modest Vasil'evich Ivanov was the most important naval officer to collaborate with the Soviet regime in its first days. A veteran of Port Arthur, Ivanov had commanded the cruiser *Diana* during the World War. He survived the Kronstadt massacre (he was there on leave), and in May the 2nd Cruiser Brigade elected him as commander. Discipline in this brigade was so lax that Lebedev was nearly lynched there at the end of July, and as a result Ivanov was dismissed. He returned, however, on his own initiative and with the support of his men. After the Bolshevik takeover he received a summons to the Smolny, where Lenin, himself, interviewed him on 1 November. Lenin asked if he was a socialist. 'Yes, I think so,' replied Ivanov, 'but, of course, not an important one. A "May Socialist".' The captain certainly found himself in uncharted waters, as he himself later recalled.

I am a naval officer who took part in all of Russia's wars. . . . I was never interested in politics. Because of my military upbringing and comparatively extensive combat experience I had a habit of looking down on all who were not part of naval life. For me Lenin, Trotsky, Kamenev were simply journalists, always writing something I could not understand (or, more correctly, was not interested in), somewhere abroad; they were civilians and therefore I involuntarily looked down on them.

Sitting in front of Lenin he involuntarily thought, 'Here am I, an old sailor. . . . what do I have in common with these journalist fellows'. But he agreed to serve the 'journalists', and on 4 November he was named Assistant Navy Minister and acting head of a 'Supreme Board (*kollegiia*) of the Navy Ministry'. When Verderevsky refused to accept Ivanov's appointment Sovnarkom ordered Ivanov to replace him; shortly afterwards Dybenko was put in general charge of the Navy, with Ivanov as Director (*Upravliaiushchii*) of the ministry.[2]

Why did such a senior officer collaborate with the Bolshevik state? In an open letter Ivanov described himself as a man 'who stands for popular sovereignty as represented by the committees'; he had taken his post because he hoped 'to find a common language between sailors and officers'. On 20 November he told a meeting of officers that he alone was defending the interests of the navy. The officers' attempt to remain in isolation, uncontaminated by the new regime, would lead to disaster: 'In the future structure of life you are dead men'. 'We cannot expect help from elsewhere. We must save the fleet ourselves.' But he was isolated, and most officers probably shared Timirev's opinion of him as 'unprincipled, ambitious in the extreme, and envious'.[3]

On 7 November Sovnarkom officially established the 'Supreme Naval Board', consisting of Dybenko, Ivanov, and a Black Sea sailor. The new structure was further developed by the '1st All-Russian Congress of the Sailors of the Navy' (18–25 November). At Dybenko's suggestion it chose the 'Naval Section of the C.E.C.' (also known as the 'Legislative Council of the Navy Department'), consisting of thirteen Bolsheviks and seven non-Bolsheviks. The Naval Section replaced the Admiralty Council as the navy's legislative body; it was also the direct descendent of Tsentroflot and of the Naval Revolutionary Committee (abolished by the congress). The executive of the Naval Section was the Supreme Board.[4]

A surprising final change at the centre was the enhanced power of the Naval General Staff. Captain E. A. Berens was elected Chief of N.G.S. in place of Count Kapnist. He had fought aboard the *Variag* at Chemulpo in 1904 and during the war was naval attaché in Rome (in 1906 he had been a member of the court which condemned the *Pamiat' Azova* mutineers, but perhaps this fact was not generally known in 1917). Fedor Raskol'nikov was made Berens's commissar, and under these two men the N.G.S. became more important than it had ever been before. An early Soviet source stated that 'the main working organ of Naval Administration and Command from the moment of the October Revolution was the Naval General Staff'. On 15 January 1918 Sovnarkom gave the N.G.S. direct control over naval operations.[5]

In the Baltic the Soviet *Gleichschaltung* proceeded more slowly. Neither the officers nor the committees were ready for drastic action. Razvozov, the C.-in-C., was reluctant to resign, although he had no sympathy with political extremism; in early December he rejected it with the following – rather naive – words:

> They want me to think like them, to believe in socialism, in their ideals. We don't even know what these are. Common dining rooms, common wives, common homes?! . . . I don't believe in this socialism which we have now. . . .

But in early November he still had hopes: 'No, we haven't hit bottom yet: we have all been waiting for something which is just about to happen – a little while longer and all this nonsense will be over [and] something acceptable will begin.' Throughout the month he was sustained by a belief that the Constituent Assembly, scheduled for the 28th, would restore order. In the meantime he refused to recognise Soviet power. Tsentrobalt, for its part, was reluctant to lose Razvozov. When he threatened to step down over the sending of the *Oleg* and *Pobeditel'* to Petrograd, Tsentrobalt refused to accept his resignation. 'The introduction of elective command is still at the preparatory stage,' reported Razvozov to the N.G.S. on 13 November, 'and evidently even Tsentrobalt does not imagine itself capable of the practical realisation of elective command.' But on the same day he began prefacing his printed orders with the phrase: 'In agreement with the Central Committee of the Baltic Fleet'. On 6 November Tsentrobalt resolved to order the C.-in-C. to recognise the charter adopted by the second fleet congress. Nothing happened at first, but on the 17th the committee, by electing an Executive Bureau to work with the Staff, took the first step towards the implementation of the charter.[6]

As soon as it had consolidated its position in Petrograd, the new regime decided to put the Baltic Fleet in order. On 19 November Modest Ivanov arrived at Helsingfors and hoisted his flag aboard the *Grazhdanin*. Razvozov, unwilling to recognise the new 'minister', refused to present himself. Both officers went to the yacht *Shtandart* to confer with Tsentrobalt. 'A meeting took place,' recalled Rengarten, 'highly painful and ridiculous in its contents, and coarse and stormy in form.' Although Tsentrobalt generally supported Ivanov, it decided to put off any decision until the following day.[7]

The next morning Ivanov again ordered the C.-in-C. to come to the *Grazhdanin*, and the Baltic admirals held a council of war. Some officers, like Rear-Admiral Zarubaev, still had hopes. Others favoured resignation. Bakhirev, the defender of Moon Sound, was typically outspoken about the new government and its agents: 'We don't recognise you, and that's that. Go to the devil.' (*Ne priznaem vas i – shabash. K chertovoi materi stupaite.*) Razvozov however finally decided to go to his Canossa and was just about to leave, when a cutter arrived with Ivanov aboard. All the officers retired to the *Krechet*'s wardroom, where they worked out a compromise, after Ivanov explained that he was not a member of the government. A statement was issued to the effect that the earlier disagreements had been based on a misunderstanding. At the Tsentrobalt meeting that afternoon, Ivanov supported Razvozov, and all the major commanders – except Captain A. A. Ruzhek, head of the minelayers – threatened to resign if their C.in-C. was dismissed. Despite bitter attacks by Izmailov and the Bolshevik Vasily Gnedin, Tsentrobalt resolved to keep the C.-in-C. pending the introduction of elective command. Ivanov and Razvozov kissed and shook hands amid wild applause.[8]

Foolishly, perhaps, Razvozov left the fleet at the end of November for a tour of inspection of the Gulf of Bothnia, and his enemies used his absence to stage a coup. Dybenko arrived on 3 December and told a meeting of ship committees that the Staff and the post of Commander-in-Chief had been abolished. Instead several officers would be invited to serve in Izmailov's Military Section. Izmailov then announced that Captain Ruzhek had been 'hired' as 'competent individual' to the Operations Section and that on 5 December the red flag was to be raised.[9]

This state of affairs was most unsatisfactory to the officer corps. On the night of 4 December 300 officers led by Graf held a protest meeting in the Officers Club and resolved that they would all resign if the new command system was introduced. The mood, as reported to Rengarten, was 'All for one, and one for all!' The meeting was enlivened by the appearance of Izmailov, 'the insolent stupid commissar bluejacket' as Graf later described him, with two other comrades. The officers laughed – unwisely – at their appeals. Izmailov had the last laugh. He called a meeting of all officers in the Mariia Palace on the following afternoon and broke their united front. When a final meeting was held in the Officers Club on the 6th, the officers rejected the resolution of Graf's meeting by a vote of 557 to 151 (44 abstentions). They decided that they wanted Razvozov kept on, but that if he went they would merely reserve their 'freedom of action'. 'Thus,' lamented Rengarten, 'the whole edifice of the officers' unanimity collapsed.'[10]

This was really the end of the old Baltic Fleet. Some officers from the Staff attempted a 'strike', based on the resolution of 4 December, but without success. Many officers decided to leave with Razvozov, including Bakhirev, Timirev, and Graf. The action of Timirev, now the commander of the 1st Cruiser Brigade, was probably typical. Ignoring Ruzhek, he took his brigade to its winter station at Reval, and by 15 January received permission to retire – without pension rights.[11]

Several factors lay behind the final defeat of the officer corps. According to Cromie fear weighed heavily on Razvozov's mind; 'He is of the opinion that the men are quite mad, and the slightest spark will start a conflagration'. The postponement of the Constituent Assembly showed that it was a weak reed to lean on. The officers lacked the will, organisation, and solidarity to withhold their labour. Rengarten summed up the motivations of those who elected to work under the new system: 'it is a question of conviction, on the one hand, and consciousness of their weakness (responsibilities to their families, unsuitability for other work, etc.)'.[12]

SOVIETISATION

By the beginning of December both the central naval administration and the Baltic Fleet command were controlled by the Soviet government. The next step was the satisfaction of the pent-up demands of the lower deck. The armistice signed in December encouraged these demands. 'The war is ending,' wrote one officer. 'The closeness of peace can be felt in the air. New interests of peacetime replace the wartime interests with which the country has lived since the outbreak [of war]'.[13]

One attempt to work out the new naval system took the form of the 'All-Russian Naval Conference', which convened on 29 December. But this asked for too much and claimed excessive power for itself, and on 21 January the exasperated Naval Section gave it five days to disperse. The delegates agreed, but only after protesting that 'in this intrusion we see an encroachment on [the rights of] the representatives of the toiling people'. The obvious body to work out the new regulations was the navy's legislative organ, the Naval Section itself. But it was too large for efficient work, and by late January it was actually struggling for power with Dybenko's Supreme Board. The Board won, because in a sweeping reorganisation the Naval Section was abolished.[14]

A decree of 30 January gave sole control over the 'People's Commissariat for Naval Affairs' to the 'Board of the People's Commissariat for Naval Affairs' formerly the Supreme Naval Board. The Board now consisted of three Bolsheviks – Dybenko, Vakhrameev, and Raskol'nikov – and a merchant navy officer from the Black Sea. (Ivanov was removed; his new – and minor – responsibility was the liquidation of the navy's foreign contracts.)[15] The transformation of the navy was being undertaken not by a democratic congress nor by a large 1917-style committee, but by a small Bolshevik-dominated board.

What kind of fleet would the Board control? One answer had been provided in 'Regulations on the Democratisation of the Navy' issued on 8 January by Dybenko and Ivanov. The Regulations were the high-water mark of naval democracy; they ended all ranks and gave to every 'fleet serviceman' the title of 'seaman (*moriak*) of the Red Fleet of the Russian Republic'. Among the 'seamen', the 'command staff' (*komandnyi sostav*), were to manage the operational and technical spheres. The command staff and the committees elected by the 'non-command staff' (*nekomandnyi sostav*) were to share in the general administration of the unit, but the committees alone had the power to make political decisions. The decree provided a method of election for various levels of command staff from a ship's specialist (e.g. the gunnery 'officer') to the 'Chief of the Naval Section of the [Fleet] Central Committee' (i.e. the *de facto* C.-in-C.). Ships' officers were elected by the crew, 'flagmen' (*flagmany*) by the committees and commanders of the units under them (for example, the commander of the Destroyer Division would be elected by his flotilla commanders and flotilla committees). And a commander could be subject to 'recall' (*otvod*) if one-third of his electors raised a challenge and two-thirds approved this challenge.[16]

The regulations were not quite as extreme as they seemed. The re-election of the present command staff, for example, was to be carried out passively through challenges rather than through a general election. (The grounds for this were that the command staff were already, *de facto*, elected.) And election and recall were indirect, through committees, except at ship level. Nomination came from above. The fleet committee, moreover, had to approve all elections from the level of an assistant commander of a ship (i.e. the first officer). And the Supreme Board had to approve the election of the Chief of the Naval Section; in six weeks' time this was to prove directly relevant to the Baltic.

The 'Decree on the Organisation of the Workers' and Peasants' Red Fleet', in retrospect a document of greater importance, was issued by Sovnarkom on 29 January: 'The Navy, which is [now] based on general military conscription under tsarist laws, is declared dissolved and a Socialist Workers' and Peasants' Red Navy is organised'. The essence of the decree was worked out by a commission which Tsentrobalt had created on 9 January; in charge was former Sr Lieutenant K. I. Vasilevsky. The growing demands of the lower deck accelerated the commission's work, and a project was completed on the 25th. Sovnarkom issued it in a somewhat modified form. There were four parts: general regulations, a copy of an application form, a draft contract and a table of pay-rates.[17]

The regulations stipulated that each ship would control the intake of its own personnel. Volunteers would sign a contract binding themselves to a certain term of service, and contract-breakers and deserters would be punished (another version of the contract stipulated imprisonment for up to five years). There was a significant difference between the Tsentrobalt project and the final decree as to the nature of service; the navy was to be organised not on a 'free-hire' (*vol'nonaemnyi*) basis but on a 'volunteer' (*dobrovol'cheskii*) one. The former term had been used in the old navy for civilians hired on a contract basis, and it was not rigorous enough.[18] Supply was also decentralised; it was to be handled on a local basis, through co-operatives. This was presumably due to a breakdown of the conventional supply organs and a lingering distrust of dishonest supply officers.

Pay, probably the most important point, was to range from 955r. a month for the Chief of the N.G.S. to 180r. for a new recruit; an ordinary sailor was to be paid 210r. All personnel received an extra cost-of-living 'regulator' of 160r. On the surface, this was very generous. The last rise, on 6 June 1917, had created a pay scale for qualified seamen ranging from 85r to 30r; the new scale for non-command staff ran from 420r. to 370r. (including the 'regulator'). But this increase of from 494 to 1233 per cent meant little, given the runaway inflation. And pay was in rubles, which were worth very little in Finland; the sailors there had asked for Finnish marks.

Tsentrobalt grudgingly accepted Sovnarkom's version of the decree, but many sailors were unsatisfied. The 4th Submarine Flotilla resolved that no one wanted to stay on under the new regulations, due to the 'unclarity of the decree and the low pay'. Graf recalled that the project worked out by the Bolshevik 'sages' was completely unrealistic – they simply did not have enough money. It would in fact appear that many sailors were not paid at all in February and March.[19]

The original task of the Vasilevsky commission, as Tsentrobalt saw it, had been 'to keep the largest possible number of experienced seamen in the fleet'. But half the fleet had left by the time the decree was issued, and the other half did not think much of it, so a drastic reduction of the fleet's strength had to be accepted. On 31 January Dybenko and the Board divided the ships of the Baltic Fleet into three categories. Category I, including the dreadnoughts and 'Noviks', was to be kept in service, while ships in Categories II and III were to be put into reserve or storage. Furthermore, Tsentrobalt announced that all training units were to be disbanded by 15 April.[20]

SOVKOMBALT

Legislation could do little to help the Baltic Fleet, where things were getting worse and worse. There were demands for leave and immediate demobilisation. Many ratings simply deserted or overstayed their leave. The food shortage was such that in the middle of November Tsentrobalt sent a threatening message to Kronstadt demanding flour. There were not enough uniforms. Cash was in short supply; on 24 January Tsentrobalt announced that it needed 215 million rubles for expenses from November to February: 'If the money has not been delivered by 10 February [23 February, n.s.] Tsentrobalt will be forced to issue an order disbanding the fleet and, as a result, surrendering its responsibilities'. It was at about this time that the chairman of Tsentrobalt approached the British naval attaché with the proposal that he should finance the fleet (the Foreign Office rejected the idea).[21] Tsentrobalt could not even be sure of the obedience of its own electors. To reduce coal and food consumption it had decided to send four of the oldest and least valuable ships – the *Grazhdanin, Avrora, Diana* and *Rossiia* – back to Kronstadt, where supply was better. The order was given on 15 December, but all the crews, except that of the *Avrora*, refused to carry it out; a general meeting was required to convince them. Even then the ships did not arrive at Kronstadt until the 27th, after which the *Avrora* and *Diana* went on to Petrograd against orders.[22]

Tsentrobalt itself was changing. As early as the beginning of November Razvozov had said that the presence of 15 anarchists in the C.C.B.F. showed that the Bolsheviks were losing their grip. By mid-November the fourth session had ceased to be a docile supporter of the new government, and this was even more true of the fifth and final session, which lasted six weeks (15 January to 4 March). At its first meeting the fifth session voted nearly unanimously to remove Dybenko as the Baltic representative on the Supreme Board. The immediate cause was the refusal of the People's Commissar to come to Helsingfors and account for his actions. Vasily Marusev, Aleksei Baranov, Andrei Shtarev, and Vladimir Polukhin, all important fleet activists (and all except Shtarev Bolsheviks), had complained about Dybenko's dictatorial attitude. 'He sat like a lord and smoked a cigarette and paid little attention to them,' reported one sailor who went with a delegation to see him in January. Another issue was Dybenko's inability to supply the fleet with revolvers. They had been requested as early as 1 November, and on 11 January the fourth session presented an ultimatum. In any event Dybenko arrived in Helsingfors on 19 January, with the help of Raskol'nikov satisfactorily explained his actions, and received a vote of confidence from Tsentrobalt.[23] But the affair must have made it clear that the fleet's central committee, in addition to being unable to cope with the serious problems, was also too independently-minded.

The Bolsheviks found an alternative to Tsentrobalt in the form of its Military Section. The chairman of Vobalt, Nikolai Izmailov, was to be the central personality in the fleet from the beginning of December – when he engineered the overthrow of Razvozov and began to oversee the day-to-day running of the fleet – until the beginning of March. Izmailov, a 25-year-old diver from the Kronstadt training ship *Afrika*, had been a delegate to the Kronstadt Soviet before coming to Tsentrobalt. As the eldest son of a village carpenter from Penza Province, it was not surprising that he gravitated towards the Socialist-Revolutionaries; he was to remain a Left S.R. until the summer of 1918. Izmailov was not by nature a diplomatic person; Dybenko described him as 'strong, although sometimes excessively sharp and hot-tempered'. He was temporarily suspended from Tsentrobalt in September for striking one of the moderate delegates in the face. Nevertheless, Izmailov's forceful character must have seemed to the Soviet government just what was needed to bring the Baltic Fleet under control.[24]

Aleksandr Antonovich Ruzhek, Razvozov's successor and the 'senior officer' from December to March, was no rival to Izmailov. He was the least qualified of the Baltic commanders; February 1917 had found him in command of ten obsolete destroyer-minesweepers. He was more passive than his predecessor or his successors. Graf described Izmailov's attitude: 'He simply slighted his assistant "Comrade Ruzhek", despite the fact that the latter cringed and fawned before him in every possible way.'[25]

On 30 January the Supreme Board assigned five commissars to run the Baltic Fleet: Izmailov, E. S. Blokhin, A. S. Shtarev, A. N. Kabanov, and V. Dolgov. All these men were veterans of Tsentrobalt, none of them were Bolsheviks. Six days later, on 18 February (n.s.) Sovnarkom confirmed the appointment of Izmailov as 'commissar of the Baltic Fleet' and of Blokhin, Shtarev, and the Left S.R. P. I. Shishko as his assistants (Kabanov and Dolgov were dropped).[26]

Many people saw this as a violation of popular sovereignty. Seaman 2nd Cl. P. M. Skurikhin, an Anarchist-Communist, put this clearly to Tsentrobalt on 14 February:

> From yesterday's teletype message I understood that we are now to consider ourselves dissolved and [that] commissars have already been assigned in our place. We have nothing against personalities, but we oppose the principle of assignment. . . . For my part, I consider that there must be no assignment and that the central organ of the Baltic Sea must exist as before. I consider that no one can dissolve this organ, since the masses created it and the masses can dissolve it.

Four days later he spoke in reply to the Bolshevik Kamashko: 'Kamashko passionately defended the assignment of commissars from above. What was the people's blood shed for if not for elected commanders?' The crew of the *Petropavlovsk* passed a resolution condemning Blokhin, who was their Tsentrobalt deputy. On 14 February (1 February, o.s.) by a vote of 20 to 1 (7 abstentions), Tsentrobalt dismissed Izmailov and Blokhin 'for exceeding their authority' and ordered them arrested. The two commissars had a 'fighting squad' at their disposal, however, and it proved physically impossible to hold them.[27]

The opponents of Tsentrobalt also had persuasive arguments. Eight days before their appointments, Izmailov and Blokhin had reported to the Supreme Board that Tsentrobalt was 'an institution which, given the transition to a volunteer basis, is completely unnecessary and which is an unnecessary drain on the state treasury'. The report also demanded an increase in discipline, which was to be enforced by a proposed 'Military Board':

> 8. All command staff and crews on ships are strictly and unquestioningly to subordinate themselves to the Military Board, which must act in the interest of the Russian Republic.

9 The non-execution of orders will incur trial or punishment, imposed by the Military Board at its discretion.

10. The Military Board works out a scheme of duty and practical exercises for the fleet which all seamen of the free fleet of the Russian Republic must strictly obey.

11. No orders of the Military Board of the Baltic Fleet are subject to discussion by the crews.

'Only with such an administration of the fleet,' declared Vobalt, 'is it possible to preserve its battle-readiness and its ability to defend the interests of the Russian Republic and of the revolution.'[28]

Izmailov made more specific criticisms in a speech to Tsentrobalt on 31 January:

We see how 150 ships burn coal to no purpose and waste the people's money for nothing, and [Tsentrobalt] pays for requisitioned ships [?colliers], which we are now getting rid of. And if Razvozov were still here he would even now be paying the money. It is we [presumably Vobalt] who stopped the construction of concrete fortifications which were built and then blown up. The Council of Twenty [i.e. the Naval Section] had to dissolve itself because there was only squabbling there and little work and there is no need to discuss why we who sit in one place for thirty minutes cannot really be in charge. And I consider that we must dissolve ourselves and that the sections must remain and continue to work and take charge. We can see what the administration of Tsentrobalt has led us to.

Blokhin supported Izmailov, as Tsentrobalt's minutes show:

Comrade Blokhin says that things can't go on the way they have been, when all orders are debated and rejected and resolutions are introduced: 'If [we] issue an order to a ship it accepts it if it likes it; if it doesn't like it [the ship] recalls its representative. Enough of words. We must get down to business. Enough of elected organisations. We must dissolve ourselves.'[29]

The point of view of the government was put most clearly by Aleksandra Kollontai, who was a member of Sovnarkom and very close to Dybenko. She attended the Tsentrobalt meeting on 19 February and gave it her conclusions:

From all the speeches I have heard I can only conclude that some kind of dark forces are working behind you, which are trying to split the masses and to undermine both your authority and that of the Council of People's Commissars.

Now you don't want to recognise the commissars who have been assigned. But the old fleet is now liquidating itself and giving way to the new socialist fleet, and therefore your organ is now only a liquidator. A new elected organ will be created when the ships have been manned, but in the interim period responsible individuals are needed. [The] C[ouncil] [of] P[eople's] C[ommissars] has assigned commissars, but you won't recognise them and thus [you] undermine the people's organisations. They say here that the revolution must be [further] developed, but I think that the time has come to fortify what we have already won.[30]

The 'appointees' finally prevailed. Probably the threatening international situation helped: on 16 February the Germans announced their plans to launch a new offensive, and two days later they attacked. Tsentrobalt had, on the 14th, set up its own commissions to run the fleet, but five days later it agreed to give up its powers to the commissars – if the fleet approved of them; at the same time it protested at the methods used by Sovnarkom. Izmailov, 'Main Commissar of the Baltic Fleet', and Ruzhek, 'Chief of the Naval Section', announced on the 22nd that two days earlier they had taken over the administration of the fleet. Then, on 1 March, Tsentrobalt *denied* that it had dissolved itself and resolved moreover not to do so until a central committee was no longer necessary. 'You created Tsentrobalt,' it announced to the fleet, 'and you alone can dissolve it.' Nevertheless on 4 March, the day after the signing of the Peace of Brest-Litovsk, Izmailov informed the committee that he had taken over on the previous day; he gave it three days to remove itself from the *Shtandart* and elsewhere. Tsentrobalt capitulated. A plenary meeting of ship committees was held on the 6th, and it agreed to the dissolution.[31]

Tsentrobalt's replacement was the 'Council of Commissars of the Baltic Fleet', or *Sovkombalt*, which comprised the nominees of the Naval Board plus one sailor from each of the six battleships. The stress on the battleships rather than the light forces came because the former were seen as more reliable. I. M. Ludri, a prominent naval commander between the wars, stated that 'the most revolutionary were the heavy (capital) ships; one could also say that they were the best organised and best disciplined, especially in the period after October'. The new regime, as Ludri put it, was 'the original dictatorship of the heavy ships'.[32]

The confusion did not end with Tsentrobalt. On 12 March, eight days after the founding of the Council of Commissars, something really remarkable took place. Aleksandr Razvozov, the C.-in-C. who had been sacked on 5 December, was elected to be Chief of Vobalt 'by a huge majority' at a meeting of all ship committees, the Local Naval Committee, Sovkombalt, and the former officers. Elective command had finally been instituted.

The causes of Razvozov's election were related to the war with Germany. Izmailov had left the fleet, probably because he disagreed with the Soviet capitulation.[33] Dybenko had been dismissed as People's Commissar for his actions in the last days of the war. And the fleet itself faced its greatest danger since 1914. At the end of February the 1st Cruiser Brigade and other ships had arrived in Helsingfors with 4,000 refugees after Estonia was overrun by the Germans. The danger in Finland seemed equally serious; civil war was raging, and the Swedes and Germans had landed in the Aland Islands. The decision to start evacuating the fleet to Kronstadt through the ice was what really brought home the gravity of the situation. On 12 March four dreadnoughts and three cruisers, 'reliable' heavy ships, left Helsingfors for Kronstadt; that same day Razvozov was put in charge of the ships that remained. It was probably important that Razvozov was a former destroyer officer; the largest group of ships in Helsingfors was now the Destroyer Division, and Graf said that this division took the initiative in the admiral's election. The increased specific weight of the smaller ships also explains the broadening of Sovkombalt on the 12th to include ten of their representatives.[34]

Sovkombalt tried to justify the handing over of power to one man, and a former admiral at that: 'This is, of course, a step back for the revolution, but the moment and the masses demand it, since the Germans will take no account of democratic organisations'. One writer used an historical analogy; he compared Razvozov to Riurik, who was summoned by the inhabitants of 9th-century Russia to restore order to their land. It was not only the committees that needed a crisis to convince them. Razvozov, reported Cromie, had refused to take command in February, but he 'accepted during the Helsingfors panic, when the Huns took the Alands, on condition that he had absolute power'.[35]

The Riurik of the Baltic Fleet lasted only a week. Fedor Raskol'nikov came out from Petrograd and arrested Razvozov when he refused to recognise Soviet power (the admiral had assumed command on the condition that he did not have to recognise the Soviet regime). According to Graf, Razvozov was immediately released at the demand of the crews, and Raskol'nikov then called a meeting of men hostile to Razvozov and deposed him. In any event, the Board of the naval commissariat issued the following order on the 20th:

> Military Seaman Razvozov is removed from his post and retired from service for unwillingness to consider himself bound by the decrees of the Council of People's Commissars and for refusal to subordinate himself to the Board of the Naval Commissariat.

Reaction was mixed. The crew of the *Respublika* accused 'citizen Razvozov and his associates' of 'spitting in the face of democracy' by proposing to exchange the St Andrew's flag for the Red flag. But other sailors tried to arrest Raskol'nikov![36]

In the end Sovkombalt elected a replacement but Blokhin, speaking at a meeting on the 23rd, still insisted on the right of the fleet to choose its own commander:

> if the instructions don't suit us, then we will make corrections and forward them to the naval board for confirmation; if the naval board will not confirm them, then we will send them to the Council of People's Commissars; [and] if it doesn't get through there, then the Council of Commissars [of the Baltic Fleet] will choose a commander itself, give him authority, and work with such a person.

On the 25th Sovkombalt, claiming to speak for the 'broad sailor masses', again protested against Razvozov's dismissal and arrest.[37]

The government's opposition was to Razvozov as an individual. It accepted the election on 22 March of ex-Captain A. M. Shchastny, in conditions similar to the election of his predecessor. Sovnarkom issued a 'Provisional Statement on the Administration of the Baltic Fleet' on 29 March. Power was entrusted to a diarchy of the 'Chief of Naval Forces' and the 'Main Commissar'. The former was to have 'full responsibility' for operations and their preparation. The latter was to be the head of political and social activities. Both were to have advisers, in the first case the 'Council of Flagmen' and in the second Sovkombalt. Both were (in principle) appointed from the centre rather than elected, so the principle of electivity had once again been rejected. In an interview he gave in early April Trotsky, now People's Commissar for Military and Naval Affairs, explained what lay behind this change: 'The sailors themselves insisted on the necessity of enlisting a specialist and giving him the widest powers'. The change, he insisted, was not opposed by the government, for 'the experience of democratic self-administration shows us the necessity of appointing to executive positions people with special knowledge and with special experience [and of] giving these people the necessary power'.[38]

10 The Ice Crossing: Operations After October

Russia will either transfer her warships to Russian ports and keep them there until the conclusion of a general peace, or disarm them immediately.

Treaty of Brest-Litovsk

INVASION

The war at sea was on a limited scale after Moon Sound. In mid-October the Germans sent a dreadnought and a cruiser to shell the 12th Army's coastal flank from the Gulf of Riga, but this was only a demonstration. Admiral Schmidt's Task Force was disbanded on 21 October and his ships sent to the North Sea. The Russians for their part kept up a few patrols (losing the destroyer *Bditel'ny* in the process), but by mid-December the Baltic Fleet was frozen into its bases.[1] As part of the armistice of 5 December a demarcation line was drawn across the Baltic from Sweden to Vorms Island; on the German side were Ezel', Dago, Moon, and the western half of the Gulf of Riga.

The peace talks began amicably enough, but on 5 January the Germans demanded territory as far east as their troops had then advanced. This would have meant the loss of the Baltic islands, but the rest of Estonia would have been left in Soviet hands. The Bolshevik leaders, however, disagreed over whether or not to accept the terms and approved Trotsky's famous formula of 'Neither war nor peace'. The Russian delegation walked out of the talks on 28 January; the Central Powers were told that Russia was leaving the war, demobilising her army, *and* refusing to sign a peace treaty. The Soviet Main C.-in-C. made the following announcement on the 29th: 'Peace. The War is over. Russia fights no more. The cursed war is over. . . . The demobilisation of the present army is announced.'[2] Unfortunately the Germans were not impressed, and at mid-day on 18 February (5 February, o.s.) they launched a general offensive.

The first major political debate since the October Revolution began. The 'right' now urged acceptance of the German terms. The 'left' advocated revolutionary war; this group included the Left S.R.s as well as a number of those on the left of the Bolsheviks, the 'Left Communists'. Both sides had their supporters in the Baltic. The Anarchist-Communist *Vol'nyi Kronshtadt* had even opposed the initial talks with the Germans. On 30 January the Kronstadt Soviet welcomed the decision to break off negotiations, and on 21 February (8 February, o.s.), a coalition of S.R.-Maximalists and Anarchists, supported by the Left S.R.s., defeated the Bolsheviks by a vote of 95 to 65 (13 abstentions) on the issue of peace. The Kronstadt Soviet, it was resolved,

> categorically states that revolutionary Soviet Russia cannot conclude peace and make any sort of compromise with the imperialists of either Austria–Hungary and Germany or with the Anglo-French and others. The only path for revolutionary toiling Russia is armed uprising against the oppressors.

(The unsuccessful Bolshevik resolution said that 'at such a dangerous moment it is necessary to use all measures which can put a limit to the offensive of the German army'.)[3]

Helsingfors was more cautious, despite some heavy-weight support for revolutionary war. On 24 February, at a plenary meeting of the democratic organisations, the sailor Pavel Shishko, a founder-member of the Left S.R. C.C., rejected any compromise: 'Let the Germans go where they want, the revolution in the West will save us; but let our socialist revolution remain pure and unsullied.' More surprising was the personal intervention of the People's Commissar for Naval Affairs: 'Dybenko in his speech expressed a protest against the conclusion of a separate obscene peace, which would enslave Russia for long years in the claws of a rapacious Germany.' But the combination of Left S.R. and left Communist made little impression. The meeting voted for peace by 157 to 18 (30 abstentions).[4]

The advocates of revolutionary war were soon to have a chance to prove themselves. The first threat emerged before 18 February, on the 14th, when Swedish troops landed in the Aland Islands. The landing made the government much more conscious of the danger from the sea, and on the 15th Dybenko explained the naval situation to Sovnarkom. This produced results of a kind. Sovnarkom issued a general order for the dreadnoughts and 'Noviks' to defend the Central Position and for the older ships to be withdrawn to Kronstadt and Petrograd. Dybenko sent a signal to Vobalt enquiring how the evacuation was progressing and 'whether it is possible to count on some significant part of the fleet being ready at any given moment to proceed to the Central Position and defend it in the event of an attack by the German fleet'. And Lenin himself had a conversation by Hughes machine with Tsentrobalt regarding the Aland landing:

What measures of defence and repression have been taken by
Tsentrobalt? . . . We are extremely anxious. We will not permit the
thought that Tsentrobalt and our revolutionary fleet were inactive.
Await answer. Lenin.[5]

The response was not encouraging. Tsentrobalt did issue the order,
'Prepare ships for battle with the enemies of labour and freedom', but the
reply of Vobalt to Dybenko's enquiry was negative: 'Neither the fleet nor
individual ships are able to go to the Central Position, as the fleet is in the
process of transition to free-hire manning [announced four days pre-
viously] and the ships of the active fleet are refitting'. A supplementary
reply held the order to defend the Central Position to be 'in complete
contradiction to the announcement of the Brest peace delegation on the
end of the war, and to the transfer of the fleet to [a] free-hire [basis]'.
Discipline at Abo was so poor that the ships there could not be used against
the Swedes in the Aland Islands. A shipload of Finnish Red Guards was
sent, and thåt was all. Within a few days the islands were officially given
up. [6]

Estonia was invaded on 18 February. The E.C. of the Estliand Region
had declared that 'German *junkers* and other predators' would 'find behind
every bush, behind every hill, armed workers, agricultural labourers,
landless peasants . . . ready to lay down their lives for the real liberty,
equality, and fraternity of the toilers'. In reality the German 8th Army
advanced very quickly. Northern Estonia was over-run by von
Seckendorff's 'Northern Corps', a motley force from Ezel' and Dago.
Despite a few skirmishes with sailors and Red Guards, the chief obstacle
turned out to be the deep snow. Special spearhead detachments were sent
ahead, and by the 23rd these were on the outskirts of Reval.[7]

The old Northern Front had evaporated, and the few remaining Soviet
troops had no idea where the Germans were. It had been hoped to form
naval partisan detachments, but many sailors fled to Petrograd. The Red
high command was under no illusions about the chances of defending
Reval. The Northern Front simply ordered that the town should be held
long enough to secure the withdrawal of the forward troops. Krylenko (the
Main C.-in-C.) and the Board of the naval commissariat both ordered the
withdrawal of the fleet. On 23 February the C.E.C. accepted the German
terms of the 21st ('Livonia and Estonia are to be immediately cleared of
Russian forces and of the Red Guard and they are to be occupied by
German policing forces as long as the local authorities are not in a position
to guarantee calm and as long as order has not been restored'); with this
Soviet Russia was obliged to give up Reval.

The authorities on the spot gave contradictory orders and aggravated an
already confused situation. Izmailov, Main Commissar of the Baltic Fleet
and a Left S.R., ordered Reval to hold out at any cost and promised 5,000

sailors as reinforcements. The E.C. of the Estliand Region, its back to the wall, forbade evacuation. By the time it became clear to everyone that the town could not hold out, it was too late to evacuate men and stores by railway. As there was no money, the dockers refused to load ships, and they even went so far as to arrest the Port Commander. The situation on the 24th was described in a signal by the local commander, former Captain B. B. Zherve:

> There are no organised armed forces in the town, armed people are engaged in looting in the port and in the warehouses. There is no information about the enemy.

> There is absolutely no authority in the town since the Soviet of Deputies and the [Estliand] Regional [Executive] Committee have dissolved themselves.

As if all this was not enough, the Estonian nationalists went into action, and on the night of 24–25 February their 'Liberation Committee' in Reval declared Estonia an independent republic. The last ship, the *Admiral Makarov*, left at midday on the 25th, after German cyclists had entered the town. The German historian of the campaign described how 'amidst the jubilation of the population, who sang "*Es braust ein Ruf wie Donnerhall*" and heartily cheered His Majesty, the German Kaiser, the commander of the Northern Corps entered the city' (this was, one presumes, the German population). The warehouses and many of the coastal batteries had not been destroyed; von Seckendorff captured a wealth of equipment, including 626 guns, 251 of them heavy.[8]

It had at first been hoped to hold the southern flank of the Central Position, the navy-manned heavy batteries on Vul'f Island. Had Vul'f been held, and had the Red Finns won their civil war, it might have been possible to prevent an enemy breakthrough into the eastern Baltic. In fact, the mood of the demobilised and unpaid sailor-gunners was such that the batteries had to be abandoned.[9]

But on the positive side, 5 cruisers, 8 submarines, 12 minesweepers, and 31 auxiliaries escaped with the aid of the *Ermak* and 4 smaller ice-breakers; they carried 4,000 refugees and some stores. It was a difficult task, as the ice was very thick and the cruisers retained only a third of their original complements. But only one vessel, the submarine *Edinorog*, was lost.[10]

Since the weather, internal disorganisation, demobilisation, and refits made the fleet useless for defending the Central Position, all that the Baltic sailors could do in this short Soviet – German war was to fight as 'partisans'. On 23 February the C.E.C. had agreed to evacuate Estonia, but there were those who did not accept such a peace. Among them was Pavel Dybenko, who had formed a detachment of sailors and placed them at the disposal of the 'Extraordinary Staff for the Defence of Petrograd'. The Staff sent him to the most threatened area, the Narova River, which was the natural defence line for Petrograd, and the border between Estonia and Russia proper. Meanwhile Dybenko and other leaders of the fleet had, evidently on their own initiative, worked out a plan for a counter-offensive into the territory given up to Germany. Dybenko was to advance along the railway *beyond* the Narova and, with the support of the Helsingfors-based *Respublika*, recapture Reval. Raskol'nikov, the Assistant People's Commissar and another opponent of the peace terms, ordered Izmailov to send the battleship to Reval with 1,000 men. In fact, the Baltic Fleet command decided to send both the *Respublika* and the *Riurik*, but on the morning of 2 March the crew of the *Riurik* refused to move; so neither ship sailed. (It was also claimed later that Dybenko had failed to send a prearranged signal to Helsingfors.)[11]

In any event Dybenko had his hands full. German flying columns advanced along the Estonian railways, and by Thursday 28 February they were just outside the border town of Narva. Dybenko, with 1,600 sailors and Red Guards, reached the town on Friday evening. West of Narva his forces collided with the Germans, and at midway on Saturday Dybenko and his staff fled back through Narva in panic. They only stopped at the next major town, Iamburg. Dybenko refused the order of the local commander, former General Parsky, to go back and secure Narva. The town was captured undamaged on Sunday. Even worse, on Tuesday the sailors decided to move on to Gatchina, and this forced Parsky to leave Iamburg. Although Dybenko and his men returned on Thursday morning, Petrograd ordered them to the rear; Parsky had announced that only with the *removal* of the rowdy sailors could he secure his sector. Dybenko for his part sent a sarcastic signal: 'Command of the Detachment has been transferred to His Excellency, General Parsky'.[12]

Dybenko was removed from his post as People's Commissar, and in May he was tried by the Moscow Revolutionary Tribunal. The defence, led by the Left S.R. Shteinberg, alleged that 'the trial was staged because Dybenko had become dangerous and he had to be removed'. In the end Dybenko was acquitted of the charge of misconduct. He did however lose his position among the leaders of the new Russia.[13]

The attempt at a 'revolutionary defence' of Estonia was a farce. During the two-week campaign the Germans captured 17,000 Russians and 1,500 guns; they lost 20 dead and 89 wounded.[14]

The Soviet government signed the humiliating peace of Brest-Litovsk on 3 March. The treaty involved massive territorial concessions and, more relevant to this study, it completely destroyed what was left of the Russian position in the Baltic. Article V, demobilising the army, stated that 'Russia will either transfer her warships to Russian ports and keep them there until the conclusion of a general peace, or disarm them immediately'. Article VI stipulated, in addition to the Russian evacuation of Estonia and other places, that

> Finland and the Aland Islands will also immediately be cleared of Russian troops and the Russian Red Guard, and the Finnish ports of the Russian fleet and of Russian naval forces. So long as the ice makes impossible the transfer of warships to Russian ports, only limited forces will remain on board them.

The capitulation did not completely still the adherents of revolutionary war. 'Revolutionary spirit is created by struggle,' argued the Left S.R. rating Aleksandr Brushvit at Kronstadt. Iarchuk called the Bolsheviks 'liquidators' and the treaty a 'death sentence'. But despite these arguments the Kronstadt Soviet voted to approve peace by a vote of 101 to 58 (26 abstentions). Everyone could see, as Artemy Liubovich put it to the Kronstadt Soviet, that the 'objective conditions' did not favour revolutionary war.[15] At Kronstadt the masses 'voted with their feet', fleeing in large numbers when the Germans attacked. The same was true at Reval and Helsingfors. The extreme left lacked the mass support required for revolutionary war. The task now was simply to save what could be saved.

EXODUS

As early as 27 January former General M. D. Bonch-Bruevich, the chief of staff to the Main C.-in-C., had complained of the poor leadership of the Finnish Regional Committee: 'In general it is necessary to recognise that the Sveaborg Fortress . . . may soon lose its significance, and the fleet will be isolated'.[16] This may have contributed, with the Swedish landing in the Aland Islands and the danger of war with Germany, to Sovnarkom's review of naval policy and to the Board's order of 17 February to Vobalt on the evacuation of the less important ships.

The evacuation, known as the 'Ice Crossing', was actually carried out in exactly the opposite way, between 12 March and 11 April, with the most valuable ships leaving first. Even while the verbal battle over the appointed commissars was raging in Tsentrobalt, Ruzhek (the *de facto* C.-in-C.) contradicted Dybenko by ordering the evacuation of the four dreadnoughts first. Ruzhek resigned when a plenary meeting overturned this plan, but Tsentrobalt was won over, the plan was accepted. Confirmatory orders arrived from the N.G.S. in Petrograd on 2 March: 'Transfer to . . . Kronstadt that part of the ships which is still able to go to sea and which, given the state of the ice, can be transferred there, i.e. the 1st and 2nd Battleship Brigades and, perhaps, the cruisers'. Despite a resolution by a plenary session that two dreadnoughts should stay behind to protect the small ships, all four were included in the first detachment, which left Helsingfors on the 12th.[17]

In overall command was former Rear-Admiral Zarubaev, commander of the dreadnought brigade. His convoy, aided by two large ice-breakers, consisted of the best ships in the active fleet: the four dreadnoughts and the cruisers *Riurik, Admiral Makarov,* and *Bogatyr'*.

Thick ice blocked the 180 miles between Helsingfors and Kronstadt. The Russian navy had some experience of movement through the ice, but with several ice-breakers to each ship (e.g. two ice-breakers led the *Riurik* from Kronstadt to Reval in January 1917); in the crisis of 1917–18 some specialists suggested that the big ships could only be moved one at a time. The first detachment had to stop each evening as darkness approached, and each night the column became frozen into the ice. But in the morning the ice-breakers broke the ships out, and the journey was made without losses. The convoy arrived at Kronstadt on 17 March.[18]

Ten days after the first detachment left, Aleksei Mikhailovich Shchastny was elected to command the fleet. Shchastny was only 37 and during the war had reached the rank of captain. He had been first officer of the *Poltava* and then captain of the destroyer *Pogranichnik,* before joining the Baltic Staff in the Maksimov era. A more dynamic man than Ruzhek, one of his first steps was to urge that the officers be given more power. Shchastny was also a covert anti-Bolshevik. He told Lieutenant Fedotov at the beginning of the year that 'the Bolsheviki are German agents, they are going to try to hand the fleet to the Germans so that they can use it against the Allies. Something is going to happen, however, which will stop them. . . . The Baltic Fleet made the bolshevik revolution possible, the Baltic Fleet will bring bolshevik power to an end.' He apparently was connected with a secret anti-Bolshevik organisation in the fleet. But he was also an astute politician, and Rengarten once called him 'the most cunning of the cunning'.[19]

Shchastny was going to need all of his cunning to extricate the fleet. German minesweepers finally broke through the Forward Position on the last day of March, and on 4 April a Task Force, commanded by Rear-Admirel Meurer and including the dreadnoughts *Westfalen* and *Posen,* sailed past the unmanned Russian batteries into Gange. Four American-built 'AG'-class submarines were found scuttled in the harbour. Von der Goltz's 'Baltic Division', 9,000 strong, was landed to help the White Finns.[20]

Shchastny's main problem was a lack of ice-breakers to move the fleet from Finland to Russian ports. The *Truvor* was in dockyard hands. Three other big ice-breakers had been hijacked by the White Finns (the crews were Finnish): the *Sampo* in January, and the *Tarmo* and *Volynets* in March. There was also the *Ermak,* the world's largest ice-breaker, but she remained at Kronstadt for over a week after convoying the first detachment, and when she finally tried to return to Helsingfors her route was blocked by the *Tarmo* and coastal batteries (both captured by the White Finns). The Baltic command had on 12 March ordered the preparation of a second convoy, consisting of the *Republika*, *Andrei Pervozvanny*, two mine-layers, and a transport. The ships were ready by the 23rd, but it was felt that they could not move without ice-breakers. In view of this, Shchastny had reported on 31 March that 'the evacuation of ships is completely impossible at the moment'.[21]

Early on 3 April Shchastny warned the Board and the N.G.S. of the German approach. He requested diplomatic intervention on behalf of the fleet and 'instructions on what is to be done with the fleet in Helsingfors'. 'Due to the lack of ice-breakers,' he added, 'the fleet cannot be evacuated'.[22]

Shchastny meanwhile sent a delegation of four former officers and two ratings to parley with the invaders. They had very few cards to play. About all they could do was threaten to use Helsingfors as a hostage; they had been instructed to say that 'the fleet reserves freedom of action including measures which would entail a threat to the safety of the town'. The result of the negotiations was the 'Gange Agreement' of 5 April. By this the Germans guaranteed the safety of the fleet if certain conditions were met: ships and stores were not to be damaged, only skeleton crews were to be left, and breechlocks were to be removed. As a sign of their neutrality the Russian ships were to fly a red and white flag as the Germans approached; during the German occupation they were to fly the St Andrew's flag. By these terms Meurer put the Baltic Fleet completely at the mercy of the Germans. (Ironically, it was Meurer who was sent to Rosyth eight months later to conduct the initial negotiations for the surrender of the High Seas Fleet.) A supplementary wireless message from the German Foreign Ministry on the 5th demanded disarmament of Russian warships in Helsingfors by midday on the 12th, the expected date of Goltz's arrival.[23]

On 4 April, despite the pessimistic reports of 31 March and 3 April, and before he received a reply to his request for instructions from the Board, Shchastny sent off a second detachment. This was now planned to consist of the *Andrei Pervozvanny*, the *Respublika*, and three submarines. Two small ice-breakers were available, and the battleships had armoured hulls and ice-breaker bows; the submarines were to be towed. At the last moment, and on their own initiative, the two remaining heavy ships, the *Baian* and *Oleg*, joined the convoy. One submarine was forced to return, but the other vessels ploughed on. Only 90 miles were covered in the first three days, but near Gogland the convoy made a rendezvous with the *Ermak*, which this time was escorted by the *Riurik*. The ships reached Kronstadt on the 10th.[24]

The real problem now was the remaining vessels, about 250 light warships and auxiliaries. The central authorities had to make a difficult decision. There were apparently two alternatives: (1) to fulfil the German demands and disarm the fleet or (2) to scuttle it; Shchastny's reports apparently precluded the third alternative of evacuation. Sovnarkom came to a decision on 6 April:

> [Resolved.] To order the Board of the Naval Commissariat to issue immediately an order to the chief of naval forces of the Baltic Sea on the fulfilment of the conditions of the German wireless message of 5 April and of points 5 and 6 of the Brest treaty and on the presentation to the Council of People's Commissars by 11 April of a copy of the report on the removal of breechblocks and firing-pins from the ships.

Vakhrameev forwarded this resolution to the Baltic at 7.30 a.m. on the 7th and ordered that it be fulfilled by the 11th. The possibility of further evacuation was mentioned only in passing: 'Continue where possible the removal of ships from Helsingfors to Kronstadt.' The other possible alternative, scuttling the fleet, seems to have been rejected. The possibility had been raised as early as 2 March, with an N.G.S. directive that 'measures must be taken on all ships without exception so that in the event of a real danger of their being captured they may be quickly and reliably destroyed'; a similar order was given on the 20th. Councils of war held in Helsingfors on 3 and 4 April decided to proceed with detailed preparations; the destroyers, submarines, minelayers, and minesweepers were to be moved out into the roadstead and prepared for scuttling. The signal for action would come from the *Krechet*: three flags by day, three red lights by night.[25] But Vakhrameev's signal of 7 April made no mention of the possibility of scuttling, and it would appear that the central authorities accepted that the ships would have to be left disarmed in German-occupied Helsingfors. In fact the centre gave no firm directions and the final decision was left to Shchastny.

Shchastny's decision was neither to leave the fleet to the Germans nor to scuttle it. The fleet would be withdrawn through the ice. It was a difficult decision. There were still too few ice-breakers, and many ships were in the middle of their winter refits. Coal, fuel oil, and provisions were in short supply. The demobilisation had been completed by a Sovkombalt order of 5 March; anyone who wanted to could leave. By the end of the month most ships had only a fraction of their normal complements. On the destroyer *Zabaikalets*, an extreme case, the crew consisted of 4 officers and 8 men, compared with an establishment of 7 officers and 92 men. The destroyers generally had from one-third to one-quarter of their normal crews.[26]

Cromie reported the difficult situation in Helsingfors:

> The number of men leaving the Fleet and fortress during February and March was appalling: Dreadnoughts had four instead of eleven hundred, T.B.D.s averaged seven, in the *Pamiat Azova* they had to engage eighteen Finns as stokers in order to heat and light the ships.

There was no pretence of morals anywhere: the ships were full of girls day and night, officers embezzled public money and organized the sale of Government stores, which were eagerly sought ashore, where famine prices reigned. Our sailors got their pleasure for ten lumps of sugar.

Russian sources agreed that morale was bad. 'Most of the personnel who had been accepted on a free-hire basis were not suited to their tasks,' recalled P. D. Bykov, a participant, 'and in any event they were not trained and did not know their ships.' 'Part of the command and non-command staff offered passive and sometimes even active opposition to the evacuation of the ships, not showing the required energy in their work or refusing altogether to go [and] deserting their ships.' 'Of discipline only a ghost remained and [the crews] fulfilled all orders haphazardly.' Another early Soviet writer, P. Stasevich, was equally critical: 'that part of the sailors which was ready to sacrifice their lives . . . was not very great'. When news arrived of the landing at Gange, sailors fought one another to get on trains leaving Helsingfors; Sovkombalt had to ask the Finnish Red Guards to post sentries at the Helsingfors railway station to stop deserters. One of the reasons Shchastny moved the fleet out into the roadstead was to prevent men jumping ship. And it was not just the ratings who deserted; many former officers decided not to return to revolutionary Russia. Some had refused to leave Reval, and at least 33, including 14 destroyer captains and 2 flotilla commanders, the commander of a submarine flotilla, and the chief of the Minelayer Detachment, were to desert before the departure of the final detachment. The captain of the *Strashny* fled with 17,000 rubles. The position of the officers became worse after these desertions; as Bykov recalled: 'The authority of the command staff, particularly after some of them left their ships at Reval, was broken'.[27]

Despite all these problems, the evacuation went ahead. According to a Soviet article published in 1922 it was Shchastny who took the initiative on removing the bulk of the remaining ships from Finland, despite the Board's order of 7 April – and despite his pessimistic signals of 31 March and 3 April. I. F. Shpilevsky, a member of Sovkombalt, recalled that when a joint meeting of Sovkombalt and the command staff met to consider the problem it was agreed 'by a very insignificant majority' to carry on with the evacuation.[28]

The ships were made ready for sea at short notice. According to Graf, the sailors had heard rumours that they would be hanged by the Germans and 'worked as they had never worked before, even in the old days' (after the railway lines were cut in early April the sea became the only way home).[29] But the main factor was no doubt a combination of surviving professionalism and revolutionary spirit.

The fleet began to leave on 7 April, and the last ships – including the *Krechet* – left on the 11th. This 'third detachment' consisted of 45 destroyers, 3 torpedo boats, 10 submarines, 5 minelayers, 7 minesweepers,

11 patrol boats, and 81 auxiliaries and minor warships. Most ships, in six groups, followed the so-called 'Strategic Channel' through the skerries. This was longer and had more navigational hazards than the route through the open sea, but there was less danger from moving ice. Convoy discipline was weak; ships passed one another out of turn, snarls developed, and the whole convoy was delayed. Some ships fired at the ice-breakers to get their assistance. Quite a few ships, including 21 destroyers and all the submarines, received serious damage from the ice, from groundings, and from collisions. On the whole, however, the Ice Crossing was a success, for not one of the ships in the third detachment was lost; the last vessel arrived in Kronstadt on 22 April. It is true that a number of ships had to be left behind: 37 under the St Andrew's flag, 38 under the civilian flag, and 10 under the Red Cross flag. Only 7 out of about 50 minesweepers escaped.[30] Nevertheless the movement through dangerous ice of so many ships, including the valuable 'Noviks' and submarines, was a tremendous achievement.

Just after the Gange Agreement the *Westfalen* and *Posen* steamed through the abandoned Central Position to Reval. On the afternoon of 11 April Meurer left Reval for Helsingfors with his two battleships and the *Sampo*: by dusk his crews could see the Sveaborg Cathedral. Late on the 12th, after the fog had lifted, a landing party went ashore on Skatudden. There was fierce fighting with Red Guards in Market Square, but by the 14th the Germans and White Finns were firmly in control of Helsingfors, the main base of the revolutionary Baltic Fleet.[31]

The German invasion showed that the fleet could offer serious resistance neither on land nor at sea. General Bonch-Bruevich told Lenin that in his expert opinion Petrograd was threatened by a German landing and that the Soviet capital should be moved;[32] this took place on 11 March, and the naval danger may well have been a factor.

The one success was the Ice Crossing. Émigré officers do not hestitate to give Shchastny the credit: 'This remarkable voyage . . . only succeeded thanks to the energy of . . . Shchastny, assisted by the officers and by some sailors who had remained loyal.'[33] The fact that Shchastny was put in front of a firing squad in June 1918 has tended to obscure his role in Soviet accounts. N. S. Kroviakov, in an otherwise useful book on the Ice Crossing published in 1955, gives a most distorted view of the captain as a man who wanted to *hold back* the evacuation or to destroy the fleet: 'The inspiration for the operation and the general leadership of its execution belonged to the Soviet government, to the C.C. of the Party, and personally to V. I. Lenin.' Nevertheless, one Soviet article written in 1922 for *Morskoi sbornik* (the official naval journal) acknowledged Shchastny's contribution: 'It must be recognised that the fleet was preserved for the Republic only thanks to the exceptional energy, decisiveness, and firm will of the Commander-in-Chief'. More surprisingly, an article written in 1963 in

Voenno-istoricheskii zhurnal, without mentioning Shchastny by name, noted that 'the post of commander-in-chief . . . played a positive role in the organising of the transfer of the fleet'.[34] It is doubtful whether so many ships would have left had there not been an energetic fleet commander prepared, as Shchastny was, to take the initiative without instructions from the centre. One should not forget, however, that the evacuation of the first and second detachments, with the most valuable ships, was carried out or prepared before Shchastny's election. And the episode was a credit to all the Baltic sailors who took part.

The Ice Crossing saved many ships for Soviet Russia. Failure would have been a second Tsu-shima. The survival of the Baltic Fleet allowed it to fight in Russian internal waters and in defence of Petrograd in 1918 and 1919; it was the destroyers and small craft which were most important in the Civil War. And later the 'Noviks' and submarines served with the dreadnoughts as the nucleus of the Soviet Navy of the 1920s and 1930s.

Conclusion

In keeping with the classical dramatic unities, the end of the heroic period of the revolutionary Baltic Fleet came with the return of the last ships to the place where the naval revolution had first erupted – Kronstadt.

The men of the fleet dispersed and went on to other things. Some of the well-known sailor activists died fighting for Soviet power in the Civil War – among them Khokhriakov, Markin, and Zhelezniakov. Eizhen Berg, an anarchist artificer from the *Sevastopol'*, was one of the 26 Baku commissars. Others were the victims of Soviet power. Ivan Balakin was Tsentrobalt's commissar on the *Samson* and *Zabiika* during the October uprising; a year later he was executed as a mutineer. Petr Perepelkin, another Tsentrobalt man and a member of the July delegation, was shot as one of the leaders of the 1921 Kronstadt anti-Communist mutiny. Pavel Dybenko recovered from his disgrace to become the first commandant of Kronstadt after the 1921 mutiny. He rose to command the Leningrad Military District (i.e. a very important Army Group) but perished with other Red Army leaders in 1937. A number of Baltic veterans died in 1938, including Grigorii Kireev (chairman of the Helsingfors Sailors Club), Petr Kurkov (chairman of the *Avrora* committee), Avgust Loos (chairman of the 2nd Depot committee), and Andrei Tupikov (Tsentrobalt commissar aboard the *Slava* at Moon Sound).[1] Nikolai Izmailov survived, but he spent 16 years in prison camps and in exile before his 'rehabilitation' in 1956.

The Bolshevik civilian activists were, as a group, unfortunate. Roshal' and Zhemchuzhin died early in the Civil War. Kingisepp was executed by the Estonian government in 1922. Many more perished in Stalin's purges, including Antipov, Antonov-Ovseenko, Anvel't, Liubovich, Sheinman, Smilga, Smirnov (as C.-in-C. of the Black Sea Fleet), and Stark. Raskol'nikov died mysteriously in Nice in 1939, after publicly denouncing Stalin and refusing to return to the Soviet Union. The only important ones still alive in the 1950s were Flerovsky and Zalezhsky. Members of other parties fared as badly. Prosh'ian died of illness in 1918 and received a personal obituary from Lenin. Anatoly Lamanov, a student who was the non-partisan leader of the Kronstadt Soviet during the 'honeymoon', was shot after the 1921 mutiny. Iarchuk and V. I. Lebedev, two extremes of the Russian socialist movement, both ended up as émigrés.

Few officers who continued in Soviet service were to see the resurrection of the Russian Navy. Rengarten, who finally went over to the Reds, died of typhus during the Civil War. Maksimov died in 1924, Berens in 1928. Modest Ivanov survived the inter-war years, only to starve to death in the siege of Leningrad. But Commander L. M. fon-Galler, first officer of the *Slava* at Moon Sound, was deputy commander of the Soviet Navy during the war of 1941–5 (he was arrested in 1947 and died in prison in 1950). Those officers who resisted Soviet power also suffered. Razvozov died of tuberculosis in gaol in 1920, and Bakhirev and Pilkin perished in Red prisons at about the same time. Prince Cherkassky was killed fighting in the White army. Those officers who were able to emigrate at the end of the Civil War, including Dudorov, Fedotov, Graf, Rusin, and Timirev, found themselves cut off from their profession as well as their country.[2] The case of Rear-Admiral Stark, commander of the Destroyer Division, was probably typical; his wife died in Petrograd, but he and his children escaped aboard. Stark reached Paris where he became, in succession, a taxi driver, a lorry driver, and a bank clerk; he died in Paris in 1950. The fate of Verderevsky, C.-in-C. and Navy Minister, was more unusual – and happier. He emigrated to France but was granted honorary Soviet citizenship in 1945 for his part in the Resistance.

The mass of Baltic sailors shared the experiences of other citizens of Soviet Russia. Many enjoyed a well-earned retirement in the 1950s and 1960s, including A. V. Baranov, Khovrin, Pronin, and Vakhrameev. Others like them, now all old men in their eighties, are honoured as leading veterans of the Great October Socialist Revolution.

The sailors really deserved their reputation as revolutionary militants. Politically, they were more 'advanced' than that other key force, the soldiers. Dybenko explained this in emotional terms by talking of the sailor as 'an eternally mutinous soul'. A more rational answer would take into account a certain corporate pride, which Dybenko himself acknowledged: 'The sailor always felt that he was superior to the soldier, to the worker, and therefore he felt obliged to be in the vanguard'.[3] And this, as well as a receptiveness to revolutionary propaganda, can be explained by the social background of the sailors. That they supported the R.S.D.W.P.(b.) more than any other party is accounted for, before October, by the energy of Bolshevik agitation and by the disorganisation and the self-compromising policies of the other socialist parties; after October, it is explained by the fact that the Bolsheviks represented Soviet power.

The popularity of the Bolsheviks should not be exaggerated, however. An optimistic estimate might put 'card-carrying' party membership in October at anywhere between five and ten thousand sailors, no more than 10 to 15 per cent of the fleet. The Bolsheviks did receive 56 per cent of the vote in the Constituent Assembly elections, but this was at a time when a pro-Bolshevik vote was a vote of confidence in Soviet power. The Bolsheviks relied heavily on the support of other parties, especially the Left S.R.s. Even those sailors who appeared to support Bolshevism were not unthinking instruments. The representative from Helsingfors mentioned this in late September 1917 at a Bolshevik conference in Finland: 'The sailors still look on themselves as an independent revolutionary force, as their own kind of special "party" and not as prone to subordination to party directives'.[4] And it was the need for allies and an inability to regiment the sailors that made the Bolsheviks careful to stress the defensive nature of key political actions.

The extent to which the sailors' political stance was sometimes a negative 'protest vote' became more clear in the months after October, when some sailors turned against Bolshevism. But the Bolsheviks *did* express, more than any other organised party, the wishes of the sailors – especially from the high summer of 1917. Unlike the other parties they were prepared to give the sailors what they wanted, and they alone had the will and strength to translate opinion into action.

The struggle did not revolve solely around party politics. Equally important was the desire to democratise everyday life. The collapse of the old administrative structure was to be expected, given that the officers were identified with the autocracy. The bloodshed of February was rather more surprising, but it is understandable in the light of the events of 1905–6 (moreover the massacres of February and March were the only major incidents of violence within the fleet in our 14-month period).

Commander Cromie had a low opinion of naval democracy; 'You cannot imagine how foolish these people can be,' he wrote to a British colleague in late April 1917.[5] But the Russian ratings believed that a fleet run on democratic lines would be more effective than the fleet of the old regime. The Bolsheviks played their part in democratisation, and at the highest level there may have been an element of calculation. But the attitude of the Bolshevik ratings – even of the few underground veterans – was more straightforward. For them, as for their non-Bolshevik comrades, naval democracy was not just a tool towards a greater political objective but a genuine and achievable aim, like 'workers' control'. And they remained convinced of the feasibility of this aim, at least until the beginning of 1918.

Two things led to a change, the victory of the Bolsheviks and the continuing breakdown of the fleet. Both the new Bolshevik leadership in Petrograd and the ratings who had gained administrative experience in 1917 became aware of the shortcomings of the *komitetshchina*. The times were too dangerous for continued experiment; the first priority was now – rightly – the survival of the Soviet state. This change of attitude became clear by mid-winter of 1917–18, and it was then that Berens, the Chief of the N.G.S., told Dmitry Fedotov of a recent conversation with Lenin: 'What amazed me,' said Berens, 'was that when I proposed certain basic principles for the organisation of service and discipline . . ., Lenin turned to me and said: "Why, all this is much too loose-jointed. We want real discipline and you will revise all your propositions accordingly. We are building now. The destruction period is over!" '6

What had indeed been a period of destruction was, for the sailors, one of creativity, in terms both of politics and of self-administration. But when it was fighting for its life the Soviet government had to give technical efficiency and political reliability priority over popular sovereignty. Gradually the old forms returned. The committees were abolished and the 'appointees' took over. Political activity came to mean controlled Communist activity, and after the 1921 mutiny the independent political tradition was snuffed out. By the end of the Civil War the impetus for change had been lost. In 1935 ranks were reintroduced including, from May 1940, the rank of admiral. The Soviet Navy by then had more in common with the navy of the Tsar in terms of its 'conventional' organisation and its apolitical status than it did with the revolutionary Baltic Fleet. The years 1917 and 1918 were a forgotten time of experiment.

Appendix 1

BALTIC FLEET PERSONNEL

1. Numbers

In early 1917 there were 4,339 commissioned officers, about 1,000 doctors and civilian officials, and 1,245 warrant officers in the fleet.

Officially, the 'other ranks' at this time comprised some 82,625 ratings, including 2,466 long-service men, 704 volunteers, 65,411 sailors (1909 – 16), 14,044 reservists (1904 – 8). The 'official' total for May – June was 78,617, while that for November was 78,122. V. V. Petrash estimated, on the basis of the elections to the second fleet congress and to the Constituent Assembly, that in November the actual number of ratings serving in the Baltic Sea was about 60,000. Some 5,000 serving on the land front and another 3,000 in lake flotillas can be accounted for. This leaves a deficit of about 10,100, nearly 15 per cent of the 'official' total, which Petrash evidently accounts for by saying that 'not a few sailors were on leave or on missions'.[1]

Naval Militia (*Ratniki morskogo opolcheniia*) made up 10,341 men. These were reservists from the classes of 1899 – 1903. Of 19,000 in the whole navy, 8,265 were working in Navy Department factories and shipyards.[2]

There were 19,022 soldiers in units attached to the Baltic Fleet.[3]

2. Social Composition

Soviet historians have debated the precise class nature of the fleet. V. V. Petrash and S. S. Khesin were among the first to use archival material from the Central Naval Archive (*TsGAVMF*).[4] D. A. Garkavenko presented even more complete data in a later article,[5] but some of his conclusions have been challenged. One of the central questions of the debate was the cause of the greater militancy of the Baltic Fleet compared to the Black Sea Fleet. Khesin, in his first article, suggested that there was little difference between the two fleets and that the key factor was proximity to Petrograd. Garkavenko submitted the figures to closer scrutiny, primarily by clarifying what the Navy Department had meant by 'miscellaneous' professions. He then concluded that the vital factors were class composition and Bolshevik agitation, in that order.[6] Khesin later struck back, reasserting the weakness of the sailors in class terms.[7] As a result of this debate a large amount of information has been published. The following list gives the professions of the 57,109 sailors drafted into the Baltic Fleet in the years 1899 – 1905 and the 40,130 drafted in 1914 – 16; it shows how the already high proportion of urban workers was increased in the years immediately before the revolution.[8]

	1899–1905 (%)	1914–16 (%)		1899–1905 (%)	1914–16 (%)
Farmers (*khlebopashtsy*)	46.7	23.2	Blacksmiths	2.1	2.9
Miscellaneous	17.3	19.8	Clerks	1.5	2.4
Seamen			Boilermen	1.2	2.7
(*sudokhodtsy*)	6.1	11.8	Housepainters	1.2	1.8
Metal craftsmen			Oilers	1.0	2.1
(*slesari*)	5.6	9.0	Lathe operators	0.7	1.0
Carpenters			Foundrymen	0.6	1.6
(*plotniki*)	2.8	3.3	Coppersmiths	0.5	0.3
Stokers	2.7	3.8	Caulkers	0.2	0.6
Tradesmen			Telegraphists	0.1	0.6
(*torgovtsy*)	2.5	2.6	Electricians	–	1.6
Fishermen	2.5	2.9			
Joiners (*stoliari*)	2.4	2.3		100	100
Machinists (*mashinisty*) and asst. machinists	2.2	3.6			

D. A. Garkavenko attempted, through a series of complicated calculations, to work out the class character of the fleet. First he analysed the Navy Department's 'miscellaneous' category, which – he maintained – included a large number of hidden 'proletarians'. Then he broke professions down into classes; A. G. Rashin's *Formirovanie rabochego klassa Rossii* (M, 1958) was used, for example, to determine that 52 per cent of 'joiners' were 'building workers' (and 'proletarians') while the other 48 per cent were 'artisans' (and 'petty bourgeoisie'). The following are the figures for all ratings in the fleet (i.e. the classes of 1904–16) in 1917:[9]

	numbers	%
Factory workers *(fabrichno-zavodskie rabochie)*	24,572	30.8
Building *(stroitel'nye)* workers	5,008	6.3
Ship workers *(sudorabochie)*	5,065	6.3
Workers in light industry	1,968	2.5
Unskilled workers	6,043	7.6
Total proletarians	42,656	53.5
Semi-proletarians	7,451	9.3
Peasants	19,850	24.9
Artisans *(remeslenniki)*	3,056	3.8
Tradesmen	1,702	2.1
Employees	4,144	5.2
Miscellaneous	915	1.1
Total	79,774	100

The difference between Garkavenko's calculations and those of Khesin (based on the 1914–16 intake) are shown in the following:[10]

	Garkavenko	Khesin
Proletarians	53.5%	25.4%
Semi-proletarians	9.3%	25.9%
Peasants and petty bourgeoisie	37.2%	48.6%
	100 %	100 %

Appendix 2

BALTIC FLEET ORDER OF BATTLE[1]

(Named ships survived in Soviet hands, unless otherewise noted. Bases: A – Abo, G – Gange, H – Helsingfors, K – Kronstadt, L – Lapvik, P – Petrograd, R – Reval.)
   C.-in-C., Baltic Fleet *Krechet*

A. *Active Fleet*

   1st Battleship Brigade (H): *Gangut, Petropavlovsk, Poltava, Sevastopol'*
   2nd Battleship Brigade (H and L): *Andrei Pervozvanny, Imp. Pavel I (Respublika), Slava* (sunk 4.x.17), *Tsesarevich (Grazhdanin)*
   1st Cruiser Brigade (R): *Riurik, Adm. Makarov, Baian, Bogatyr', Oleg*
   2nd Cruiser Brigade (H and A): *Gromoboi, Rossiia, Avrora* (P), *Diana*
   Destroyer Division (R): *Novik;* **4th Flotilla,** *Gen. Kondratenko, Okhotnik* (sunk 13.ix.17), *Pogranichnik, Sibirsky Strelok;* **5th Flotilla**, *Amurets, Emir Bukharsky, Finn, Gaidamak, Moskvitianin, Ussuriets, Vsadnik;* **6th Flotilla**, *Donskoi Kazak, Steregushchy, Strashny, Turkmenets Stavropol'sky, Ukraina, Voiskovoi, Zabaikalets;* **11th Flotilla**, *Grom* (sunk 1.x.17), *Orfei, Pobeditel', Zabiiaka;* **12th Flotilla**, *Azard, Desna, Letun* (decmsnd., K), *Samson;* **13th Flotilla**, *Avtroil* (cmsnd. 30.vii.17), *Iziaslav* (cmsnd. 17.vi.17); **14th Flotilla**, *Kapitan Izyl'met'ev* (cmsnd. late 1917), *Lt. Il'in* (cmsnd. late 1917); **15th Flotilla**, *Gavriil* (cmsnd. late 1917), *Konstantin* (cmsnd. 19.v.17) (two more 'Noviks', *Miklukha-Maklai* and *Svoboda,* joined the fleet in the winter of 1917–18); 7 transports, 13 auxiliaries
   Submarine Division: **1st Flotilla** (R), *Bars* (sunk 15.v.17), *Gepard* (recmsnd. 25.vii.17, sunk 15.xi.17), *Tur* (cmsnd. 10.viii.17), *Vepr, Volk;* **2nd Flotilla** (R), *L'vitsa* (sunk 29.v.17), *Pantera, Rys' Tigr;* **3rd Flotilla** (R), *Iaguar* (cmsnd. 25.x.17), *Kuguar* (cmsnd. 1917), *Leopard* (cmsnd. 1917), *Zmeia* (cmsnd. 12.iv.17); **4th Flotilla** (R and G), *AG 11, AG 12, AG 16* (all scuttled 3.iv.18), *AG 14* (sunk vi.17), *AG 15* (sunk 8.vi.17, raised, scuttled 3.iv.18); **5th Flotilla** (R), *Edinorog* (cmsnd. 1917, sunk 25.ii.18), *Ugor'* (cmsnd. 1.v.17) (one further 'Bars' class, *Ersh*, joined the fleet in the winter of 1917–18); **6th Flotilla** (A), *Kasatka, Makrel', Minoga, Okun', Fel'dmarshal Graf Sheremet'ev (Keta);* (Other operational boats were the British submarines: *C32* was wrecked on 8.x.17, *E1, E8, E9, E19, C26, C27,*

and *C35* were scuttled in the spring of 1918); **Submarine Training Detachment** (R), *Beluga, Peskar', Shchuka, Sterliad'* (all scuttled Reval, ii.18); 3 depot ships, 5 transports, 4 auxiliaries

Baltic Sea Mine Defence:

(a) **Patrol Boat Division** (H): **7th Destroyer Flotilla**, *Boevoi, Burny, Inzh.-Mekh. Dmitriev, Inzh.-Mekh. Zverev, Vnimatel'ny, Vnushitel'ny, Vynoslivy*; **8th Destroyer Flotilla**, *Iskusny, Krepky, Legky, Likhoi, Lovky, Metky, Molodetsky, Moshchny*; **9th Destroyer Flotilla**, *Del'ny, Deiatel'ny, Dostoiny, Gromiashchy, Rastoropny, Raziashchy, Sil'ny, Storozhevoi, Stroiny* (sunk 8.viii.17), *Vidny*; **1st Patrol Boat Flotilla**, *Grif, Ruslan* (both prob. cptrd.), *Iastreb, Vladimir, Voron*; **2nd P. B. Flotilla**, *Barsuk* (foundered 5.x.17), *Gornostai, Kunitsa, Sobol', Vydra*; **4th P.B. Flotilla**, *Kobchik, Korshun*; two flotillas of small craft – Patrol Launches *Nos. 1 – 12, 16 – 17*, Base Launches *Nos. 1 – 6* (all prob. cptrd. H)

(b) **Minesweeper Division:** *Ust'-Narova*, M/sw. *No. 4*, one auxiliary; (b1) **1st Minesweeper Detachment** (H): *Provodnik*; **1st Flotilla**, Torpedo Boats *Nos. 212, 214 – 220, 222* (all cptrd. H), *No. 213*; **2nd Minesweeper Flotilla** (10th Destroyer Flotilla), *Podvizhny, Rezvy, R'iany* (all cptrd.), *Poslushny* (wrecked 9.xi.17), *Prochny, Prytky, Retivy*; **3rd Flotilla**, *Zashchitnik* (cmsnd. 6.vi.17, cptrd.), *Cheka, Minrep, Udarnik* (cmsnd. 6.vi.17), *Zapal*; **4th Flotilla**, M/sw. *Nos. 18–19*, Motor M/sw. *Nos. 1 – 9* (probably all cptrd.), *Gruz, Kapsiul', Kometa, Krambol* (b2) **2nd Minesweeper Detachment** (R): M/sw. *No. 2* (cptrd.); **5th Flotilla**, M/sw. *Nos. 3, 8, 23, 24, 103*; **6th Flotilla**, M/sw. *Nos. 5, 10* (prob. both cptrd.), *Nos. 9, 11, Patron, Plamia, Planeta*; **7th Flotilla**, M/sw. *Nos. 14 – 17* (prob. all cptrd.); **8th Flotilla**, *Alesha Popovich, Bogatyr', Dobryna, Mikula, Potok, Sviatagor'* (prob. all cptrd.), *Il'ia Muromets* (sunk 10.viii.17)

(c) **Minelayer Detachment:** *Svir'* (H, cptrd.), *Amur, Lena, Msta, Narova* (all H); *Ural, Volga* (both R); *Il'men'* (A, cptrd.); 7 auxiliaries

(d) **Netlayer Detachment** (H): 5 auxiliaries; **1st Flotilla,** *Bureia, Irtysh* (prob. both cptrd.), *Zeia*, 2 auxiliaries; **2nd Flotilla,** *Lovat', Sheksna*, 1 auxiliary; **3rd Flotilla**, *Pripiat'*, 2 auxiliaries

Skerries Detachment: Skerries Flotilla (A), gunboats *Bobr, Gil'iak* (both cptrd.), *Groziashchy, Khivinets, Khrabry*, 26 patrol boats, 13 auxiliaries and small craft; **Patrol Areas**

Gulf of Bothnia Detachment: Gulf of Bothnia Flotilla, despatch vessels *Berkut, Kondor, Posadnik, Voevoda* (all cptrd.), *Abrek*; **Patrol Areas; Nikolaishtadt**

Aviation Division (R): seaplane carrier *Orlitsa*, 22 auxiliaries (there were 97 aircraft in the Baltic Fleet in early 1917)

Signals Service: destroyers *Lt. Burakov* (sunk 30.vii.17), *Prozorlivy* (cptrd.), *Porazhaiushchy*

B. Auxiliaries

Transport Flotilla: 4 auxiliaries; **1st Flotilla** (H), 7 transports; **2nd Flotilla** (R), 7 transports; **3rd Flotilla** (K), 8 transports; **4th Flotilla** (H), 7 transports

Transport Detachment: 15 colliers, 7 oilers, 6 ammunition ships, 3 refrigerator ships, 7 special service ships

Training Detachments (K): **Artificers School**, Shore Detachment, *Okean*, *Lastochka*, 6 auxiliaries; **Gunnery Training Detachment**, Shore Detachment, *Imp. Aleksandr II (Zaria Svobody)*, *Verny*, *Argun';* **Torpedo and Mining Training Detachment**, Shore Detachment, *Nikolaev (Osvoboditel')*, *Terek*, *Khoper*, 1 auxiliary; **Diving School**, *Afrika*; **Medical Orderlies School; Boys School**

Baltic Sea Pilot and Light Department: 2 lightships, 10 auxiliaries

Finnish Pilot and Light Department: ice-breakers *Murtaja* (cptrd.), *Sampo* (cptrd. i.18), *Tarmo* (cptrd. 21.iii.18), 4 lightships, 59 auxiliaries

Special Surveying Section: 40 auxiliaries

C. Naval Fortresses

Petr Veliky (Reval): ex-battleship *Petr Veliky*, 4 ice-breakers – *Gerkules* (prob. cptrd.), *Tsar' Mikhail Fedorovich (Volynets)* (cptrd. 23.iii.18), *Ermak*, *Gorod Revel'*, 33 auxiliaries

Sveaborg: 14 auxiliaries

Abo-Oland Fortified Position

Moon Sound Fortified Position: 2 auxiliaries

Rear Fortified Position: 2 auxiliaries

D. Ports

Appendix 3

DEMOCRATIC ORGANISATIONS

(Abbreviations: A, Anarchists; B, Bolsheviks; In, 'Internationalists'; LSR, Left S.R.s; M, Mensheviks; Mx, Maximalists; NP, Non-Partisans; SR, Socialist-Revolutionaries; TNS, *Trudovaia Narodno-sotsialisticheskaia partiia*)

1. Kronstadt

A. Kronstadt Town Duma (elected 23 – 26.vii.17)[1]

	Total population				Naval votes	
	Votes	%	Seats	%	Naval votes	%
B	10,214	36.3	25	36.8	2,653	58.3
SR	10,910	38.8	27	39.7	1,514	33.3
M	950	3.4	2	2.9	63	1.4
NP	2,174	7.7	5	7.4	120	2.6
TNS	2,086	7.4	5	7.4	94	2.1
Nationalists	1,104	3.9	3	4.4	98	2.2
Homeowners	533	1.9	1	1.5	7	0.0
Former councillors	116	0.4	0	0	0	0
Void	67	0.2	0	0	1	0.0
Total	28,154	100	68	100	4,550	100

B. Kronstadt Soviet of Workers' and Soldiers' Deputies

Session	B	%	SR	%	M	%	NP	%	A	%	Mx	%	Total
1st (10.iii.17)[2]	11	4.1	108	40.3	72	26.9	77	28.7	0	0	0	0	268
E.C.	na	na	na	na	na	na	na	na	0	0	0	0	na
2nd (5.v.17)[2]	93	31.2	91	30.5	46	15.4	68	22.8	0	0	0	0	298
E.C.	9	30.0	9	30.0	5	16.7	7	23.3	0	0	0	0	30
3rd (11.viii.17)[3]	96	33.7	73	25.6	13	4.6	96	33.7	7	2.5	0	0	285
E.C.	10	33.3	8	26.7	1	3.3	10	33.3	1	3.3	0	0	30
4th (26.i.18)[4]	139	46.2	64	21.3	6	2.0	21	7.0	15	5.0	56	18.6	301
E.C.	na	na	na	na	na	na	na	na	na	na	na	na	na
5th (1.iv.18)[5]	58	29.3	43	21.7	15	7.6	26	13.1	11	5.6	45	22.7	198
E.C.	na	na	na	na	na	na	na	na	na	na	na	na	na

2. *Finland*

A. Helsingfors Soviet of Deputies of the Army, Navy, and Workers (until 21 April called the 'Soviet of Deputies of the Army, Navy, and Workers of Sveaborg Port').

Information about this important body is fragmentary. It had no party factions and was divided into army, navy, and worker factions. A 1st Session met on 4 March, and by April the soviet included some 530 members, of whom 43 (8.1%) were Bolsheviks.[6] The 2nd Session was elected on 19 April. Available figures from various sources list 80 Bolsheviks, 125 S.R.s (all left-inclined), 17 Mensheviks, and 48 non-partisans; Raskol'nikov claimed that in May there were 125–30 Bolsheviks (23.4–24.3%) out of 535 members. The E.C. elected on 22 April consisted of 62 full members (27 army, 25 navy, 3 merchant navy, 7 workers) and 11 candidates.[7] The 3rd Session was elected in August. It was evidently dominated by the R.S.D.W.P. (b.), as the Bolshevik Aron Sheinman was elected chairman of the E.C. The Helsingfors Soviet dissolved itself on about 3 March 1918.[8]

B. Regional Congresses of the Army, Navy, and Workers of Finland, and the Regional Committee of the Army, Navy, and Workers of Finland

Congress	B	%	SR	%	LSR	%	M	%	NP	%	Total
1st (17–19.iv.17)[9]	6	5.7	na	na	na	na	na	na	na	na	106
Committee	0	0	na	na	na	na	na	na	na	na	11
2nd (20–24.v.17)[10]	19	12.9	na	na	na	na	na	na	na	na	147
Committee	4	16.0	9	36.0	1	4.0	8	32.0	3	12.0	25
3rd (9–12.ix.17)[11]	63	49.2	na	na	na	na	na	na	na	na	128
Committee	37	56.9	0	0	26	40.0	2	3.1	0	0	65
4th (25–27.xi.17)[12]	82	70.1	0	0	32	27.4	0	0	3	2.6	117
Committee	30	69.8	0	0	13	30.2	0	0	0	0	43

3. Reval

A. Reval Soviet of Workers' and Forces' Deputies

Sesion	B	%	SR	%	M	%	NP	%	In	%	Total
1st (3.iii.17)[13]	60	na	na	na	na	na	na	na	0	0	na
E.C.	na	na	na	na	na	na	na	na	0	0	na
2nd (13.v.17)[14]	58	29.4	87	44.2	29	14.7	23	11.7	0	0	197
E.C.	6	30.0	9	45.0	3	15.0	2	10.0	0	0	20
3rd (c.l.viii.17)[15]	74	41.6	66	37.1	9	5.1	21	11.8	8	4.5	178
E.C.	8	40.0	8	40.0	1	5.0	2	10.0	1	5.0	20
4th (c.10.xii.17)[16]	na	na	22	11.0	na	na	na	na	0	0-	c.200
E.C.	na	na	5	na	na	na	na	na	0	0	na

B. Reval Town Duma (elected early August 1917)[17]

	Votes	%	Seats	%
B	21,572	30.9	31	30.7
SR	15,145	21.7	22	21.8
M	8,282	11.9	12	11.9
Est. Rad. Socialist	12,612	18.0	18	17.8
Est. Homeowners	4,464	6.4	6	5.9
German	3,187	4.6	5	5.0
Union of Reval Russian Orgs.	2,010	2.9	3	3.0
Kadet	478	0.7	1	1.0
Other	2,123	3.0	3	3.0
Total	69,873	100	101	100

4. Constituent Assembly

A. Baltic Electoral District[18]

(1) Navy:	Kron.	Rev.	Hels.	Gange-Lapvik	Nik-shtadt	Abo-Oland	Total
Registered electors	10,512	7,425	28,088	2,820	1,702	6,749	57,296
Ballot papers	6,540	5,417	22,370	2,515	1,217	5,411	43,470
%voting	62.2	73.0	79.6	89.2	71.5	80.2	75.9
List/Votes							
1 (LSR)	1,439	3,548	13,871	1,501	814	5,313	26,486
%	11.2	33.5	31.7	30.7	33.9	49.6	31.1
2 (B)	10,296	5,309	23,754	2,923	1,252	4,099	47,633
%	80.3	50.1	54.4	59.7	52.1	38.2	56.0
3 (Off.)	173	423	1,112	79	69	255	2,111
%	1.3	4.0	2.5	1.6	2.9	2.4	2.5
4 (RSR)	785	1,083	4,641	343	223	955	8,030
%	6.1	10.2	10.6	7.0	9.3	8.9	9.4
5 (NP)	128	229	320	51	46	100	874
%	1.0	2.2	0.7	1.0	1.9	0.9	1.0
Total	12,821	10,592	43,698	4,897	2,404	10,722	85,134

Baltic Electoral District (contd.)

(2) Army:	Kron.	Rev.	Hels.	Gange-Lapvik	Nik-shtadt	Abo-Oland	Total
Registered electors	20,111	41,278	34,969	1,600		5,999	103,957
Ballot papers	13,934	24,931	24,088	1,570		4,877	69,400
% voting	69.3	60.4	68.9	98.1		81.3	66.8
1 (LSR)	2,539	10,117	14,510	2,052		5,315	34,533
%	9.2	20.5	29.8	63.1		54.9	24.9
2 (B)	23,633	31,417	22,891	778		3,834	82,553
%	85.3	63.8	47.0	23.9		39.6	59.6
3 (Off.)	114	1,090	635	34		52	1,925
%	0.4	2.2	1.3	1.0		0.5	1.4
4 (RSR)	1,276	5,969	10,410	374		439	18,468
%	4.6	12.1	21.4	11.5		4.5	13.3
5 (NP)	139	644	238	15		38	1,074
%	0.5	1.3	0.5	0.5		0.4	0.8
Total	27,701	49,237	48,684	3,253		9,678	138,553

B. Civilian Vote at Kronstadt (According to Bolshevik *Golos pravdy* and Trudovik *Trud i zemlia*):[19]

	Golos pravdy		Trud i zemlia):[19]	
	Votes	%	Votes	%
Bolshevik	12,319	68.2	11,684	67.7
Kadets	2,351	13.0	2,336	13.5
SR	1,195	6.6	1,112	6.4
Narodnye sotsialisty	1,072	5.9	1,070	6.2
Orthodox Union	399	2.2	399	2.3
Estonian	303	1.7	237	1.4
Menshevik (United)	300	1.7	294	1.7
Ukrainian and Jewish organisations	95	0.5	94	0.5
Finnish socialists	16	0.1	16	0.1
Co-operative Group	13	0.1	13	0.1
Total	18,063	100	17,255	100

C. Civilian Vote at Reval:[20]

	Votes	%
Bolshevik	22,003	47.5
Est. Trudovik Party	13,855	29.9
Est. Democratic Bloc	4,735	10.2
Est. S. D. W. P. (Mensh.)	2,689	5.8
Est. Radical-Democratic Party and Peasant Union	1,136	2.5
SR	1,135	2.4
Estonian SR	787	1.7
Total	46,340	100

Bibliography

I. OFFICIAL SOURCES

A. Public Record Office, London
Adm.116/1862   Includes Baltic Fleet order of battle for 1917
Adm.137/1249, 1388, 1389   Reports of naval representatives in Russia; copies of documents sent to the Admiralty by the F.O.
Adm.137/1570   Reports of F. N. A. Cromie
F.O.371/3011, 3018, 3315, 3325, 3329   Reports of naval representatives in Russia

B. Sota-arkisto (Military Archives), Helsinki. Venäläinen Kokoelma (Russian Collection)
1426   Baltic Staff orders on personnel
1636   Rules, protocols, and appeal of 1st Congress of Baltic Fleet
2866   Orders of Baltic C.-in-C., September – December, 1916
3178   Membership lists, draft charter, protocols, and decrees of Tsentrobalt, April – July, 1917
3184   Orders of Baltic C.-in-C., January – December, 1917; decrees of Tsentrobalt, May – June, September – November, 1917
3220   Protocols of Helsingfors Soviet, July 1917 – January 1918; protocols of Tsentrobalt, October – November, 1917
3221   Protocols of Helsingfors Soviet Sailors' Section
3224   Orders of Baltic C.-in-C., 1917
3901   Ship committee documents; Staff draft charter for Tsentrobalt; list of deputies to Helsingfors Soviet
3910   Regulations on Disciplinary Courts
7374   Regulations on Ship Committees, regulations on Local Naval Committees
13828   Circulars of Baltic C.-in-C.

C. Valtionarkisto (National Archives), Helsinki
Viaporin sotasatama 2   Project for organisation of Tsentrobalt; list of members of organising commission

D. Helsinki University Library
The library contains an unbound collection of printed Prikazy Nachal'nika Morskogo Shtaba Verkhovnago Glavnokomanduiushchago (Orders of the Chief of the Naval Staff of the Supreme C.-in-C.)

II. CONTEMPORARY NEWSPAPERS AND JOURNALS

A. Central
Armiia i Flot Svobodnoi Rossii/*Armiia i Flot Rabochei i Krest'ianskoi Rossii*
  (official)
Delo naroda (S.R.)
Edinstvo (Menshevik)
Ezhenedel'nik Morskogo sbornika/*Svobodnyi flot*/*Revoliutsionnyi flot* (official)
Izvestiia Petrogradskago Soveta rabochikh i soldatskikh deputatov (official)
Izvestiia VTsIK (official)
Morskoi sbornik (official)
Novaia zhizn' (independent socialist)
Pravda (Bolshevik)
Tsentroflot (official)
Vestnik Vremennago Pravitel'stva (official)
Zemlia i volia (S.R.)

B. Kronstadt
Golos pravdy/*Proletarskoe delo*/*Golos pravdy* (Bolshevik)
Izvestiia Kronshtadtskago Soveta rabochikh i soldatskikh deputatov (official)
Kotlin (independent)
Kronshtadtskaia iskra (Menshevik)
Kronshtadtskii vestnik (independent)
Trud, zemlia, i more/*Trud i zemlia* (Trudovik)

C. Helsingfors
Finliandskaia gazeta (official)
Golos Sotsial-Demokrata (Menshevik)
Izvestiia Gel'singforsskago Soveta deputatov armii, flota i rabochikh/*Izvestiia*
  (official)
Moriak (Sailors Club)
Narodnaia niva (Right S.R.)
Obshchee delo (Kadet)
Russkii vestnik (independent)
Sotsialist-revoliutsioner (Left S.R.)
Volna/*Priboi* (Bolshevik)
Za Rossiiu (independent)

D. Reval
Bor'ba (Left S.R.)
Iskra (Menshevik)
Izvestiia Revel'skago Soveta rabochikh i voinskikh deputatov (official)
Revel'skii nabliudatel' (independent)
Shtorm (Sailors Club)
Utro pravdy/*Zvezda*/*Utro pravdy* (Bolshevik)

Voennaia gazeta: Svobodnoe slovo ofitsera, soldata i matrosa/Svobodnoe slovo soldata i matrosa (independent)

III. SECONDARY SOURCES: BOOKS AND ARTICLES

This list is selective. It includes important works devoted primarily to the Baltic Fleet as well as certain relatively minor sources which were cited more than once. Well-known general works in English are excluded, as are general surveys, protocols, and collections of documents published in the Soviet Union since 1956 (including congress protocols, Lenin's collected works, and the series *Velikaia Oktiabr'skaia sotsialisticheskaia revoliutsiia: Dokumenty i materialy*). The notes contain full references for these works and also for the numerous minor works cited only once.

Aleksandrov, G. S., 'Iz zapisok ochevidtsa', *SS*, no. 13 (13.iv.17), 2f, no. 14 (14.iv.17), 2f.

Aleksandrov, V. I. (resp. ed.), *Voenno-morskoi revoliutsionnyi komitet: Sbornik dokumentov* (L, 1975).

Aleksandrovskii, G. D., 'Agoniia Morskogo Uchilishcha v Petrograde', *Kolybel' flota: Navigatskaia shkola – Morskoi korpus: K 250-ti letiiu so dnia osnovaniia shkoly matematicheskikh i navigatskikh nauk, 1701–1951 g.* (Paris, 1951), 238–41.

Antonov-Ovseenko, V. A., 'Baltflot v dni kerenshchiny i Krasnogo Oktiabria (Beglye vospominaniia)', *Proletarskaia revoliutsiia*, 1922, no. 10, 118–30.

——'Povest' oktiabr'skikh dnei (Iz vospominanii tov. Antonova-Ovseenko)', *Krasnoarmeets*, 1920, no. 28–30, 18–23.

——(N. Antonov), 'V Baltflote (iiun'-iiul' 1917 goda)', *Petrogradskaia pravda*, no. 157 (16.vii.1922), 6.

——'V oktiabr'skie dni (Otryvki iz vospominanii V. A. Antonova-Ovseenko)', *Krasnoarmeets*, 1919, no. 10–15, 28–32.

——*V semnadtsatom godu* (M, 1933).

Avtukhov, V., 'Kornilovshchina', *Morskoi sbornik*, 1924, no. 8, 1–16.

Bakhmetev, E., 'Oktiabr' i fevral' '; *Krasnyi baltiets*, 1920, no. 6, 35–42.

Baranov, A. V., 'Oktiabr'skie dni v Petrograde', *PLKF*, 239–50.

Baranov, S. N., *Veter s Baltiki* (M, 1967).

B'erkelund, B., 'Pervye dni revoliutsii v Baltiiskom flote', *Voennaia byl'*, no. 107 (1970), 20–6.

Blinov, A. M., 'Matrosskie komitety Baltiiskogo flota v Oktiabr'skom vooruzhennom vosstanii', *Lenin i Oktiabr'skoe vooruzhennoe vosstanie v Petrograde*, eds. I. I. Mints, *et al.*, 300–16.

——'Pervye revoliutsionnye organy vlasti v Kronshtadte v 1917 godu', *Voennye moriaki . . .*, ed. S. F. Naida, 133–47.

Bogdanov, A. V., *Moriaki – baltiitsy v 1917 g.* (M, 1955).

Bonch-Bruevich, M. D., *Vsia vlast' Sovetam: Vospominaniia* (M, 1964).
Bonch-Bruevich, V. D., *Vospominaniia o Lenine*, 2nd edn. (M, 1969).
Breslav, B. A., '15 let tomu nazad', *Katorga i ssylka*, 1932, no. 11/12, 46–68.
Bubnov, A. [D.], *V tsarskoi stavke: Vospominaniia admirala Bubnova* (New York, 1955).
—— 'Vliianie opyta voiny s Iaponiei na reformy v russkom flote', *Morskiia zapiski*, vol. xviii (1960), no. 3 (53), 32–40.
Bykov, P., 'Perekhod flota iz Gel'singforsa v Kronshtadt zimoiu 1918 goda', *Morskoi sbornik*, 1923, no. 11, 13–29.
Chugaev, D. A. (ed.), *Protokoly i postanovleniia Tsentral'nogo komiteta Baltiiskogo flota: 1917–1918* (M – L, 1963).
[Cromie, F. N. A.], 'Documents on British Relations with Russia, 1917–1918 (II): F. N. A. Cromie's Letters, March 27th to July 11th, 1917', ed. D. R. Jones, *Canadian-American Slavic Studies*, vii (1973), no. 3, 350–75.
—— 'Documents on British Relations with Russia, 1917–1918 (III): F. N. A. Cromie's Letters, September 27th to December 2nd, 1917', ed. D. R. Jones, *Canadian-American Slavic Studies*, vii (1973), no. 4, 498–510.
—— 'Documents on British Relations with Russia, 1917–1918 (iv): F. N. A. Cromie's Letters, January 19th to August 14th, 1918', ed. D. R. Jones, *Canadian-American Slavic Studies*, viii (1974), no. 4, 544–62.
Dingel'stedt, F. N., 'Vesna proletarskoi revoliutsii (Iz vpechatlenii agitatora o marte 1917 g.)', *Krasnaia letopis'*, 1925, no. 1 (12), 191–214.
Drezen, A. K. (ed.), 'Baltflot v iiul'skie dni 1917 g.', *Krasnyi arkhiv*, 1931, vol. 3 (46), 69–109.
—— 'Baltiiskii flot ot iiulia k Oktiabriu 1917 g.', *Krasnaia letopis'*, 1929, no. 5 (32), 157–212.
—— 'Baltiiskii flot v gody pod''ema (1910–1913)', *Krasnaia letopis'*, 1930, no. 3 (36), 126–63, no. 4 (37), 123–56.
—— (ed.), *Baltiiskii flot v Oktiabr'skoi revoliutsii i grazhdanskoi voine* (M – L, 1932).
—— 'Bor'ba za sovetizatsiiu Baltiiskogo flota', *Krasnaia letopis'*, 1929, no. 6 (33), 115–68.
—— (ed.), *Burzhuaziia i pomeshchiki v 1917 godu: Chastnye soveshchaniia chlenov Gosudarstvennoi dumy* (M – L, 1932).
—— (ed.), 'Flot posle Oktiabr'skoi pobedy', *Krasnyi arkhiv*, 1932, vol. 4 (53), 63–99.
—— (ed.), 'Oktiabr' i flot (po novym dokumentam)', *Krasnyi flot*, 1926, no. 10/11, 11–24.
—— 'Tsentral'nye matrosskie i ofitserskie organizatsii Baltiiskogo flota v 1917 g.', *Krasnaia letopis'*, 1929, no. 3 (30), 43–104.
Dublitskii, B., 'Baltiiskii flot v Iiul'skie dni 1917 g.' *Krasnaia letopis'*, 1922, no. 2/3, 352–5.
Dudorov, B. P., 'Vitse-admiral A. I. Nepenin (Opyt biografii)', *Morskiia*

zapiski, vols. XIV – XX (1956 – 62).

Dybenko, P. E. 'Baltflot v Oktiabr'skie dni (Vospominaniia)', *Pravda*, no. 252 (3784) (3.xi.1927), 6.

—— 'Baltiiskii flot v dni velikogo Oktiabria', *Oktiabr' v Petrograde: Sbornik statei*, ed. O. A. Lidak (L, 1933), 256 – 82.

—— *Miatezhniki: Iz vospominanii o revoliutsii* (M, 1923).

—— *Oktiabr' na Baltike: Vospominaniia* (Tashkent, 1934).

—— *V nedrakh tsarskogo flota* (M, 1919).

Egorov, A., *Baltflot v gody reaktsii: 1900 – 1913* (M, 1928).

Egorov, I. V., 'Matrosy-bol'sheviki nakanune 1917 g.', *OSh*, 11 – 17.

Fedotov, D., 'The Russian Navy and the Revolution', *United States Naval Institute Proceedings*, XLVIII (1922), 896 – 916.

—— (D. Fedotoff White), *Survival: Through War and Revolution in Russia* (Philadelphia, 1939).

Flerovskii, I. P., 'Iiul'skii politicheskii urok', *Proletarskaia revoliutsiia*, 1926, no. 7 (54), 57 – 90.

—— 'Kronshtadt v Oktiabr'skoi revoliutsii', *Proletarskaia revoliutsiia*, 1922, no. 10, 130 – 51.

—— 'Kronshtadtskaia respublika', *Proletarskaia revoliutsiia*, 1926, no. 11 (58), 29 – 55, no. 12 (59), 113 – 84.

Fraiman, A. L. (resp. ed.), *Baltiiskie moriaki v bor'be za vlast' Sovetov (Noiabr' 1917 – dekabr', 1918)* (L, 1968).

—— *Forpost sotsialisticheskoi revoliutsii: Petrograd v pervye mesiatsy Sovetskoi vlasti* (L, 1969).

—— *Revoliutsionnaia zashchita Petrograda v fevrale – marte 1918 g.* (M – L, 1964).

Gagern, E. von (ed.), *Der Krieg in der Ostsee: Von Anfang 1916 bis zum Kriegsende (Der Krieg in der Ostsee*, vol. III; *Der Krieg zur See, 1914 – 1918)* (Frankfurt/Main, 1964).

Garkavenko, D. A., 'Sotsial'nyi sostav matrosov russkogo flota v epokhu imperializma', *Istoriia SSSR*, 1968, no. 5, 36 – 56.

Gel'mersen, G. M. fon-, 'Stranitsy istorii', *Voennaia byl'*, no. 101 (1969), 36f.

Gordienko, I., 'V Kronshtadte v 1917 g.: Iz pervogo perioda Fevral'skoi revoliutsii', *Krasnaia letopis'*, 1926, no. 1 (16), 44 – 57.

Graf, G. K., *Na "Novike": Baltiiskii flot v voinu i revoliutsiiu* (Munich, 1922).

Grechaniuk, N. *et al.*, *Baltiiskii flot: Istoricheskii ocherk* (M, 1960).

Greger, R., *Die Russische Flotte im Ersten Weltkrieg 1914 – 1917* (Munich, 1970).

Guliaev, N. I., 'Korabel'nye inzhenery i inzhener-mekhaniki flota', *Morskiia zapiski*, vol. XX (1962), no. 3/4 (57), 73 – 93.

Gur'ev, K., 'Oktiabr'skii pokhod krasnykh moriakov', *Krasnyi flot*, 1922, no. 8, 122 – 8.

Iarchuk, E., *Kronshtadt v russkoi revoliutsii* (New York, 1923).

[Il'in-Zhenevskii, A. F. and I. P. Flerovskii] ('I-Zh' and 'A. F.'),

'Bol'shevistskie gazety Kronshtadta i Gel'singforsa v 1917 g.', *Krasnaia letopis'*, 1927, no. 3 (34), 83–107.

[Il'in-Zhenevskii, A. F.] (A. F. Ilyin-Genevsky), *From the February Revolution to the October Revolution, 1917* (London, 1931).

Isakov, I. I. (resp. ed.), *Morskoi atlas: Voenno-istoricheskie karty* (3 vols., M, 1957–8).

—— *Rasskazy o flote* (M, 1962).

Iunga, E., *Ledovyi pokhod: Istoricheskii ocherk* (L, 1949).

Ivanov, M., 'Moia pervaia vstrecha s tov. Leninym', *Krasnyi flot*, 1926, no. 2, 65f.

—— 'Pis'mo v redaktsiiu', *Revoliutsionnyi flot*, no. 16 (28) (17.xii.17).

Ivanov, N. Ia., *Kornilovshchina i ee razgrom: Iz istorii bor'by s kontrrevoliutsiei v 1917 g.* (L, 1965).

Izmailov, N. F., *Baltiiskii flot v Oktiabr'skie dni* (M, 1957).

—— *Baltiitsy shli Leninskim kursom: Vospominaniia veterana* (Kaliningrad, 1970).

—— and A. S. Pukhov, *Tsentrobalt*, 2nd edn. (Kaliningrad, 1967).

—— 'Tsentrobalt v Oktiabre', *Komsomol'skaia pravda*, no. 248 (29.x.1927), 2.

Katkov, G. 'The Russian Navy and the Revolution: 1905–1921', *The Soviet Navy*, ed. M. G. Saunders (London, 1958), 84–92.

Kaupisch, H. (ed.), *Die Befreiung von Livland und Estland (18. Februar bis 5. März 1918) (Der grosse Krieg in Einzeldarstellungen*, no. 39) (Oldenburg, 1918).

Khesin, S. S., 'Lichnyi sostav russkogo flota v 1917 godu', *Voenno-istoricheskii zhurnal*, 1965, no. 11, 99–104.

—— *Matrosy revoliutsii: Uchastie voennykh moriakov v bor'be za uprochenie Sovetskoi vlasti (Oktiabr' 1917 g. – mart 1918 g.)* (M, 1958).

—— *Oktiabr'skaia revoliutsiia i flot* (M, 1971).

—— 'Russkii flot i sverzhenie samoderzhaviia', *Sverzhenie samoderzhaviia: Sbornik statei*, eds. I. I. Mints, *et al.* (M, 1970), 184–93.

—— 'Russkii flot nakanune Oktiabria', *Istoricheskie zapiski*, vol. 81 (1968), 68–100.

—— 'Tsentrobalt (K 50-letiiu sozdaniia)', *Voenno-istoricheskii zhurnal*, 1967, no. 4, 120–5.

—— 'V. I. Lenin i Baltiiskii flot v dni Oktiabria', *Voenno-istoricheskii zhurnal*, 1969, no. 7, 120–5.

—— 'V. I. Lenin i organizatsiia Krasnogo flota', *Voprosy istorii*, 1970, no. 2, 3–17.

Kholodniak, A., *'Avrora' (Boevoe i revoliutsionnoe proshloe kreisera 'Avrora')* (L, 1925).

Khomchuk, N., 'O Ledovom pokhode korablei Baltiiskogo flota v 1918 godu', *Voenno-istoricheskii zhurnal*, 1963, no. 2, 120–4.

Khovrin, N. A., *Baltiitsy idut na shturm* (M, 1966).

—— 'V Oktiabr'skie dni v Pitere', *OSh*, 123–5.

—— 'V 1917 godu vo flote (Vospominaniia matrosa)', *Krasnaia letopis'*, 1926, no. 5 (20), 55–75.

Kirby, D. G., 'A Navy in Revolution: The Russian Baltic Fleet in 1917',*European Studies Review*, iv, no. 4 (1974), 345–58.

Kiuru, M. Kh., *Boevoi rezerv revoliutsionnogo Petrograda v 1917 g.: Iz istorii russkikh bol'shevistskikh organizatsii v Finliandii* (Petrozavodsk, 1965).

Kolbin, I. N., 'Baltiitsy v Oktiabr'skie dni', *OSh*, 118–23.

—— 'Iiul'skie dni i kontr-revoliutsiia na Kronshtadte', *Krasnyi flot*, 1927, no. 12/13, 4–9.

—— 'Kronshtadt organizuetsia, gotovitsia k boiu', *OSh*, 23–50.

—— 'Kronshtadt ot fevralia do kornilovskikh dnei', *Krasnaia letopis'*, 1927, no. 2 (23), 134–62.

—— *1917 god v Kronshtadte* (M, 1930).

Kondakov, D., 'Uchastie Kronshtadta v vystupleniiakh 3–5 iiulia', *Petrogradskaia pravda*, no. 149 (17.vii.1921), 2.

Kononov, G., 'Kronshtadtsy', *Moriak*, no. 11 (2.ix.17), 242.

Korolev, G., 'Proshlye dni', *Krasnyi flot*, 1924, no. 2, 25–9.

Kosinskii, A. M., *Moonzundskaia operatsiia Baltiiskogo flota 1917 goda* (M, 1928).

Kostenko, V. M., 'V "Klube samoubiits" (Pamiati pogibshikh pri ispolnenii sluzhebnago dolga)', *Morskiia zapiski*, x (1952), no. 1/2, 37–51.

Kostiukov, 'Kak my opozdali ko vziatiiu Zimnego dvortsa', *Krasnyi baltiets*, 1920, no. 6, 45f.

Krasnov, P. N., 'Na vnutrennem fronte', *Arkhiv russkoi revoliutsii*, vol. 1 (1921), 97–190.

Kronshtadt na 1916 god: Spravochnaia kniga (Kronstadt, 1916).

Kroviakov, N. S., 'K istorii "Ledovogo pokhoda" Baltiiskogo flota v 1918 g.', *Istoricheskie zapiski*, vol. 52 (1955), 3–48.

—— *'Ledovyi pokhod' Baltiiskogo flota v 1918 godu (K istorii pervoi strategicheskoi operatsii Sovetskogo Voenno-Morskogo Flota)* (M. 1955)

Kudelli, P. F., (ed.), *Oktiabr'skii shkval (Moriaki Baltiiskogo flota v 1917 godu)* (L, 1927).

—— (ed.), *Pervyi legal'nyi Peterburgskii komitet bol'shevikov v 1917 g.: Sbornik materialov i protokolov zasedenii Peterburgskogo komiteta RSDRP(b) i ego Ispol'nitel'noi komissii za 1917 g.* (M–L, 1927).

Kurkov, P. I., 'Kreiser "Avrora": Vospominaniia uchastnika', *PLKF*, 259–62.

Lamanov, P. N., 'V Kronshtadte posle Iiul'skikh dnei: Ultimatum vremennogo pravitel'stva', *Krasnaia letopis'*, 1927, no. 3, 23–34.

Liven, A. A., *Dukh i distsiplina nashego flota* (St Petersburg, 1908).

Longley, D. A., 'Officers and Men: A Study of the Development of Political Attitudes among the Sailors of the Baltic Fleet in 1917', *Soviet Studies*, vol. xxv, no. 1 (1973), 28–50.

Ludri, I. M., 'Sudovye komitety', *OSh*, 77–86.

Lukashevich, S., 'Materialy dlia istorii russkogo flota: Kratkaia khrono-
logiia revoliutsionnogo dvizheniia v russkom voennom flote', *Morskoi
sbornik*, vol. CDXIII (1920), no. 6/7, 34–46.

Lukin, A., 'Razstrel Shchastnago', *Posledniia novosti*, no. 3377 (21.vi.1930),
3f.

Lur'e, M. L. (ed.), 'Kronshtadtskie moriaki v iiul'skom vystuplenii 1917
goda', *Krasnaia letopis'*, 1932, no. 3 (48), 76–105.

M. Iu., 'Fevral' v Kronshtadte (Po vospominaniiam uchastnika)',
Leningradskaia pravda, no. 59 (12.iii.1927), 4.

Matveev, F. P. (ed.), *Petrogradskii Sovet rabochikh i soldatskikh deputatov:
Mart – mai 1917 g.: Iz zapisnoi knizhki deputata 176 pekhotnogo polka* (M –
L, 1932).

Mawdsley, E., 'The Baltic Fleet in the Russian Revolution, 1917–1921'
(Ph.D. Thesis, London University, 1970).

Mazurenko, K. I., 'Na "Slave" v Rizhskom zalive: 1915–17 gg.', *Morskiia
zapiski*, vol. IV (1946), no. 2, 89–106, no. 3/4, 144–87.

Medvedev, V. K., 'Kronshtadt v iiul'skie dni 1917 g.', *Istoricheskie zapiski*,
vol. 42 (1953), 262–75.

Mel'gunov, S. P., *Kak bol'sheviki zakhvatili vlast': Oktiabr'skii perevorot 1917
goda* (Paris, 1953).

——*Na putiakh k dvortsovomu perevorotu: Zagovory pered revoliutsiei 1917 goda*
(Paris, 1931).

Mil'nichuk, S., 'Vospominaniia matrosa', *Proletarskaia revoliutsiia*, 1922,
no. 11, 146–60.

Mints, I. I. (ed.), *Lenin i Oktiabr'skoe vooruzhennoe vosstanie v Petrograde:
Materialy Vsesoiuznoi nauchnoi sessii, sostoiavsheisia 13–16 noiabria 1962 g. v
Leningrade* (M, 1964).

Moiseev, S. P., *Spisok korablei russkogo parovogo i bronenosnogo flota: S 1861 po
1917* (M, 1948).

Mordvinov, R. N. (ed.), *Baltiiskie moriaki v podgotovke i provedenii Velikoi
Oktiabr'skoi sotsialisticheskoi revoliutsii* (M – L, 1957).

——*Kursom 'Avrory': Formirovanie Sovetskogo Voenno-Morskogo Flota i nachalo
ego boevoi deiatel'nosti (Noiabr' 1917 – mart 1919 gg.)* (M, 1962).

Mus'iakov, P. I., *Nikolai Izmailov* (M, 1964).

N. N., 'Organizatsionnoe postroenie Krasnogo flota (Kratkii istoricheskii
obzor ego za vremia s 1917 po oktiabr' 1922 g.)', *Morskoi sbornik*, 1923,
no. 1, 3–20.

Naida, S. F., 'Bor'ba revoliutsionnykh moriakov russkogo flota za pobedu
sotsialisticheskoi revoliutsii', *Voennye moriaki . . .*, ed. S. F. Naida, 41–
132.

——*Revoliutsionnoe dvizhenie v tsarskom flote, 1825–1917* (M – L, 1948).

——(ed.), *Voennye moriaki v bor'be za pobedu Oktiabr'skoi revoliutsii* (M,
1958).

Nelaev, V. A., *Pavel Dybenko* (M, 1965).

Nevolin, A., 'Stranitsy iz istorii kreisera "Avrora" (Vospominaniia starogo avrorovtsa)', *Voenno-istoricheskii zhurnal*, 1960, no. 11, 71–80.

Novikov, I., 'Pered Oktiabr'skim perevorotom v Gel'singforse', *Krasnyi baltiets*, 1921, no. 1, 51–6.

—— 'Vospominaniia uchastnika iiul'skogo i oktiabr'skogo perevorotov v 1917 godu', *Krasnyi baltiets*, 1920, no. 6, 23–34.

Ol'derogge, G. B., *Modest Ivanov* (M, 1969).

Pankratov, N. R., 'Bor'ba bol'shevikov za matrosskie massy Baltiiskogo flota v period Fevral'skoi revoliutsii', *Sbornik trudov uchilishcha* (Chernomorskoe vysshee voenno-morskoe uchilishche im. P. S. Nakhimova), no. 5 (1957), 3–22.

Pavlov, A. N., 'K iubileiu "bezkrovnoi" ', *Morskiia zapiski*, vol. xii (1954), no. 3, 9–20.

Pavlovich, N. V. (ed.), *Flot v pervoi mirovoi voine* (2 vols., M, 1964).

Petrash, V. V., *Moriaki Baltiiskogo flota v bor'be za pobedu Oktiabria* (M – L, 1966).

—— 'Moriaki-baltiitsy v Oktiabr'skie dni', *Oktiabr'skoe vooruzhennoe vosstanie v Petrograde: Sbornik statei*, eds. S. I. Avvakumov, *et al.* (M – L, 1957), 214–58.

—— 'Sostav Baltiiskogo flota i uchastie voennykh moriakov v Oktiabr'skom vooruzhennom vosstanii', *Lenin i Oktiabr'skoe vooruzhennoe vosstanie v Petrograde*, ed. I. I. Mints, 317–30.

—— 'V. I. Lenin i moriaki Baltiiskogo flota v 1917 g.', *V. I. Lenin v Oktiabre i v pervye gody Sovetskoi vlasti*, eds. A. L. Fraiman, et al. (L, 1970), 39–53.

—— 'Vybory v Uchreditel'noe sobranie po Baltiiskomu izbiratel'nomu okrugu', *Gorod Lenina v dni Oktiabria i Velikoi Otechestvennoi voiny 1941 – 1945 gg.: Sbornik statei*, eds. S. N. Valk, *et al.* (M – L, 1964), 64–82.

Petrov, M. A., *Podgotovka Rossii k mirovoi voine na more* (M – L, 1926).

Petrov, M. A., 'Moriaki Revel'skoi bazy v bor'be za sverzhenie samoderzhaviia i pobedu Oktiabr'skoi revoliutsii', *Voennye moriaki. . .*, ed. S. F. Naida, 147–67.

—— *Uchastie moriakov Baltiiskogo flota v bor'be za Sovetskuiu vlast' v Estonii (1917 g.)*, Avtoreferat kandidatskoi dissertatsii (Tallin, 1956).

Piat' let Krasnogo flota (Petrograd, 1922).

Pitkin, V. A., 'Dva admirala (Ocherki)', *Morskiia zapiski*, vol. ix (1951), 53–68.

Piterskii, N. A. (resp. ed.), *Boevoi put' Sovetskogo Voenno-Morskogo Flota* (M, 1967).

Pronin, A. G., 'Moi vospominaniia', *PLKF*, 249–58.

Protokoly pervago s"ezda Partii Levykh Sotsialistov-Revoliutsionerov (Internatsionalistov) (n.p., 1918).

Pukhov, A. S., *Moonzundskoe srazhenie: Revoliutsionnye moriaki Baltiki na zashchite Petrograda v 1917 godu* (L, 1957).

—— 'Vosstavshaia Baltika', *Pervyi den' novogo mira*, ed. V. F. Sulin, 7–40.

Raskol'nikov, F. F., *Kronshtadt i Piter v 1917 godu* (M – L, 1925).

—— 'Lenin v Oktiabre', *Krasnyi flot*, 1924, no. 2, 20f.

180   *The Russian Revolution and the Baltic Fleet*

—— *Rasskazy Michmana Il'ina* (M, 1934).

—— 'Revoliutsionnyi Kronshtadt', *Morskoi sbornik*, vol. CDIII (1918), no. 1, 45–58.

[Rengarten, I. I.], 'Baltiiskii flot nakanune Oktiabria (Iz dnevnika I. I. Rengartena)', ed. A. K. Drezen, *Krasnyi arkhiv*, 1929, vol. 4 (35), 5–36.

—— 'Fevral'skaia revoliutsiia v Baltiiskom flote (Iz dnevnika I. I. Rengartena)', ed. A. K. Drezen, *Krasnyi arkhiv*, 1929, vol. 1 (32), 88–124.

—— 'Oktiabr'skaia revoliutsiia v Baltiiskom flote (Iz dnevnika I. I. Rengartena)', ed. A. K. Drezen, *Krasnyi arkhiv*, 1927, no. 6 (25), 34–95.

'Revoliutsionnye otriady matrosov v kontse 1917 i nachale 1918 gg.', *Krasnyi flot*, 1922, no. 2, 91–6.

S. P. B., 'Boevaia deiatel'nost' Baltiiskogo flota posle Oktiabr'skoi revoliutsii (Istoricheskii ocherk)', *Morskoi sbornik*, 1922, no. 1/2, 57–81.

Sapozhnikov, V. I., *Podvig Baltiitsev v 1918 godu* (M, 1954).

Shatsillo, K. F., *Russkii imperializm i razvitie flota: Nakanune pervoi mirovoi voiny (1906–1914 gg.)* (M, 1968).

Shliapnikov, A., *Kanun semnadtsatogo goda: Vospominaniia i dokumenty o rabochem dvizhenii i revoliutsionnom podpol'e za 1914–1916 g. g.* (M – Petrograd, 1923).

—— *Semnadtsatyi god* (4 vols., M – Petrograd, 1923).

Shpilevskii, I. F., *Bratva (Baltiiskie moriaki v Grazhdanskoi voine): Vospominaniia* (L, 1929).

Sidorov, A. L. (ed.), *Revoliutsionnoe dvizhenie v armii i na flote v gody pervoi mirovoi voiny: 1914–fevral' 1917: Sbornik dokumentov* (M, 1966).

Sistematicheskii sbornik postanovlenii izdannykh po Narodnomu komissariatu po morskim delam s 25 oktiabria 1917 g. po 31 dekabria 1918 g. (M, 1919).

Sivkov, P. Z., *Kronshtadt: Stranitsy revoliutsionnoi istorii* (L, 1972).

—— *Moriaki Baltiiskogo flota v bor'be za vlast' Sovetov v 1917 godu* (M, 1946).

Smilga, I., 'Istoricheskaia noch': Otryvok iz vospominanii I. Smilgi', *Krasnoarmeets*, 1919, no. 10–15. 23f.

Sokolov, A., 'Komissiia dlia vyrabotki polozhenii, kasaiushchikhsia voenno-morskogo byta', *EMS*, no. 2 (3.vi.17), 10f.

Solov'ev, I. and T. Fedorova, 'K istorii vozniknoveniia bol'shevistskikh organizatsii na Baltiiskom flote', *Voenno-istoricheskii zhurnal*, 1966, no. 11, 10–19.

Sorokin, F., *Gvardeiskii ekipazh v fevral'skie dni 1917 goda* (M, 1932).

Spisok lichnago sostava sudov flota, stroevykh i administrativnykh uchrezhdenii Morskogo vedomstva (St. Petersburg, 1916).

Stasevich, P., 'Ledovyi pokhod Baltiiskogo flota', *OSh*, 129–44.

Stoliarenko, M. A., *Syny partii – Baltiitsy (Rabota partii bol'shevikov v Baltiiskom flote 1907–fevral' 1917 g.)* (L, 1969).

Sukhanov, N., *Zapiski o revoliutsii* (7 vols., Berlin-Petrograd-Moscow, 1922–3).

Sulin, V. F. (ed.), *Pervyi den' novogo mira: Vospominaniia i materialy ob uchastii moriakov Baltiiskogo flota v Oktiabr'skom vooruzhennom vosstanii* (Tallin, 1970).

Suslov, 'Sutki na "Andree Pervozvannom" ', *IGS*, nos. 68–71 (7–10.vi.17), 73 (13.vi.17).

Svod morskikh postanovlenii: Kniga desiataia: Morskoi ustav (St Petersburg, 1914).

Tarsaidze, A. G., *Morskoi Korpus za chetvert' veka, 1901–1925* (New York, 1944).

Timirev, S. N., *Vospominaniia morskogo ofitsera: Baltiiskii flot vo vremia voyny i revoliutsii (1914–1918 g.g.)* (New York, 1961).

1917–1922 god v Kronshtadte (Kronstadt, 1922).

Vakhrameev, I. I., *Vo imia revoliutsii: Vospominaniia* (M, 1957).

Vasil'ev, V. V., 'Revoliutsionnoe proshloe "Komsomol'tsa" (Vospominaniia okeantsa)', *Krasnyi flot*, 1922, no. 8, 77–82.

Velikaia Oktiabr'skaia sotsialisticheskaia revoliutsiia v Estonii: Sbornik dokumentov i materialov (Tallin, 1958).

Vinokurov, I. N., *et al.*, *Kronshtadt: Kratkii putevoditel'* (L, 1963).

Vishnevskii, E., 'Matrosskaia fraktsiia Gel'singforsskogo soveta (Tsentrobalt – organizator matrosskikh mass)', *OSh*, 50–77.

Vl. S., 'Iiul'skie dni i flot', *Krasnyi flot*, 1925, no. 7, 5–8.

Vladimirova, V., *Kontr-revoliutsiia v 1917 g. (Kornilovshchina)* (M, 1924).

Der Weltkrieg 1914 bis 1918: Die Kriegführung im Sommer und Herbst 1917: Die Ereignisse ausserhalb der Westfront bis November 1918 (Der Weltkrieg 1914 bis 1918, vol. xiii) (Berlin, 1942).

Zalezhskii, V. N., *Bor'ba za Baltiiskii flot* (M – L, 1925).

―― 'Gel'singfors vesnoi i letom 1917 goda', *Proletarskaia revoliutsiia*, 1923, no. 5 (17), 117–89.

Zashchuk, I. I. *Russkii flot: Spravochnaia knizhka dlia sukhoputnykh ofitserov* (St Petersburg, 1912).

Zinger, M., *Brat "Avrory"* (Minsk, 1957).

Zver'kov, I., 'Zasluzhennaia kara ili revoliutsionnye dni Kronshtadta', *Trud i zemlia*, nos. 100 (22.viii.17), 104 (26.viii.17), 107 (30.viii.17), 109 (1.ix.17), 113 (6.ix.17).

Notes

CHAPTER 1

•

1 A. A. Liven, *Dukh i distsiplina nashego flota*, 120.

2 V. V. Petrash, *Moriaki Baltiiskogo flota v bor'be za pobedu Oktiabria*, 17–19.

3 Sota-arkisto (Helsinki), Venäläinen Kokoelma, File 3221 (hereafter cited as VK 3221, etc.), Prikaz Komanduiushchago flotom Baltiiskago moria (hereafter cited as Prikaz Komflota) no. 889 (23.xi.16).

4 N. Piterskii, 'Boevaia podgotovka flota v voennoe vremia (Po opytu imperialisticheskoi voiny 1914–1918 gg.)', *Morskoi sbornik*, 1937, no 6, 57f.

5 A. L. Sidorov (ed.), *Revoliutsionnoe dvizhenie v armii i na flote v gody pervoi mirovoi voiny*, 437; S. S. Fabritskii, *Iz proshlago: Vospominaniia Fligel'-Ad''iutanta Gosudaria Imperatora Nikolaia II* (Berlin, 1926), 142; M. Petrov, 'Krizis russkogo morskogo komandovaniia', *Morskoi sbornik*, 1926, no. 8/9, 10.

6 B. P. Dudorov, 'Vitse-admiral A. I. Nepenin', *Morskiia zapiski*, xix (1961), no. 1/2 (54), 105.

7 Ibid., no. 3/4 (55), 66f.

8 D. Fedotov, 'The Russian Navy and the Revolution', *United States Naval Institute Proceedings*, xlviii (1922), 900f; Prikaz Komflota no. 976 (12.xii.16).

9 G. Kononov, 'Kronshtadtsy', *Moriak*, no. 11 (2.ix.17), 242; V. Poshekhov, 'Noch' pod l-e marta 1917 g. v Kronshtadte', *Krasnyi baltiets*, 1920, no. 1, 34. For other comments on Viren see: E. Bakhmetev, 'Oktiabr'' i fevral'', *Krasnyi baltiets*, 1920, no. 6, 37; G. K. Graf, *Na 'Novike'*, 291; S. N. Timirev, *Vospominaniia morskogo ofitsera*, 80f. As early as 1911 revolutionary sailors had discussed a plan for assassinating Viren (A. Drezen, 'Baltiiskii flot v gody pod''ema', *Krasnaia letopis'*, 1930, no. 3 (36), 160).

10 Petrash, *Moriaki*, 15f; Graf, 291f; Sidorov (ed.), 377; *Izvestiia Kronshtadtskago Soveta* (hereafter cited as *IKS*), no. 100 (20.vii.17), 2; A. K. Drezen (ed.), *Burzhuaziia i pomeshchiki v 1917 godu*, 80.

11 Timirev, 73–6; Prikaz Komflota no. 922 (28.xi.16), no. 958 (7.xii.16); Dudorov, *Morskiia zapiski*, xix (1961), no. 1/2 (54), 108f.

12 Liven, 119f; Kononov, 242.

13 Petrash, *Moriaki*, 30–2; I. I. Isakov, *Rasskazy o flote*, 42; Sidorov (ed.), 317, 328, 371.

14 S. S. Khesin, 'Russkii flot nakanune Oktiabria', *Istoricheskie zapiski*, vol. 81 (1968), 80.

15 Petrash, *Moriaki*, 19; A. Drezen, 'Tsentral'nye matrosskie i ofitserskie organizatsii Baltiiskogo flota v 1917 g.', *Krasnaia letopis'*, 1929, no. 3 (30), 68–70; Suslov, 'Sutki na "Andree Pervozvannom"', *Izvestiia Gel'singforsskago Soveta* (hereafter cited as *IGS*), no. 71 (10.vi.17), 2f.

16 Drezen, 'Baltiiskii flot v gody pod''ema', 145; D. A. Garkavenko, 'Sotsial'nyi

sostav matrosov russkogo flota v epokhu imperializma', *Istoriia SSSR*, 1968, no. 5, 52; B. M. Kochakov, 'Sotsial'nyi sostav soldat tsarskoi armii v period imperializma', *Iz istorii imperializma v Rossii*, resp. ed. M. P. Viatkin (L, 1959), 350, 364; S. S. Khesin, 'Lichnyi sostav russkogo flota v 1917 godu', *Voenno-istoricheskii zhurnal*, 1965, no. 11, 101, 103.

17 Available data do not permit an exact comparison, but the differences were significant. In the army, 65% were under 30, 30% were 30 to 39, and 5% were over 39 (N. N. Golovine, *The Russian Army in the World War* (New Haven, 1931), 51). In the Baltic Fleet, 79.5% were under 29, and 16.6% were 29 to 33 (Petrash, *Moriaki*, 17, 21).

18 Sidorov (ed.), 315–405; N. A. Khovrin, *Baltiitsy idut na shturm*, 13–46; K. Orlov, *Zhizn' rabochego-revoliutsionera* (L, 1925), 27–32; V. Zalezhskii, *Bor'ba za Baltiiskii flot*, 3–11; A Shliapnikov, *Kanun semnadtsatogo goda*, 47–58; 'Delo o revoliutsionnoi organizatsii sredi matrosov na lineinykh korabliakh "Imp. Pavel I", "Imp. Aleksandr II", i "Tsesarevich"', *Krasnyi baltiets*, 1920, no. 5, 27–36, no. 7, 51–64; I. Solov'ev and T. Fedorova, 'K istorii vozniknoveniia bol'shevistskikh organizatsii na Baltiiskom flote', *Voenno-istoricheskii zhurnal*, 1966, no. 11, 18.

19 N. Khovrin, 'V 1917 godu vo flote', *Krasnaia letopis'*, 1926, no. 5(20), 55; Khovrin, *Baltiitsy*, 43; Sidorov (ed.), 382f; Shliapnikov, *Kanun*, 56–8.

20 Sidorov (ed.), 435; *Zemlia i volia*, no. 48 (21.v.17), 2f.

21 Solov'ev and Fedorova, 15; Sidorov (ed.), 404; Petrash, *Moriaki*, 47; M. Kh. Kiuru, *Boevoi rezerv revoliutsionnogo Petrograda v 1917 g.*, 8; Graf, 289.

22 Fedotov, 916; Suslov, *IGS*, no. 68 (7.vi.17), 2.

23 I. F. Shpilevskii, *Bratva*, 22, 27; Prikaz Komflota no. 985 (15.xii.16).

24 D. Fedotoff White, *Survival*, 77; [I. I. Rengarten], 'Fevral'skaia revoluitsiia v Baltiiskom flote', ed. A. K. Drezen, *Krasnyi arkhiv*, 1929, vol. 1 (32), 91–8; S. P. Mel'gunov, *Na putiakh k dvortsovomu perevorotu*, 159. Shul'gin, a member of the Duma, recalled hearing of a naval plan to kidnap the empress, but he dismissed this as 'idle talk' (*Dni* (Belgrade, 1925), 127).

25 *Revel'skii nabliudatel'*, no. 54 (7.iii.17), 2; Graf, 355.

26 Graf, 356f.

27 Fedotov, 910.

28 S. S. Khesin, *Oktiabr'skaia revoliutsiia i flot*, 36–9; M. A. Stoliarenko, *Syny partii–baltiitsy*, 164f; 'Kak nachalos' vosstanie v fevrale 1917 g. na kreisere "Avrora"', *Krasnyi baltiets*, 1921, no. 11/12, 47–52.

29 *IKS*, no. 100 (20.vii.17), 2 (this letter was published unofficially after February in the *Mozhaiskii Telegraf*, but there seems no reason to doubt its authenticity); Sidorov (ed.), 404f; I. Kolbin, 'Kronshtadt organizuetsiia, gotovitsia k boiu', *Oktiabr'skii shkval* (hereafter cited as *OSh*), ed. P. F. Kudelli, 25f.

30 Graf, 293–6; Kolbin, 'Kronshtadt organizuetsiia', 27–9; I. Zver'kov, 'Zasluzhennaia kara ili revoliutsionnye dni Kronshtadta', *Trud i zemlia*, no. 100 (22.viii.17), 2f; R. N. Mordvinov (ed.), *Baltiiskie moriaki v podgotovke i provedenii Velikoi Oktiabr'skoi sotsialisticheskoi revoliutsii* (hereafter cited as *BMPP*), 19–21; A. A. Sergeev (ed.), 'Fevral'skaia revoliutsiia 1917 goda (Dokumenty stavki verkhovnogo glavnokomanduiushchego i shtaba glavnokomanduiushchego armiiami severnogo fronta)' *Krasnyi arkhiv*, 1927, vol. 2 (21), 19.

31 Various figures have been given, but those of Petrash, based on archival sources, have been accepted for the number of officers killed and imprisoned. Petrash also states that in the Baltic Fleet as a whole 4 officers committed suicide

and 11 disappeared and are presumed to have deserted; a considerable proportion of these must have been from Kronstadt (*Moriaki*, 52f). Some 33 ratings – mostly warrant officers and senior petty officers – were killed in the Baltic Fleet; probably from one-half to one-third died at Kronstadt (Khesin, 'Russkii flot nakanune Oktiabria', 80). Many n.c.o.s were arrested at Kronstadt. It was stated in the Kronstadt Soviet that 39 naval and army officers had been killed and 236 arrested (*IKS*, no. 16 (6.iv.17), 2). In late May the Provisional Government's commissar reported that 51 military personnel had been killed, including 40 army and naval officers – but he could not be certain of his figures; 500 people had been arrested, including 230 officers (A. K. Drezen (ed.), *Burzhuaziia i pomeshchiki*, 80). On the rebel side, 2 sailors and 5 soldiers were killed and buried as 'martyrs to the revolution' (*Kotlin*, no. 53 (8.iii.17), 2).

32 Bakhmetev, 40; Zver'kov, *Trud i zemlia*, no. 113 (6.ix.17), 2; Khovrin, *Baltiitsy*, 63f. In fact, the Duma's Military Commission did order 800 soldiers from two regiments to Kronstadt to restore order, but they never actually went (F.D. (ed.), 'Fevral'skaia revoliutsiia v Petrograde (28 fevralia – 1 marta 1917 g.)', *Krasnyi arkhiv*, 1930, vol. 4/5(41/42), 68).

33 N. Tochenyi, 'Kronshtadtsy i vremennoe pravitel'stvo', *Voennye moriaki v bor'be za pobedu Oktiabr'skoi revoliutsii*, ed. S. F. Naida, 316.

34 *BMPP*, 16f; Prikaz Komflota no. 156 (1.iii.17).

35 Dudorov, *Morskiia zapiski*, xix (1961), no. 3/4(55), 71; Rengarten, 'Fevral'skaia revoliutsiia', 95, 119.. The émigré S. P. Mel'gunov tried to use Nepenin's remarks as evidence of his participation in an officers' plot against the Tsar. Mel'gunov admitted however that Rengarten's account was the only hard evidence available and that no further conclusions could be made about this 'interesting page in the history of the fleet' because the participants had all been killed (*Na putiakh*, 158–62). In fact, this was not true, as one member of the circle of 'progressive' officers in the Baltic Staff, Commander F. Iu. Dovkont, was still alive in 1956, and he denied any links with liberals at the centre and particularly with Zhitkov, the editor of *Morskoi sbornik*. Nepenin's biographer added that none of the admiral's links were particularly liberal, and he was probably quite correct in describing Mel'gunov's accusations as 'more than erroneous and unfair' (Dudorov, *Morskiia zapiski*, xix (1961), no. 3/4(55), 72–9).

36 Rengarten, 'Fevral'skaia revoliutsiia', 103, 105; *BMPP*, 29f: Prikaz Komflota no. 265/op. (3.iii.17), no. 267/op. (3.iii.17); Suslov, *IGS*, no. 69 (8.vi.17), 2, no. 70 (9.vi.17), 2; Graf, 254–7; K. I. Mazurenko, 'Na "Slave" v Rizhskom zalive', *Morskiia zapiski*, iv (1946), no. 3/4, 166; M. Zinger, *Brat 'Avrory'*, 7.

37 Timirev, 93; *BMPP*, 17f, 29; Suslov, *IGS*, no. 68 (7.vi.17), 2f; *Vestnik Vremennago Pravitel'stva*, no. 174(220) (11.x.17), 3.

38 Rengarten, 'Fevral'skaia revoliutsiia', 105; Suslov, *IGS*, no. 68 (7.vi.17), 2.

39 I. Novikov, 'Pered Oktiabr'skim perevorotom v Gel'singforse', *Krasnyi baltiets*, 1921, no. 1, 52f; G. S. Aleksandrov, 'Iz zapisok ochevidtsa', *Svobodnoe slovo matrosa i soldata* (hereafter cited as *SS*), no. 13 (13.iv.17), 2; Suslov, *IGS*, no. 68 (7.vi.17), 3, no. 69 (8.vi.17), 2f, no. 70 (9.vi.17), 2f, no. 71 (10.vi.17), 2f, no. 73 (13.vi.17), 2f; Prikaz Komflota no. 967 (11.xii.16); Graf, 272–8, 282–7; Rengarten, 'Fevral'skaia revoliutsiia', 106; *BMPP*, 29–31; Mazurenko, *Morskiia zapiski*, iv (1946), no. 3/4, 167–9; Shpilevskii, *Bratva*, 30–6. Petrash states that 42 officers were arrested (probably from both army and navy) and gives a high figure of 45 naval officers killed (*Moriaki*, 52f). Other sources give a slightly lower figure of 38 –

39 naval officers killed (Graf, 288; Timirev, 95; A. Shliapnikov, *Semnadtsatyi god*, vol. 1, 137). Probably half the 33 Baltic ratings killed were at Helsingfors. There were only two 'martyrs to the revolution' in Helsingfors, one of whom was a Tatar mess steward from the *Andrei* who was accidentally killed by the crew (*IGS*, no. 7 (19.iii.17), 2; Boris B'erkelund, 'Pervye dni revoliutsii v Baltiiskom flote', *Voennaia byl'*, no. 107 (1970), 22). Another mutineer was killed by his own ricochet (Graf, 285).

40 Suslov, *IGS*, no. 73 (13.vi.17), 2; *BMPP*, 31; Shpilevskii, *Bratva*, 35f; Aleksandrov, *SS*, no. 13 (13.iv.17), 2f.

41 *BMPP*, 32; A. N. Pavlov, 'K iubileiu "bezkrovnoi"', *Morskiia zapiski*, xii (1954), no. 3, 13, 19; Zinger, 7.

42 *BMPP*, 31f; Dudorov, *Morskiia zapiski*, xx (1962), no. 1/2 (56), 47f; Rengarten, 'Fevral'skaia revoliutsiia', 106, 123f; *Revel'skii nabliudatel'*, no. 54 (7.iii.17), 1f.

43 *BMPP*, 33f; Rengarten, 'Fevral'skaia revoliutsiia', 108.

44 *BMPP*, 34; Rengarten, 'Fevral'skaia revoliutsiia', 108f; Dudorov, *Morskiia zapiski*, xx (1962), no. 1/2 (56), 55f.

45 Pavlov, 16–18.

46 *BMPP*, 39f.

47 *Revel'skii nabliudatel'*, no. 50 (2.iii.17), 3; *BMPP*, 24–8. Some sources state that naval officers were killed at Reval; Petrash gives a figure of 5, and an official report gave one of 3 (*Moriaki*, 52; Shliapnikov, *Semnadtsatyi god*, vol. 1, 137). No detailed information is available, but it does not seem that any naval officers were killed aboard their ships in the period from 1 to 3 March. Perhaps the casualties were officers normally based at Reval who died elsewhere. According to Petrash, 8 officers – possibly from both the army and the navy – were arrested in Reval (*Moriaki*, 53).

48 A. Th. Kerensky, *The Catastrophe: Kerensky's Own Story of the Russian Revolution* (London, 1927), 158.

49 Khovrin, 'V 1917', 57.

50 Bakhmetev, 36.

51 *Vestnik Vremennago Pravitel'stva*, no. 174(220) (11.x.17), 3.

CHAPTER 2

1 V. Zalezhskii, *Iz vospominanii podpol'shchika* (Kharkov, 1931), 182; A. M. Kosinskii, *Moonzundskaia operatsiia Baltiiskogo flota 1917 goda*, 43.

2 *IKS*, no. 53 (24.v.17), 1.

3 Khovrin, 'V 1917', 63; *IGS*, no. 31 (22.iv.17), 3; no. 99 (14.vii.17), 4.

4 *IKS*, no. 85 (1.vii.17), 1, no. 116 (8.viii.17), 3.

5 *Zemlia i volia*, no. 47 (20.v.17), 3, no. 48 (21.v.17), 3; *Narodnaia niva*, no. 102 (25.viii.17), 4; Zalezhskii, *Bor'ba*, 26; F. F. Raskol'nikov, *Kronshtadt i Piter v 1917 godu*, 89.

6 *Kronshtadtskaia iskra*, no. 2 (2.viii.17), 3; *Delo naroda*, no. 119 (5.viii.17), 4; V. A. Antonov-Ovseenko, *V semnadtsatom godu*, 159; *Zemlia i volia*, no. 48 (21.v.17), 3; G. Korolev, 'Proshlye dni', *Krasnyi flot*, 1924, no. 2, 26; Khovrin, 'V 1917', 63; Raskol'nikov, *Kronshtadt*, 88; Zalezhskii, *Bor'ba*, 83; *Izvestiia Revel'skago Soveta* (hereafter cited as *IRS*), no. 19 (6.iv.17), 4.

7 *Utro pravdy*, no. 10 (20.vi.17), 4; Raskol'nikov, *Kronshtadt*, 90; V. N. Zalezhskii, 'Gel'singfors vesnoi i letom 1917 goda', *Proletarskaia revoliutsiia*, 1923, no. 5(17), 135; *IKS*, no. 78 (22.vi.17), 1.

8 *Narodnaia niva*, no. 51 (24.vi.17), 3; *Delo naroda*, no. 57 (25.v.17), 2; *IRS*, no. 182 (24.x.17), 3; *Protokoly pervago s"ezda Partii Levykh Sotsialistov-Revoliutsionerov (Internatsionalistov)*, 12.

9 *Narodnaia niva*, no. 71 (19.vii.17), 4; *IGS*, no. 28 (18.iv.17), 4; Korolev, 25.

10 *Narodnaia niva*, no. 51 (24.vi.17), 1, 3; *Sotsialist-revoliutsioner*, no. 1 (9.vii.17), 1, no. 63 (4.x.17), 4, no. 64 (5.x.17), 1.

11 *Zemlia i volia*, no. 47 (20.v.17), 3; *Trud i zemlia*, no. 81 (29.vii.17), 2; *IRS*, no. 127 (17.viii.17), 4; Antonov-Ovseenko, *V semnadtsatom godu*, 195; *Protokoly 1 – go s"ezda P.L.S. – R.*, 5, 12.

12 *IKS*, no. 98 (18.vii.17), 1.

13 'Raskol'nikov, F.F.', *Entsiklopedicheskii slovar' russkogo bibliograficheskogo instituta Granat* (hereafter cited as *Granat*), 7th edn. (M, n.d.), vol. 41, part 2, 187–92; A. P. Konstantinov, *F. F. Il'in-Raskol'nikov* (L, 1964); N. E. Saul, 'Fedor Raskolnikov, a "Secondary Bolshevik"', *Russian Review*, vol. 32 (1973), no. 1, 131–42; N. Sukhanov, *Zapiski o revoliutsii,* vol. 3, 18.

14 G. G. Roshal', 'Iz zhizni "doktora": Vospominaniia o t. S. G. Roshale', *Krasnaia letopis'*, 1922, no. 4, 313–6; *Revoliutsionnyi flot*, no. 8 (27.iii.18), 2f; N. A. Khodza, *Bol'shevistskii komissar Semen Roshal'* (M, 1952); *BMPP*, 162; *IKS*, no. 31 (26.iv.17), 2.

15 A Rakitin, *Imenem revoliutsii . . . (Ocherki o V. A. Antonove-Ovseenko)* (M, 1965); 'Antonov-Ovseenko, Vl. A.', *Granat*, vol. 41, part 1, 6–10; Khovrin, *Baltiitsy*, 91f.

16 W. S. Woytinsky, *Stormy Passage: A Personal History through Two Russian Revolutions to Democracy and Freedom, 1905–1960* (N.Y., 1961), 285.

17 Zalezhskii, *Bor'ba*, 71. Of the 21 delegates (16 different individuals) sent by the Kronstadt and Helsingfors organisations to the March – April Conference of Party Workers, the 7th Party Conference, and the 6th and 7th Party Congresses, 8 (6 individuals) were outsiders and 4 (4 individuals) may have been outsiders. The 9 Reval delegates were probably all local people. Only 4 (3 individuals) of the 30 delegates were definitely naval ratings. ('Protokoly Vserossiiskogo (martovskogo) soveshchaniia partiinykh rabotnikov: 27 marta – 2 aprel'ia 1917 g.', *Voprosy istorii KPSS*, 1962, no. 6, 148; L. Trotsky, *The Stalin School of Falsification* (N.Y., 1972), 232f; *Sed'maia (Aprel'skaia) Vserossiiskaia konferentsiia RSDRP (bol'shevikov): Petrogradskaia obshchegorodskaia konferentsiia RSDRP(b): Aprel' 1917 g.: Protokoly* (M, 1958), 326–30; *Shestoi s"ezd RSDRP(bol'shevikov): Avgust 1917 goda* (M, 1958), 300f, 303; *Sed'moi ekstrennyi s"ezd RKP(b): Mart 1918 goda: Stenograficheskii otchet* (M, 1962),201, 204f.

18 *BMPP*, 334n20; *6-oi s"ezd*, 354.

19 *Zemlia i volia*, no. 48 (21.v.17), 3.

20 P. F. Kudelli (ed.), *Pervyi legal'nyi Peterburgskii komitet bol'shevikov v 1917 g.*, 53; Zalezhskii, 'Gel'singfors', 117; *7-aia konferentsiia*, 127; D. A. Chugaev (resp. ed.), *Revoliutsionnoe dvizhenie v Rossii v mae-iiune 1917 g.: Iiun'skaia demonstratsiia* (M, 1959), 72f. For an interesting discussion of the Kronstadt organisation see: D. Longley, 'Some Historiographical Problems of Bolshevik Party History (The Kronstadt Bolsheviks in March 1917)', *Jahrbücher für Geschichte Osteuropas*, vol. 22, no. 4 (1975), 494–514.

21 *Volna*, no. 1 (30.iii.17), 1.

22 *Kotlin*, no. 59 (15.iii.17), 2; 'Protokoly . . . martovskogo soveshchaniia', *Voprosy istorii KPSS*, 1962, no. 5, 116; Khovrin, 'V 1917', 62; *IKS*, no. 19 (11.iv.17), 1.

23 *Volna*, no. 13 (14.iv.17), 4.

24 *Edinstvo*, no. 13 (14.iv.17), 3f; Zalezhskii, *Bor'ba*, 16, 51; A.F. Ilyin-Genevsky, *From the February Revolution to the October Revolution, 1917*, 45; F. Averichkin, 'V. I. Lenin i flot', *Krasnyi flot*, 1924, no. 1, 19f.

25 *Narodnaia niva*, no. 32 (2.vi.17), 2; *SS*, no. 19 (20. iv.17), 2, no. 54 (2.vi.17), 1, no. 60 (9.vi.17), 1, no. 61 (10.vi.17), 1; *Golos Sotsial-Demokrata*, no. 1 (30.vii.17), 16.

26 *Utro pravdy*, no. 7 (10.vi.17), 3, no. 8 (13.vi.17), 4; *SS*, no. 67 (17.vi.17), 4.

27 *7-aia konferentsiia*, 125; *Velikaia Oktiabr'skaia sotsialisticheskaia revoliutsiia v Estonii*, 67, 132, 175; Zalezhkii, *Bor'ba*, 48; *BMPP*, 64f.

28 *Narodnaia niva*, no. 47 (20.vi.17), 3; Antonov-Ovseenko, *V semnadtsatom godu*, 152.

CHAPTER 3

1 [F. N. A. Cromie], 'Documents on British Relations with Russia, 1917–1918 (II)', ed. D. R. Jones, *Canadian-American Slavic Studies*, VII (1973), no. 3, 355.

2 L. S. Gaponenko (resp. ed.), *Revoliutsionnoe dvizhenie v Rossii posle sverzheniia samoderzhaviia* (M, 1957), 615f; Isakov, 18; Cromie 'Documents (II)', 371; Public Record Office, Admiralty Papers, class 137, vol. 1249, 406 (hereafter cited as Adm. 137/1249, 406, etc.); VK 3221, Meeting of Helsingfors Soviet Sailors' Section (hereafter cited as HSSS) no. 60 (15.viii.17).

3 *RDR posle sverzheniia*, 657f.

4 Ibid., 633; Fedotoff White, 118.

5 *Vestnik Vremennago Pravitel'stva*, no. 19 (29.iii.17), 3.

6 Timirev, 27f; VK 3221, HSSS no. 75 (24.ix.17); Dybenko, *V nedrakh*, 15; *Moriak*, no. 4 (16.vi.17), 80; Dybenko, *Miatezhniki*, 26. Some émigré officers maintained that Maksimov was no liberal before 1917 (A. Bubnov, *V tsarskoi stavke*, 334; K. A. Popov (ed.), *Dopros Kolchaka* (L, 1925), 56; Timirev, 28, 95f).

7 VK 3184, Prikazy Komflota no. 3 (5.iii.17), no. 9 (9.iii.17), no. 15 (10.iii.17), no. 31 (14.iii.17), no. 88 (5.iv.17), no. 101 (10.iv.17), nos. 124–5 (15.iv.17), no. 126 (16.iv.17), no. 155 (25.iv.17); VK 3910, Prikaz Komflota no. 185 (30.iv.17); *IGS*, no. 5 (16.iii.17), 1; Liven, 123f.

8 L. S. Gaponenko (resp. ed.), *Revoliutsionnoe dvizhenie v Rossii v aprele 1917 g.: Aprel'skii krizis* (M, 1958), 312f.

9 *IGS*, no. 47 (11.v.17), 3.

10 *RDR v mae-iune*, 237–9; *IGS*, no. 57 (25.v.17), 1, no. 59 (27.v.17), 1; *IKS*, no. 67 (9.vi.17), 1.

11 A. Sokolov, 'Komissiia dlia vyrabotki polozhenii, kasaiushchikhsia voenno-morskogo byta', *Ezhenedel'nik Morskogo sbornika* (hereafter cited as *EMS*) no. 2 (3.vi.17), 10f: Timirev, 115; Graf, 368.

12 *EMS*, no. 2 (3.vi.17), 7–9, no. 3 (10.vi.17), 8–11; VK 3221, HSSS no. 18 (28.iv.17).

13 *EMS*, no. 2 (3.vi.17), 5–7; *IGS*, no. 106 (22.vii.17), 2, no. 165 (3.x.17), 3; *Revel'skii nabliudatel'*, no. 175 (10.viii.17), 3; A. G. Tarsaidze, *Morskoi korpus za*

chetvert' veka, 1901–1925, 24.

14 *EMS*, no. 4 (17.vi.17), 8–9, no. 12 (12.viii.17), 15f.

15 VK 3184, Prikaz Komflota no. 219 (10.v.17); *IGS*, no. 101 (16.vii.17), 2; Onipko first arrived in Helsingfors at the end of April, as commissar of the Petrograd Soviet (*IGS*, no. 34 (26. iv.17), 1).

16 VK 3221, HSSS no. 35 (8.vi.17); VK 1636, Meeting of the Congress, 8.vi.17.

17 *IGS*, no. 30 (21.iv.17), 1; *IKS*, no. 26 (20.iv.17), 2, no. 48 (17.v.17), 1; *SS*, no. 15 (15.iv.17), 4, no. 20 (21.iv.17), 1.

18 *BMPP*, 54f; *IGS*, no. 10 (23.iii.17), 1, no. 30 (20.iv.17), 1; VK 3221, HSSS no. 10 (14.iv.17); D. A. Chugaev (ed.), *Protokoly i postanovleniia Tsentral'nogo komiteta Baltiiskogo flota* (hereafter cited as *Protokoly*), 437.

19 VK 3178. This version is very similar to a draft published in *Protokoly* (pp. 436f) with modifications accepted on 28 April (pp. 35f).

20 P. E. Dybenko, *V nedrakh tsarskogo flota*; 'Dybenko, Pavel Efimovich', *Granat*, vol. 41, part I, 128–34; Khovrin, *Baltiitsy*, 17–19; *IGS*, no. 10 (23.iii.17), 4.

21 *Protokoly*, 42, 58.

22 Ibid., 47, 52, 53, 63.

23 *BMPP*, 341n52; Drezen, 'Tsentral'nye organizatsii', 94; Raskol'nikov, *Kronshtadt*, 104.

24 *Protokoly*, 429f; VK 1636, Meetings of the Congress, 30, 31.v, 1.vi.17.

25 VK 3901, 56f.

26 VK 1636, Meetings of the Congress, 29, 31.v.17; *Protokoly*, 438n12; Dybenko, *Miatezhniki*, 49; Khovrin, *Baltiitsy*, 106f; Drezen, 'Tsentral'nye organizatsii', 96–8. Dybenko's assertion that Kerensky approved the charter (*Miatezhniki*, 54) is incorrect.

27 *IGS*, no. 83 (24.vi.17), 4; VK 1636, Meeting of the Congress, 8, 15. vi.17; VK 3221, HSSS no. 39 (16.vi.17); Drezen, 'Tsentral'nye organizatsii', 99f.

28 VK 1636, Meetings of the Congress, 1–4.vi.17; VK 7374.

29 *BMPP*, 68f; *Tsentroflot*, no. 1 (25.x.17), 11.

30 *Moriak*, no. 9 (19.viii.17), 204. The court had included Timirev, captain of the *Baian*, and Podgursky, commander of the Gulf of Bothnia naval forces.

31 Timirev, 28; Petrash, *Moriaki*, 127; Drezen, 'Tsentral'nye organizatsii', 101; Cromie, 'Documents (II)', 367f, 370, 372, 'Documents (III)', 504; A. I. Denikin, *Ocherki Russkoi Smuty: Krushenie vlasti i armii (Ocherki Russkoi Smuty*, vol. 1, *vypusk* 2) (Paris, n.d.), 10; *IGS*, no. 65 (3.vi.17), 2; Bubnov, 335f.

32 Cromie, 'Documents (II)', 365, 372; VK 1636, Meeting of the Congress, 2, 3.vi.17; Zalezhskii, 'Gel'singfors', 180.

33 N. F. Izmailov and A. S. Pukhov, *Tsentrobalt*, 55f; *BMPP*, 83; Antonov-Ovseenko, *V semnadtsatom godu*, 167; *IGS*, no. 70 (9.vi.17), 1.

34 VK 3221, HSSS no. 39 (16.vi.17); Petrash, *Moriaki*, 129–31; *BMPP*, 100f, 343; *IKS*, no. 76 (20.vi.17), 3; *SS*, no. 71 (22.vi.17), 3; *Protokoly*, 74f, 81f.

35 *BMPP*, 100; *Protokoly*, 74.

36 Kerensky, *Catastrophe*, 181; *IGS*, no. 49 (14.v.17), 2.

37 Zalezhskii, *Bor'ba*, 91; *Svobodnyi flot*, no. 13/25 (13.xi.17), 5.

38 'The committees instituted by the Provisional Government,' noted one émigré source, 'could but aggravate the situation' (N. Monasterev and S. Terestchenko, *Histoire de la Marine Russe* (Paris, 1932), 321).

39 *BMPP*, 146.

40 P. E. Dybenko, *Oktiabr' na Baltike*, 28; *Perepiska sekretariata TsK RSDRP (b) s*

mestnymi partiinymi organizatsiiami: Sbornik dokumentov (M, 1957), vol. I, 133; Antonov-Ovseenko, *V semnadtsatom godu*, 156, 168.

41 VK 1636, Meeting of the Congress, 15.vi.17.

CHAPTER 4

1 *IKS*, no. 30 (25.iv.17), 4; no. 36 (2.v.17), 1.

2 *IKS*, no. 46 (14.v.17), 1, no. 50 (19.v.17), 2.

3 F. P. Matveev (ed.), *Petrogradskii Sovet rabochikh i soldatskikh deputatov*, 138, 253n60; *Izvestiia Petrogradskago Soveta*, no. 78 (30.v.17), 3; I. G. Tseretelli, *Vospominaniia o fevral'skoi revoliutsii* (2 vols., Paris, 1963), vol. I, 413–27.

4 *IKS*, no. 54 (25.v.17), 1, no. 56 (27.v.17), 1, no. 74 (17.vi.17), 2; V. Ia. Nalivaiskii (ed.), *Petrogradskii Sovet rabochikh i soldatskikh deputatov: Protokoly zasedanii Ispolnitel'nogo komiteta i Biuro Ispolnitel'nogo komiteta* (M – L, 1925), 165; Raskol'nikov, *Kronshtadt*, 68–71; Kudelli (ed.), *Pervyi legal'nyi PK*, 120.

5 *IKS*, no. 70 (13.vi.17), 1f; *Kronshtadtskaia iskra*, no. 1 (22.vii.17), 2; Raskol'nikov, *Kronshtadt*, 67; Khesin, *Oktiabr'skaia revoliutsiia i flot*, 75; Matveev (ed.), 134.

6 *IKS*, no. 57 (28.v.17), 2.

7 *BMPP*, 88f; Petrash, *Moriaki*, 143f; I. P. Flerovskii, 'Iiul'skii politicheskii urok', *Proletarskaia revoliutsiia*, 1926, no. 7 (54), 63–8; *Golos pravdy*, no. 72 (11.vi.17), cited in *BMPP*, 89.

8 *Golos pravdy*, no. 72 (11.vi.17), cited in *BMPP*, 90; Flerovskii, 'Iiul'skii politicheskii urok', 63–9; Ilyin-Genevsky, 60; Petrash, *Moriaki*, 145; *BMPP*, 94, 99; *IKS*, no. 77 (21.vi.17), 1, no. 83 (28.vi.17), 1f.

9 *IKS*, no.83 (28.vi.17), 1f, no. 86 (2.vii.17), 3.

10 D. A. Garkavenko, *Partiia, armiia i flot v fevral'skoi revoliutsii: Voennaia rabota bol'shevistskoi partii v period podgotovki i provedeniia fevral'skoi burzhuazno-demokraticheskoi revoliutsii 1917 g.* (L, 1972), 187; Drezen (ed.), *Burzhuaziia i pomeshchiki*, 85; *IKS*, no. 62 (24.v.17), 2f; *Svobodnyi flot*, no. 2 (14) (26.viii.17), 15.

11 Public Record Office, Foreign Office Papers, class 371, vol. 3018, p. 452 (hereafter cited as F.O.371/3018, 452, etc.), Buchanan to F.O., no. 859, 8.vi.17 (n.s.); A. F. Kerensky, *The Prelude to Bolshevism: The Kornilov Rebellion* (London, 1919), 136; Prikaz Nachal'nika Morskogo Shtaba Verkhovnago Glavnokomanduiushchago no. 278 (3.vi.17).

12 *BMPP*, 116, 164–7.

13 *IKS*, no. 95 (14.vii.17), 2.

14 Ilyin-Genevsky, 71–3; P. A. Polovtsev, *Glory and Downfall: Reminiscences of a Russian General Staff Officer* (London, 1935), 254.

15 *IKS*, no. 95 (14.vii.17), 3; Sukhanov, vol. 4, 513.

16 *BMPP*, 131f, 172–4; *Rech'*, no. 170 (22.vii.17), cited in R. P. Browder and A. F. Kerensky (eds), *The Russian Provisional Government, 1917* (hereafter cited as *RPG*) (3 vols, Stanford, 1961), III, 1376.

17 *IKS*, no. 92 (11.vii.17), 3, no. 94 (13.vii.17), 1–3, no. 95 (14.vii.17), 2; Raskol'nikov, *Kronshtadt*, 111f, 116f; *BMPP*, 169; V. I. Lenin, *Polnoe sobranie sochinenii*, 5th edn., vol. 34, 23f.

18 A. K. Drezen (ed.), *Bol'shevizatsiia Petrogradskogo garnizona: Sbornik materialov i*

dokumentov (L, 1932), 142; *IKS*, no. 94 (13.vii.17), 2, no. 95 (14.vii.17), 2; A. Rabinowitch, *Prelude to Revolution: The Petrograd Bolsheviks and the July 1917 Uprising* (Bloomington, 1968), 224–8, 234.

19 *BMPP*, 164f; Raskol'nikov, *Kronshtadt*, 112–4; *IKS*, no. 98 (18.vii.17), 2; E. Iarchuk, *Kronshtadt v russkoi revoliutsii*, 11; I. Kolbin, 'Iiul'skie dni i kontr-revoliutsiia na Kronshtadte', *Krasnyi flot*, 1927, no. 12/13, 4.

20 *BMPP*, 116f, 165f, 168; Raskol'nikov, *Kronshtadt*, 119.

21 Raskol'nikov, *Kronshtadt*, 136–8; *BMPP*, 170f; Sukhanov, vol. 4, 426; *IKS*, no. 89 (7.vii.17), 1f.

22 Sukhanov, vol. 4, 470.

23 *IKS*, no. 89 (7.vii.17), 1f, no. 95 (14.vii.17), 2; Raskol'nikov, *Kronshtadt*, 117, 124, *BMPP*, 168.

24 Petrash, *Moriaki*, 150; Raskol'nikov, *Kronshtadt*, 110; Iarchuk, 11.

25 *IKS*, no. 97 (16.vii.17), 2.

26 *IGS*, no. 2 (11.iii.17), 2; no. 11 (24.iii.17), 2; no. 16 (31.iii.17), 1, no. 32 (23.iv.17), 1.

27 *IGS*, no. 5 (16.iii.17), 1f, no. 39 (2.v.17), 2, no. 44 (7.v.17), 4, no. 53 (19.v.17), 4.

28 *IGS*, no. 34 (26.iv.17), 1; no. 49 (14.v.17), 1.

29 *BMPP*, 88f; *Perepiska*, vol. 1, 132f; Petrash, *Moriaki*, 145f; *RDR v mae-iiune*, 548; *IGS*, no. 88 (1.vii.17), 1.

30 *IGS*, no. 82 (23.vi.17), 4; *Narodnaia niva*, no. 49 (22.vi.17), 4, no. 50 (23.vi.17), 4; VK 3221, HSSS no. 42 (23.vi.17); *BMPP*, 101–4.

31 A. K. Drezen (ed.), 'Baltflot v iiul'skie dni 1917 g.', *Krasnyi arkhiv*, 1931, no. 3 (46), 72–6; *BMPP*, 118–21; D. A. Chugaev (resp. ed.), *Revoliutsionnoe dvizhenie v Rossii v iiule 1917 g.: Iiul'skii krizis* (M, 1959), 24f.

32 Fedotoff White, *Survival*, 168; Drezen (ed.), 'V iiul'skie dni', 94f; *BMPP*, 121f.

33 Petrash, *Moriaki*, 162; Drezen (ed.), 'V iiul'skie dni', 77–80, 91, 96, 99; *BMPP*, 121. According to Sukhanov, the leading group in the C.E.C., the so-called 'Star Chamber', did not know in advance of Dudorov's order (*Zapiski*, vol. 4, 504).

34 *RDR v iiule*, 26; Khovrin, *Baltiitsy*, 123f; *BMPP*, 122f; Drezen (ed.), 'V iiul'skie dni', 84f.

35 *BMPP*, 119, 124f.

36 Ibid., 123–5.

37 Ibid., 125–7.

38 Ibid., 131f, 142.

39 Ibid., 138f.

40 Khovrin, *Baltiitsy*, 115; *Sotsialist-revoliutsioner*, no. 37 (24.viii.17), 3, no. 49 (16.ix.17), 4. Prosh'ian and Ustinov reported on the *Petropavlovsk* ultimatum to the Helsingfors Sailors' Section (VK 3221, HSSS no. 41 (22.vi.17)).

41 N. Antonov, 'V Baltflote', *Petrogradskaia pravda*, no. 157 (16.vii.1922), 6; Korolev, 26.

42 *RDR v iiule*, 63–6; Drezen (ed.), 'V iiul'skie dni', 79, 86.

43 Drezen (ed.), 'V iiul'skie dni', 98; Antonov, 'V Baltflote', 6; Khovrin, *Baltiitsy*, 118f; *EMS*, no. 9 (22. vii.17), 13.

44 L. Trotsky, *History of the Russian Revolution* (3 vols., London, 1967), II, 63; Flerovskii, 'Iiul'skii politicheskii urok', 58.

CHAPTER 5

1 *RDR v iiule*, 40; P. N. Lamanov, 'V Kronshtadte posle Iiul'skikh dnei', *Krasnaia letopis'*, 1932, no. 3 (48), 24–5, 27–34; *Trud i zemlia*, no. 71 (18.vii.17), 4; *IGS*, no. 103 (19.vii.17), 3; *IKS*, no. 98 (18.vii.17), 1, no. 107 (28.vii.17), 1f; VK 3184, Prikaz Komflota no. 134 (20.viii.17).

2 *RDR v iiule*, 418; D. A. Chugaev (resp. ed.), *Revoliutsionnoe dvizhenie v Rossii v avguste 1917 g.: Razgrom kornilovskogo miatezha* (M, 1959), 424, 627n218; V. Vladmirova, *Kontr-revoliutsiia v 1917 g.*, 67–9, 205f; Kerensky, *Prelude*, 134, 137.

3 *IKS*, no. 102 (22.vii.17), 2, no. 108 (29.vii.17), 1, no. 112 (3.viii.17), 1.

4 Drezen (ed.), 'V iiul'skie dni', 88; *BMPP*, 129; Vl. S., 'Iiul'skie dni i flot', *Krasnyi flot*, 1925, no. 7, 7f.

5 Vl. S., 'Iiul'skie dni i flot', 8; V. A. Pilkin, 'Dva admirala', *Morskiia zapiski*, IX (1951), no. 1/4, 54; Timirev, 121; Graf, 331; Dybenko, *Miatezhniki*, 66.

6 B. Dublitskii, 'Baltiiskii flot v Iiul'skie dni 1917 g.', *Krasnaia letopis'*, 1922, no. 2/3, 355; VK 3184, Prikaz Komflota no. 7 (12.vii.17); *BMPP*, 137; *IGS*, no. 101 (16.viii.17), 2.

7 *RDR v iiule*, 63–6; *BMPP*, 138f, 347n86; Khovrin, *Baltiitsy*, 131–4.

8 Antonov, 'V Baltflote', 6; *IGS*, no. 97 (12.vii.17), 1, no. 98 (13.vii.17), 1f.

9 VK 3184, Prikazy Komflota no. 9 (12.vii.17), no. 39 (19.vii.17); *BMPP*, 140; *Protokoly*, 88.

10 Antonov-Ovseenko, *V semnadtsatom godu*, 193f; *IGS*, no. 104 (20.vii.17), 2, no. 123 (11.viii.17), 4; *BMPP*, 142; Zalezhskii, 'Gel'singfors', 176f.

11 VK 3184, Prikazy Komflota no. 7 (12.vii.17), no. 33 (19.vii.17); [I. I. Rengarten], 'Baltiiskii flot nakanune Oktiabria', ed. A. K. Drezen, *Krasnyi arkhiv*, 1929, vol. 4 (35), 5; *Protokoly*, 87.

12 *Protokoly*, 109, 162, 214; VK 3221, HSSS no. 60 (15.viii.17).

13 *Protokoly*, 91.

14 Ibid., 110; VK 3184, Prikazy Komflota no. 35 (19.vii.17), no. 40 (19.vii.17); *BMPP*, 141.

15 *BMPP*, 156; *Protokoly*, 87f, 121, 125, 137, 162.

16 VK 3184, Prikaz Komflota no. 34 (19.vii.17); VK 3221, HSSS no. 52 (27.vii.17), no. 55 (2.viii.17), no. 57 (7.viii.17), no. 60 (15.viii.17), no. 61 (19.viii.17), no. 62 (21.viii.17), no. 63 (23.viii.17); *Protokoly*, 111f, 442n29.

17 *Perepiska*, vol. 1, 13; 'Smilga, Ivar Tenisovich', *Granat*, vol. 41, part III, 62–4.

18 *6-oi s''ezd*, 74f.

19 *IGS*, no. 115 (2.viii.17), 2, no. 145 (7.ix.17), 1f; *RDR v avguste*, 255–7; *Golos Sotsial–Demokrata*, no. 7 (10.ix.17), 14.

20 *IKS*, no. 86 (2.vii.17), 2; *Revel'skii nabliudatel'*, no. 102 (13.v.17), 2; *IRS*, no. 76 (16.vi.17), 3; no. 97 (12.vii.17), 2; no. 107 (23.vii.17), 3; *Zvezda*, no. 1 (1.viii.17), 3.

21 Khovrin, 'V 1917', 62; *IGS*, no. 7 (19.iii.17),4, no. 102 (18.vii.17),4; *IRS*, no. 12 (24.iii.17), 3; *SS*, no. 39 (14.v.17), no. 73 (24.vi.17), 2, no. 87 (13.vii.17), 4; *Narodnaia niva*, no. 64 (11.vii.17), 4; *EMS*, no. 9 (22.vii.17), 13.

22 *BMPP*, 151–3; *SS*, no. 98 (26.vii.17), 3, no. 102 (30.vii.17), 4, no. 104 (2.viii.17), 4; *IRS*, no. 134 (25.viii.17), 2; *Zvezda*, no. 7 (22.viii.17), 4; *Vel. Okt. sots. revoliutsiia v Estonii*, 181.

23 L. S. Gaponenko (ed.), *Revoliutsionnoe dvizhenie v russkoi armii: 27 fevralia–24 oktiabria 1917 goda: Sbornik dokumentov* (M, 1968), 352–4, 589n188; N. Ia. Ivanov, *Kornilovshchina i ee razgrom*, 101.

24 Ivanov, 101f; Vladimirova, 133; *Posledniia novosti* no. 5818 (27.ii.1937), 4, cited in *RPG*, III, 1536.

25 Ivanov, 118, 166; Petrash, *Moriaki*, 203f; A. K. Drezen, 'Baltiiskii flot ot iiulia k Oktiabriu 1917 g.', *Krasnaia letopis'*, 1929, no. 5 (32), 198.

26 *IKS*, no. 134 (30.viii.17), 1; Petrash, *Moriaki*, 201f; *BMPP*, 351n114; Drezen, 'Flot ot iiulia', 198f; E. I. Martynov, *Kornilov (Popytka voennogo perevorota)* (M, 1927), 133; Trotsky, *History*, I, 401.

27 Vladimirova, 135; Khovrin, *Baltiitsy*, 147.

28 V. Avtukhov, 'Kornilovshchina', *Morskoi sbornik*, 1924, no. 8, 8–10; Rengarten, 'Nakanune', 14; *Protokoly*, 155, 157; *BMPP*, 189.

29 Timirev, 117f; Rengarten, 'Nakanune', 13, 17–19; *IGS*, no. 138 (30.viii.17), 3, no. 152 (17.ix.17), 1; *Protokoly*, 157f, 165, 168f.

30 *IRS*, no. 138 (29.viii.17), 1, 142 (2.ix.17), 1; Petrash, *Moriaki*, 208f; Avtukhov, 'Kornilovshchina', 10f.

31 *IKS*, no. 141 (8.ix.17), 2.

32 Timirev, 118.

33 *IKS*, no. 134 (30.viii.17), 1f; *IGS*, no. 137 (29.viii.17), 5; *Golos Sotsial– Demokrata* no. 7 (10.ix.17), 14; *IRS*, no. 146 (7.ix.17), 3.

34 *Protokoly*, 154, 164.

35 *BMPP*, 210; *Protokoly*, 192f, 198f, 201, 212; Rengarten, 'Nakanune', 28; VK 3221, HSSS no. 68 (8.ix.17).

36 *Protokoly*, 190, 197, 201, 213, 219, 221–3, 228–30, 282, 446n66.

37 *IGS*, no. 156 (22.ix.17), 1; *Golos Sotsial–Demokrata*, no. 9 (24.ix.17), 15.

38 *BMPP*, 212; Rengarten, 'Nakanune', 23–8, 31.

39 *Protokoly*, 121, 164, 212, 216f, 229; *IKS*, no. 145 (14.ix.17), 2; VK 3221, HSSS no. 66 (31.viii.17); Petrash, *Moriaki*, 77; *Perepiska*, vol. I, 294.

40 *BMPP*, 219f.

41 *Protokoly*, 430–5.

42 *BMPP*, 228–30, 234f; *Protokoly*, 243.

43 *Perepiska*, vol. I, 187f.

CHAPTER 6

1 Gaponenko (ed.), *Revoliutsionnoe dvizhenie v russkoi armii*, 35f.

2 K. F. Shatsillo, *Russkii imperializm i razvitie flota*, 89; M. A. Petrov, *Podgotovka Rossii k mirovoi voine na more*, 111, 117, 121, 133.

3 Units potentially available for service in the Baltic were as follows:

| | June 1914 | | Sept. 1917 | |
	Germany	Russia	Germany	Russia
Dreadnoughts	14	-	19	4
Battle cruisers	5	-	5	-
Pre-Dreadnoughts	20	4	19	4
Armoured cruisers	5	6	1	5
Modern light cruisers	13	-	22	-
Other light cruisers	22	4	19	4
Large destroyers	11	1	77	11–14
Other destroyers	128	58	104	52
Torpedo boats	91	16	176	16
Large submarines	20	-	85	11
Other submarines	19	12	134	9

(H. M. Le Fleming, *Warships of World War I* (London, 1961), 48–60, 115–130, 182–206, 261–73, 312–352; R. Greger, *Die Russische Flotte im Ersten Weltkrieg 1914–1917*, pp. 70–4).

4 N. B. Pavlovich (ed.), *Flot v pervoi mirovoi voine*, vol. 1, 59–247, 305–316. The Germans lost 2 (the Russians 1) armoured cruisers, 4 (0) light cruisers, 12 (2) destroyers, 2 (0) torpedo boats, 1 (2) minelayer, no (2) gunboats, 2 (2) submarines, 14 (14) small craft, and about 50 (8) merchant ships (Greger, 36–9).

5 Shliapnikov, *Semnadtsatyi god*, vol. 3, 294.

6 Khesin, 'Nakanune', 72f, 94; Adm. 137/1388, 130; A. M. Fal'kov, *Gosudarstvenno-monopolisticheskii kapitalizm i voennaia sudostroitel'naia promyshlennost' Rossii*, Avtoreferat kandidatskoi dissertatsii (L, 1960), 14.

7 *Gosudarstvennoe soveshchanie* (M–L, 1930), 207f; Khesin, 'Nakanune', 79f; Shliapnikov, *Semnadtsatyi god*, vol. 3, 137; Petrash, *Moriaki*, 29f.

8 Fedotoff White, *Survival*, 114; Cromie, 'Documents (II)', 368, 'Documents (III)', 506; A. R. Williams, *Through the Russian Revolution* (N.Y., 1967), 78.

9 Kosinskii, 34; VK 3184, Prikaz Komflota no. 114 (16.viii.17).

10 G. M. Trusov, *Podvodnye lodki v russkom i Sovetskom flote* (L, 1963), 258f; Pavlovich (ed.), vol. 1, 269f; Adm.137/1570, 235; 'Gibel' podvodnoi lodki "Bars"', *Morskoi sbornik*, CDIII (1918), no. 2/3, 145–53; Cromie, 'Documents (III)', 502, 505f.

11 I. A. Kireev, *Tralenie v Baltiiskom more v voinu 1914–1917 gg.* (M–L, 1939), 239, 241; Kosinskii, 33f, 41, 148; Adm.137/1388, 285, 297.

12 Timirev, 141; [I. I. Rengarten], 'Oktiabr'skaia revoliutsiia v Baltiiskom flote', ed. A. K. Drezen, *Krasnyi arkhiv*, 1927, no. 6 (25), 43; Kosinskii, 34.

13 Pavlovich (ed.), vol. 1, 258f; B. Arskii, 'Minnaia i boevaia sluzhba Otriada minnykh zagraditelei Baltiiskogo moria (Period 1911–1918 gg.)', *Voennaia byl'*, no. 82 (1967), 24f; B. Denisov, 'Minno-zagraditel'nye operatsii russkogo flota v Baltiiskom more v 1914–1917 gg.', *Morskoi sbornik*, 1934, no. 8, 157f, 160, 172.

14 Shliapnikov, *Semnadtsatyi god*, vol. 3, 163; Drezen (ed.), 'V iiul'skie dni', 105f; *Izvestiia Petrogradskago Soveta*, no. 186 (1.x.17), 4, cited in *RPG*, III, 1628f; Rengarten, 'Nakanune', 23.

15 *Moriak*, no. 10 (26.viii.17), 217; *Protokoly*, 146f.

16 Ernst von Gagern (ed.), *Der Krieg in der Ostsee* (hereafter cited as *Ostsee*), III, 140; Greger, 36f.

17 *Ostsee*, III, 174; Kosinskii, 13–16, 38–41, 72f, 83f, 109f.

18 Pilkin, 54, 57–64, 66–8; N. N. Kryzhanovskii, 'Admiral Mikhail Koronatovich Bakhirev i ego sovremenniki', *Morskiia zapiski*, XXI (1963), no. 58, 57–71, Graf, 301.

19 Kosinskii, 32, 44, 46; Rengarten, 'Nakanune', 32f.

20 Rengarten, 'Nakanune', 26–8, 31; Kosinskii, 55f; V. V. Romanov, 'Radiorazvedka', *Zapiski Voenno-Morskogo Istoricheskago imeni Admirala Kolchaka Kruzhka*, no. 7 (1937), 35.

21 Kosinskii, 10, 102, 150f; Pavlovich (ed.), vol. I, 290. For an account by the crew of the *Pripiat'* see: *SS*, no. 176 (29.x.17), 4.

22 Kosinskii, 79–81, 107f; *Ostsee*, III, 233–6.

23 Kosinskii, 16–18, 36–8, 54, 155f; *IGS*, no. 134 (25.viii.17), 1.

24 Kosinskii, 77f, 85–99; *Ostsee*, III, 258.

25 *Ostsee*, III, 263f; Kosinskii, 113–23; D. Malinin, 'Lineinyi korabl' "Slava" v sostave morskikh sil Rizhskogo zaliva v voinu 1914–1917 gg.', *Morskoi sbornik*, 1923, no. 6, 38–44; Timirev, 129–37; Mazurenko, *Morskiia zapiski*, IV (1946), no. 3/4, 180–6.

26 Kosinskii, 75, 128–33, 138–40, 154; *Ostsee*, III, 273f, 279f, 285.

27 A. S. Pukhov, *Moonzundskoe srazhenie*, 91f, 99; Kosinskii, 8; *Ostsee*, III, 426f; Greger, 36–8; Izmailov and Pukhov, 166f.

28 Cromie, 'Documents (II)', 366; Kosinskii, 43.

29 *BMPP*, 248.

30 Graf, 315.

31 M. Petrov, 'Istoricheskaia spravka o beregovoi oborone Baltiiskogo moria v mirovuiu voinu', *Morskoi sbornik*, 1926, no. 3, 49; Kosinskii, 25f, 67f, 76, 131, 138f.

32 Kosinskii, 156; Cromie, 'Documents (III)', 505.

33 Timirev, 109; Cromie, 'Documents (II)', 370, 372, 'Documents (III)', 503f, 506; Adm.137/1570, 78, 83, 85, 88; Kosinskii, 141, 157.

34 Shliapnikov, *Semnadtsatyi god*, vol. 3, 164; *Svobodnyi flot*, no. 12 (24) (7.xi.17), 12. One question at the time was why the British did not give more support. On the morrow of the battle Lenin himself asked whether – coupled with rumours of the evacuation of Petrograd – 'the complete inactivity of the English fleet in general, and also of the English submarines [*sic*]' testified to a plot between Kerensky and the Entente to surrender Petrograd (Lenin, *PSS*, vol. 34, 347). Kerensky did point out to the British ambassador the advantages of active British support. Such operations were considered in London – if only as a means of keeping Russian ships from falling into German hands – but they were rejected as not worth the risk. All the Admiralty would do was make a limited demonstration in the North Sea and in mid-October (o.s.) – too late – raid the Kattegat (A. J. Marder, *1917: Year of Crisis (From the Dreadnought to Scapa Flow: The Royal Navy in the Fisher Era, 1904–1919*, vol. IV) (London, 1969), 241–4; G. von Schoultz, *With the British Battle Fleet: War Recollections of a Russian Naval Officer* (London, n.d.), 306–9).

35 *BMPP*, 248.

CHAPTER 7

1 *BMPP*, 374f; Petrash, *Moriaki*, 256f; D. A. Chugaev, *et al.* (eds), *Petrogradskii Voenno-revoliutsionnyi komitet: Dokumenty i materialy* (hereafter cited as *PVRK*) (3 vols., M, 1966–7), vol. 3, 41; P. I. Kurkov, 'Kreiser "Avrora"', *Piat' let Krasnogo flota* (hereafter cited as *PLKF*), 259f; S. Mel'gunov, *Kak Bol'sheviki zakhvatili vlast'*, 96.

2 *BMPP*, 375.

3 *BMPP*, 268–70; Petrash, *Moriaki*, 255–8; A. G. Pronin, 'Moi vospominaniia', *PLKF*, 255f; Iarchuk, 28f; B. A. Breslav, '15 let tomu nazad', *Katorga i ssylka*, 1932, no. 11/12, 63–8; I. Novikov, 'Vospominaniia uchastnika iiul'skogo i oktiabr'skogo perevorotov v 1917 godu', *Krasnyi baltiets*, 1920, no. 6, 27–9; I. Pavlov, 'Avral'naia rabota 25-go oktiabria 1917 goda', *Krasnyi flot*, 1926, no. 10/11. 25f; I. P. Flerovskii, 'Kronshtadt v Oktiabr'skoi revoliutsii', *Proletarskaia revoliutsiia*, 1922, no. 10, 139; G. Usarov, '50 let tomu nazad', *Voennaia byl'*, no. 94 (1968), 99.

4 *BMPP*, 277f, 376f; Petrash, *Moriaki*, 261; Kurkov, 261f; V. A. Antonov-Ovseenko, 'Baltflot v dni kerenshchiny i Krasnogo Oktiabria', *Proletarskaia revoliutsiia*, 1922, no. 10, 127; Flerovskii, 'Kronshtadt v OR', 140; Pronin, 257f; Iarchuk, 29–31; Novikov, 'Vospominaniia', 27–31; I. I. Mints and B. V. Teterin (eds.), 'Poslednye chasy vremennogo pravitel'stva (Dnevnik ministra Liverovskogo)', *Istoricheskii arkhiv*, 1960, no. 6, 45f.

5 *BMPP*, 261–6, 270, 374f; Petrash, *Moriaki*, 249–54; I. Smilga, 'Istoricheskaia noch'', *Krasnoarmeets*, 1919, no. 10–15, 24; Dybenko, *Miatezhniki*, 81–3; Kostiukov, 'Kak my opozdali ko vziatiiu Zimnego dvortsa', *Krasnyi baltiets*, 1920, no. 6, 45f.

6 *BMPP*, 291, 305, 308f; V. E. Gatsura, 'V oktiabr'skikh boiakh 1917 g. (Iz vospominanii b. voennogo moriaka)', *Krasnoflotets*, 1928, no. 6, 2; Novikov, 'Vospominaniia', 32–4.

7 *BMPP*, 295f, 314, 358n146, 377–9; Lenin, *PSS*, vol. 35, 32–5; Raskol'nikov, *Kronshtadt*, 240; F. Raskol'nikov, 'Lenin v Oktiabre', *Krasnyi flot*, 1924, no. 2, 20f; Flerovsky, 'Kronshtadt v OR' 142, 146–50; Dybenko, *Miatezhniki*, 83–9; K. Gur'ev, 'Oktiabr'skii pokhod krasnykh moriakov', *Krasnyi flot*, 1922, no. 8, 124–8; *IGS*, no. 196 (8.xi.17), 2f; P. N. Krasnov, 'Na vnutrennem fronte', *Arkhiv Russkoi revoliutsii*, i, 167f.

8 Krasnov, 173, Dybenko, 90–4. According to Krasnov, Dybenko persuaded the gullible cossacks that he would exchange Lenin for Kerensky!

9 *BMPP*, 216f, 226f, 236, 249.

10 Ibid., 257f: Trotsky, *History*, iii, 195.

11 *BMPP*, 261–4, 268f.

12 Ibid., 287f, 296f.

13 *IGS*, no. 139 (31.viii.17), 1, no. 175 (14.x.17), 4; *BMPP*, 249; *IKS*, no. 177 (22.x.17), 2.

14 *IKS*, no. 183 (29.x.17), 3; *IGS*, no. 182 (22.x.17), 1; *IRS*, no. 180 (21.x.17), 3: *Protokoly*, 450n77; Petrash, *Moriaki*, 227. Information on the party affiliation of the fleet delegates comes from the Soviet-published *Protokoly*. Of the eleven available 'Bolsheviks' (i.e. excluding Dybenko), four (M. A. Nevsky, F. V. Olich, P. Ia. Riamo, and I. P. Sapozhnikov) did not participate in the Naval Revolutionary

Committee, the organ of those congress delegates who supported Soviet power (A. L. Fraiman (resp. ed.), *Baltiiskie moriaki v bor'be za vlast' sovetov* (hereafter cited as *BMBVS*), 312n2).

15 *BMPP*, 249.

16 *IGS*, no. 186 (27.x.17), 2; Dybenko, *Miatezhniki*, 80; *Sotsialist-revoliutsioner*, no. 74 (17.x.17), 1, no. 98 (14.xi.17), 4; *IRS*, no. 184 (26.x.17), 3.

17 *IKS*, no. 176 (21.x.17), 2, no. 182 (28.x.17), 3.

18 [V. A.] Antonov-Ovseenko, 'Krasnyi oktiabr'', *Petrogradskaia pravda*, no. 251 (5.xi.1922), 12; *BMPP*, 254, 284f; N. A. Khovrin, 'V Oktiabr'skie dni v Pitere', *OSh*, 124; Dybenko, *Miatezhniki*, 79; Smilga, 24.

19 *IGS*, no. 191 (2.xi.17), 3f.

20 *IKS*, no. 185 (31.x.17), 4; *Sotsialist-revoliutsioner*, no. 84 (28.x.17), 1; *BMPP*, 264, 314.

21 *BMPP*, 297.

22 *IKS*, no. 185 (31.x.17), 3; no. 186 (1.xi.17), 3; no. 188 (3.xi.17), 2.

23 *Protokoly*, 256, 263f, 451n81; *IGS*, no. 198 (10.xi.17), 2. In early memoirs Izmailov referred to a resolution on power in which Tsentrobalt condemned the Bolsheviks who had left Sovnarkom, opposed any coalition, and threatened to take 'power in the country into its own hands'; this resolution he refused to sign (N. Izmailov, 'Tsentrobalt v Oktiabre', *Komsomol'skaia pravda* no. 248 (29.x. 1927), 2). On the other hand, the minutes for the night of the 6th, which are published in *Protokoly*, indicate that Izmailov was the moving spirit behind a similar resolution.

24 *Moriak*, no. 17 (11.xi.17), 385; *IGS*, no. 202 (15.xi.17), 5; *IKS*, no. 200 (17.xi.17), 3.

25 *Protokoly Tsentral'nogo komiteta RSDRP(b) (Avgust 1917–fevral' 1918)* (M, 1958), 57, 86, 106.

26 *Zvezda*, no. 18 (29.ix.17), 1; *Priboi*, no. 41 (30.ix.17), 1; Lenin, *PSS*, vol. 34, 390.

27 Smilga, 23; Trotsky, *History*, III, 185.

28 Smilga, 23f; [V. A. Antonov-Ovseenko], 'Povest' oktiabr'skikh dnei', *Krasnoarmeets*, 1920, no. 28–30, 20–2; [V. A.] Antonov-Ovseenko, 'V oktiabr'skie dni', *Krasnoarmeets*, 1919, no. 10–15, 28; Antonov-Ovseenko, *V semnadtsatom godu*, 267–70, 302; Trotsky, *History*, III, 205; V. Nevskii. 'Dve vstrechi', *Krasnaia letopis'*, 1922, no. 4, 145; V. Nevskii, 'V Oktiabre (Beglye zametki pamiati)', *Katorga i ssylka*, 1932, no. 11/13 (96/7), 40; Dybenko, *Miatezhniki*, 78, 81.

29 *Protokoly*, 247; Petrash, *Moriaki*, 241; *BMPP*, 251f.

30 *IKS*, no. 169 (13.x.17), 2, no. 176 (21.x.17), 2, no. 195 (11.xi.17), 3; *Golos pravdy*, no. 107 (9.xi.17), 3.

31 I. N. Kolbin, 'Baltiitsy v Oktiabr'skie dni', *OSh*, 118f; Pronin, 250–3; Petrash, *Moriaki*, 245f; *IKS*, no. 178 (24.x.17), 1, no. 182 (28.x.17), 3, no. 189 (4.xi.17), 3f, no. 190 (5.xi.17), 4.

32 *IRS*, no. 179 (20.x.17), 3; no. 186 (28.x.17), 3; *Zvezda*, no. 25 (24.x.17), 4. Reval was to play no significant part in the Petrograd armed uprising. According to one source, M. M. Lashevich of the M.R.C. and Ia. Peters were sent to Reval on the eve of the 25th, but this seems unlikely; even more doubtful is the claim that 250 Reval sailors took part in the attack on the Winter Palace (M. A. Petrov. 'Iuzhnaia Baltika v dni Oktiabria', *Pervyi den' novogo mira*, ed. V. F. Sulin, 116).

33 *BMPP*, 254, 258f, 356n138; *Protokoly TsK*, 121.

34 I agree here with the interpretation of Robert V. Daniels (*Red October: The*

Bolshevik Revolution of 1917 (London, 1967), 161f).

35 Flerovsky, 'Kronshtadt v OR', 135f; Trotsky, *History*, III, 208; Iarchuk 27; Pronin, 254f.

36 *IKS*, no. 182 (28.x.17), 3; Breslav, 63–5; Iarchuk, 27; Pronin, 255; Kolbin, 'Baltiitsy', 119f; Trotsky, *History*, III, 237.

37 P. E. Dybenko, 'Baltflot v Oktiabr'skie dni (Vospominaniia)', *Pravda*, no. 252 (3784) (3.xi.1927), 6; *BMPP*, 264f.

38 *BMPP*, 266; Petrash, *Moriaki*, 251; Smilga, 24. In 1965 the Soviet historian Sovokin wrote an interesting letter regarding this telegram: 'In 1927 the XVth Congress of the [A.-U.C.P.(b.)] excluded I. T. Smilga from the party as an active member of the Trotskyist opposition. And then both Antonov (Ovseenko) and Dybenko altered (*peredelali*) the telegram, striking out both Sverdlov and Smilga [and] putting in their own names. This was an historical document falsified.' In a later letter Sovokin withdrew the charge of falsification and suggested that there had been two copies, one from Sverdlov to Smilga, and one from Antonov-Ovseenko to Dybenko (A. Sovokin, 'Istoriia odnoi telegrammy', *Izvestiia* no. 163 (14942) (13.vii.1965), 5; A. Sovokin, 'Eshche raz ob odnoi telegramme', *Izvestiia* no. 206 (14985) (1.ix.1965), 5). The original telegram has not survived, but there does exist a telegram from P.O. 2nd Cl. K. P. Sviridov to the Baltic Staff (!): 'I await regulations. No information.' (*BMPP*, 266). What is remarkable about this is that the message was sent from the *Amur*, which was lying in Kronstadt harbour, at midnight on the 24th; this was at a time when telephone communications between the Smolny and Kronstadt had been cut. How could Sviridov have known of the message from Sverdlov/Antonov-Ovseenko? Perhaps a courier had been sent earlier in the evening.

39 *IGS*, no. 186 (27.x.17), 2. Smilga however had favoured action at the Petersburg Committee meeting of 5 October: 'We must prepare for the congress, taking as a basis the question of an armed uprising' (Kudelli (ed.), *Pervyi legal'nyi PK*, 303).

40 [V. A.] Antonov-Ovseenko, 'Vysylai ustav – nachalos'!', *Iunyi kommunist*, 1922, no. 17/18, 26.

41 Trotsky, *History*, III, 208; Khovrin, 'V Oktiabr'skie dni', 124; Gur'ev, 124.

42 *Protokoly*, 244; Rengarten, 'Oktiabr'skaia revoliutsiia', 42, 51, 53f; *BMPP*, 304.

43 *BMPP*, 272.

44 Lenin, *PSS*, vol. 34, 265, 281f, 340f, 383f, 390.

45 G. Rovio, 'Kak tov. Lenin skryvalsia u gel'singforsskogo 'politseimeistera'', *Krasnaia letopis'*, 1922, no. 4, 304–10; Khovrin, *Baltiitsy*, 162. For an interesting discussion of the effect on Lenin of his stay in Finland see: Norman E. Saul, 'Lenin's Decision to Seize Power: The Influence of Events in Finland', *Soviet Studies*, xxiv, no. 4 (1973), 494–505.

46 Kudelli (ed.), *Pervyi legal'nyi PK*, 294–6, 298, 303, 315; *Protokoly TsK*, 96, 98, 100.

47 In addition to the depots and the *Avrora* (522 ratings), there were 3,371 men scattered around the capital in auxiliaries, training detachments, and ships under construction. The addition of 1,500 sailors working in defence factories gives a total of 9,709 (From list complied by A. S. Pukhov in *Geroi Oktiabria* (2 vols., L, 1967), vol. 2, 811–13).

48 Dybenko, 'Baltflot v Oktiabr'skie dni', 6.

49 These figures were worked out by V. V. Petrash on the basis of data collected by the M.T.C. on 28 October ('Sostav Baltiiskogo flota i uchastie voennykh moriakov v Oktiabr'skom vooruzhennom vosstanii', *Lenin i Oktiabr'skoe vooruzhennoe vosstanie v Petrograde*, eds. I. I. Mints, *et al., 325–9*).

50 V. P. Verkhos', 'K voprosu o chislennosti Krasnoi gvardii', *Voprosy istorii KPSS*, 1971, no. 10, 105n19; D. N. Collins, 'A Note on the Numerical Strength of the Russian Red Guard in October 1917', *Soviet Studies*, xxiv, no. 2 (1972), 275; Z. V. Stepanov, *Rabochie Petrograda v period podgotovki i provedeniia Oktiabr'skogo vooruzhennogo vosstaniia: Avgust – oktiabr' 1917 g.* (L, 1965), 25–8; G. L. Sobolev, 'Petrogradskii garnizon v 1917 g. (chislennost', sostav, vooruzhenie, raspolozhenie)', *Istoricheskie zapiski*, vol. 88 (1971), 76.

51 Trotsky, *History*, iii, 208; Sukhanov, vol. 7, 37; *BMPP*, 356n146.

52 According to A. S. Pukhov a total of 3,545 sailors from the Active Fleet arrived in Petrograd during this period (*Geroi Oktiabria*, vol. 2, 816–9). This, less crews and detachments on four ships (950 men) which arrived in Petrograd on 26 and 29 October, leaves 2,595 sailors from the Active Fleet arriving by rail in Petrograd from the early morning of 26 October onwards. Such a figure is not unreasonable, but it is not clear how Pukhov worked out the number of participants from each formation. A more conservative estimate would begin with the 1,800 (mostly sailors) who arrived on the first three trains and 950 on the four warships (Smilga, 24); to this would be added the unknown number in another detachment which left Helsingfors on the 29th (*BMPP*, 313f). Some 150 sailors (with 260 soldiers, 30 men from an unknown unit, and 150 Red Guards) arrived from Kronstadt on the 29th, as did the destroyer *Prozorlivy* (52 men) (*BMPP*, 305, 360n158).

53 M. N. Pokrovskii, 'Bol'sheviki i front v oktiabre – noiabre 1917 g.', *Oktiabr'skaia revoliutsiia: Sbornik statei 1917–1927* (M, 1929), 218; Sukhanov, vol. 7, 234f; *PVRK*, vol. 1, 351.

54 Krasnov, 167f.

55 Trotsky, *Stalin School of Falsification*, iii.

56 *IKS*, no. 187 (2.xi.17), 4; Mel'gunov, *Kak Bol'sheviki zakhvatili vlast'*, 107, 183f; S. T. Possony, *Lenin: The Compulsive Revolutionary* (L, 1966), 277f.

CHAPTER 8

1 *PVRK*, vol. 1, 536, vol. 2, 346, 392, 414f, vol. 3, 90f, 469; *BMBVS*, 47, 61, 67; A. L. Fraiman, *Forpost sotsialisticheskoi revoliutsii*, 109f, 113, 132, 188; I. I. Vakhrameev, *Vo imia revoliutsii*, 45–56, 69, 73.

2 *BMPP*, 286; *Moriak*, no. 22 (16.xii.17), 505; Lenin, *PSS*, vol. 50, 14; *Bor'ba*, no. 16 (6.i.18), 1; *BMBVS*, 43f.

3 *BMBVS*, 42; D. A. Chugaev (resp. ed.), *Triumfal'noe shestvie sovetskoi vlasti* (hereafter cited as *TShSV*) (2 vols., M, 1963), vol. 2, 337.

4 *BMBVS*, 67–70; Koz'min, 'Dva dnia', *Morskoi sbornik*, 1932, no. 2, 59–63; V. D. Bonch-Bruevich, *Vospominaniia o Lenine*, 161–4; Dybenko, *Miatezhniki*, 109; Fraiman, *Forpost*, 162, 200, 206f; A. K. Drezen (ed.), *Baltiiskii flot v Oktiabr'skoi revoliutsii i grazhdanskoi voine* (hereafter cited as *BFORGV*), 48–50.

5 Viktor Zh., 'Slavnyi revoliutsioner', *Krasnyi flot*, 1923, no. 1/2 (10/11), 133–6; F. Raskol'nikov, *Rasskazy Michmana Il'ina*, 18–21; V. D. Bonch-Bruevich, 168–70; Lenin, *PSS*, vol. 50, 26; *BFORGV*, 50. Dybenko, who was also present, maintained

that Lenin had wanted that day's meeting to finish of its own accord, and *then* the delegates would be forbidden to reassemble. Zhelezniakov went against Lenin's instructions – with Dybenko's approval (*Miatezhniki*, 110f).

6 *Protokoly*, 348f; *IGS*, no. 8 (12.i.18), 2; *IRS*, no. 243 (11.1.18), 3.

7 *BMBVS*, 323n93.

8 Khovrin, *Baltiitsy*, 190–4; *Golos pravdy*, no. 112 (15.xi.17), 2; Shpilevskii, *Bratva*, 58–63; M. D. Bonch-Bruevich, *Vsia vlast' sovetam*, 218–20.

9 *BMBVS*, 60; Shpilevskii, *Bratva*, 64–87; V. A. Antonov-Ovseenko, *Zapiski o grazhdanskoi voine* (M, 1924), vol. 1, 72f.

10 R. N. Mordvinov, *Kursom 'Avrory'*, 30; Fraiman, *Forpost*, 258; *BMBVS*, 317n46.

11 *BMBVS*, 318n50; Iarchuk, 39–45.

12 *BMBVS*, 64f, 317nn42, 43.

13 'Revoliutsionnye otriady matrosov v kontse 1917 i nachale 1918 g.g.', *Krasnyi flot*, 1922, no. 2, 91–6; Fraiman, *Forpost*, 262.

14 *IRS*, no. 205 (20.xi.17), 1.

15 *BMPP*, 251f; *IGS*, no. 224 (12.xii.17), 1.

16 *Ostsee*, III, 334–46.

17 *IGS*, no. 14 (19.i.18), 2, no. 19 (25.i.18), 3, no. 20 (26.i.18), 2; 'Revoliutsionnye otriady', 96; P. Bykov, 'Perekhod flota iz Gel'singforsa v Kronshtadt zimoiu 1918 goda', *Morskoi sbornik*, 1923, no. 11, 15f.

18 M. S. Svechnikov, *Revoliutsiia i grazhdanskaia voina v Finliandii: 1917–1918 gg. (Vospominaniia i materialy)* (M, 1923), 62–4; *IGS*, no. 37 (28.ii.18), 2.

19 *TShSV*, vol. 1, 413; *Krasnyi flot*, 1924, no. 1, 40; S. Zakharov, *P. D. Khokhriakov* (Sverdlovsk, 1959), 11–40; A. D. Avdeev. 'Nikolai Romanov v Tobol'ske i v Ekaterinburge (Iz vospominanii komendanta)', *Krasnaia nov'*, 1928, no. 5, 187–201.

20 *BMBVS*, 72f.

21 *Protokoly*, 258, 312, 324f, 330, 363; Petrash, *Moriaki*, 17; *IKS*, no. 203 (21.xi.17), 3, no. 46 (13.iii.18), 4; Izmailov and Pukhov, 220; N. S. Kroviakov, '*Ledovyi pokhod' Baltiiskogo flota v 1918 godu*, 109. One Soviet source maintained that, in contrast to the army, there had been virtually no desertion from the fleet by mid-January (S. S. Khesin, *Matrosy revoliutsii*, 357); the statements in Tsentrobalt seen more reliable.

22 *BMBVS*, 59f, 62, 70, 79, 317n45, 318n50; Lenin, *PSS*, vol. 50, 31; *Protokoly*, 299f, 311–13.

23 *Protokoly*, 311; *IKS*, no. 2 (4.i.18), 5; Dybenko, *Miatezhniki*, 104; *Golos pravdy*, no. 18 (25.i.18), 1.

24 S. N. Baranov, *Veter s Baltiki*, 155–61; *IKS*, no. 9 (14.i.18), 4; *IGS*, no. 33 (23.ii.18), 2; *BFORGV*, 145.

25 V. V. Anikeev and R. A. Lavrov, 'Bol'shevistskie organizatsii nakanune VII s"ezda RKP (b)', *Istoricheskii arkhiv*, 1958, vol. 3, 29; *7-oi s"ezd*, 115; *BMBVS*, 254f.

26 *SS*, no. 217 (21.xii.17), 4; *Protokoly*, 328; *IGS*, no. 23 (30.i.18), 1; *IRS*, no. 263 (16.ii.18), 1; P. Stasevich, 'Ledovy pokhod Baltiiskogo flota', *OSh*, 133f.

27 V. D. Bonch-Bruevich, 171–198; Lenin, *PSS*, vol. 50, 27; Fraiman, *Forpost*, 210f; *IKS*, no. 48 (16.iii.18), 3f.

28 *IGS*, no. 1 (3.i.18), 3; *Protokoly*, 26; Rengarten, 'Oktiabr'skaia revoliutsiia', 61.

29 *IKS*, no. 3 (5.i.18), 2; *IGS*, no. 9 (13.i.18), Supplement; *IRS*, no. 241 (8.i.18), 3; *Protokoly*, 342.

30 *IGS*, no. 233 (22.xii.17), 5; *IKS*, no. 28 (20.ii.18), 2f; *Golos pravdy*, no. 29 (21.ii.18), 1f.

CHAPTER 9

1 G. B. Ol'derogge, *Modest Ivanov*, 68; Khovrin, *Baltiitsy*, 180.

2 Ol'derogge; VK 3184, Prikazy Komflota no. 151 (2.ix.17), no. 248 (2.x.17); M. Ivanov, 'Moia pervaia vstrecha s tov. Leninym', *Krasnyi flot*, 1926, no. 2, 65f; *Dekrety Sovetskoi vlasti* (M, 1957–), vol. 1, 581.

3 M. Ivanov, 'Pis'mo v redaktsiiu', *Revoliutsionnyi flot*, no. 16 (28) (17.xii.17), 3; Rengarten, 'Oktiabr'skaia revoliutsiia', 71–5; Timirev, 156.

4 *BMBVS*, 33, 315n21; A. Drezen (ed.), 'Flot posle Oktiabr'skoi pobedy', *Krasnyi arkhiv*, 1932, no. 4 (53). 63–99.

5 V. E. Egor'ev, 'Evgennyi Andreevich Berens (Nekrolog)', *Morskoi sbornik*, 1928, no. 4, 3–7; V. V. Petrash, 'E. A. Berens', *Voenno-istoricheskii zhurnal*, 1966, no. 11, 102f; *Moriak*, no. 9 (19.viii.17), 204; N. N., 'Organizatsionnoe postroenie Krasnogo flota', *Morskoi sbornik*, 1923, no. 1, 10; *Dekrety Sovetskoi vlasti*, vol. 1, 361–3.

6 Rengarten, 'Oktiabr'skaia revoliutsiia', 53, 60f, 69, 75; Adm.137/1249, 457f, Report of B.N.L.O. Russia, 23.xi.17 (n.s.); *BMBVS*, 37; Timirev, 157; VK 3184, Prikaz Komflota no. 358 (13.xi.17); VK 3220, Meeting of Tsentrobalt, 6.xi.17; *Protokoly*, 278f.

7 Rengarten, 'Oktiabr'skaia revoliutsiia', 66; *Protokoly*, 279f; Timirev, 157–60.

8 Rengarten, 'Oktiabr'skaia revoliutsiia', 67–75; *BFORGV*, 27; *Protokoly*, 281–3; Timirev, 157–60.

9 Rengarten, 'Oktiabr'skaia revoliutsiia', 78f; Adm.137/1570, 330–2, Cromie Reports of 16 and 17.xii.17 (n.s.); VK 3184, Prikazy Komflota nos. 1–5 (5.xii.17), 6–8 (6.xii.17), 9 (7.xii.17); *Protokoly*, 300; Mordvinov, 31.

10 Rengarten, 'Oktiabr'skaia revoliutsiia', 79–91; Graf, 345f; *Revoliutsionnyi flot*, no. 16 (28) (17.xii.17), 14f; *IGS*, no. 220 (7.xii.17), 3.

11 Rengarten, 'Oktiabr'skaia revoliutsiia', 91f; *Protokoly*, 307; Timirev, 154, 169f.

12 Adm.137/1570, Cromie Report of 17.xii.17 (n.s.); Rengarten, 'Oktiabr'skaia revoliutsiia', 90, 92.

13 V. Novitskii, 'O demobilizatsii flota', *Revoliutsionnyi flot*, no. 1 (8.i.18), 2.

14 *IGS*, no. 9 (13.i.18), 2f; *IKS*, no. 4 (6.i.18), 3; *IRS*, no. 241 (8.i.18), 3; *Bor'ba*, no. 25 (15.ii.18), 2, 4; *Protokoly*, 379f, 399, 455n104; A. K. Drezen, 'Bor'ba za sovetizatsiiu Baltiiskogo flota', *Krasnaia letopis'*, 1929, no. 6 (33), 133–8.

15 Izmailov and Pukhov, 248, 250; Ol'derogge, 88f; *Revoliutsionnyi flot*, no. 5 (28.ii.18), 19.

16 *Revoliutsionnyi flot*, no. 3 (30.i.18), 17–20.

17 *Dekrety Sovetskoi vlasti*, vol. 1, 434–41; *Protokoly*, 357, 378; Izmailov and Pukhov, 247; *BMBVS*, 318n52.

18 *Dekrety Sovetskoi vlasti*, vol. 1, 434–41; *BFORGV*, 54–6; *IGS*, no. 9 (13.i.18), 3, no. 20 (26.i.18), 2. The Naval Conference had discussed the organisation of a 'free-hire fleet on the British and American model' (*Utro pravdy*, no. 8 (63) (31.i.18), 1). The term was frequently used later; in April, for example, the *Poltava* advertised for men on a 'free-hire' basis (*IKS*, no. 62 (3.iv.18), 4).

19 *Protokoly*, 399, 401; *Bor'ba*, no. 27 (19.ii.18), 3; Graf, 340.

20 *BFORGV*, 51f; *Protokoly*, 357, 385.

21 *Protokoly*, 289, 305, 382, 387; [F. N. A. Cromie], 'Documents on British Relations with Russia, 1917–1918 (IV)', ed. D. R. Jones, *Canadian-American Slavic Studies*, VIII (1974), no. 3, 547. The British naval attaché reported that he had offered to pay £300,000 a month for three months on condition that only sailors on board ships were paid ('this would help to prevent the use of landing parties for political purposes') and if he had control (F.O. 371/3315, Lindley to F.O., 25.i.18 (n.s.); for the F.O rejection see F.O. to Lindley, 1.ii.18 (n.s.)).

22 *Protokoly*, 315–17; Izmailov and Pukhov, 244.

23 Rengarten, 'Oktiabr'skaia revoliutsiia', 61; *Protokoly*, 307, 313, 333, 359, 373–5, 390, 454n100; *Shtorm*, no. 2 (18.i.18), 24; *IGS*, no. 18 (24.i.18), 4, no. 20 (26.i.18), 3. In the index to *Protokoly* only 6 members of the 5th session are listed as Bolsheviks, as compared to 19 for the 4th session.

24 *PLKF*, 219–24; Dybenko, *Miatezhniki*, 105; *Protokoly*, 204f, 212f; P. I. Mus'iakov, *Nikolai Izmailov*.

25 V. Avtukhov, 'Aleksandr Antonovich Ruzhek', *Krasnyi flot*, 1924, no. 5, 58; *BMBVS*, 56f; Graf, 346f.

26 Izmailov and Pukhov, 250f; *BMBVS*, 81f.

27 *Protokoly*, 404–6, 408–9; *Bor'ba*, no. 26 (17.ii.18), 4.

28 *BMBVS*, 74f.

29 *Protokoly*, 402f.

30 Ibid., 411f.

31 *Protokoly*, 407, 409f, 413f, 421, 425, 455nn104, 106; *BMBVS*, 84f; Izmailov and Pukhov, 182, 253, 270f.

32 *BMBVS*, 85f; I. M. Ludri, 'Sudovye komitety', *OSh*, 83.

33 One source maintained that Izmailov was replaced on 23 March (N. Khomchuk, 'O Ledovom pokhode korablei Baltiiskogo flota v 1918 godu', *Voenno-istoricheskii zhurnal*, 1963, no. 2, 122). There is, however, no evidence that he was active after 4 March; Blokhin presided over the liquidation of Tsentrobalt as acting Main Commissar. Four other facts should be mentioned: Izmailov was a delegate to the 4th Congress of Soviets (14–16 March 1918) where the Left S.R. delegates voted against the Brest peace; he was made Chief of the Main Naval Economic Administration on 24 May; in July he openly denounced the Left S.R. uprising in Moscow; and in the autumn he joined the Communist Party (*PLKF*, 222).

34 *BMBVS*, 319 n 57; Graf, 350.

35 Khomchuk, 122; *IGS*, no. 6 (15.iii.18), 3, no. 7 (16.iii.18), 3; Cromie, 'Documents (IV)', 554.

36 *BFORGV*, xiii–xiv; Graf, 350; A. Lukin, 'Razstrel Shchastnago', *Posledniia novosti*, no. 3377 (21.vi.1930), 4; *BMBVS*, 86; *IGS*, no. 15 (26.iii.18), 4.

37 *BFORGV*, xiii–xiv.

38 *BMBVS*, 87–9; *IKS*, no. 71 (13.iv.17), 1.

CHAPTER 10

1 *Ostsee*, III, 309f, 312, 319f; S. P. B., 'Boevaia deiatel'nost' Baltiiskogo flota posle Oktiabr'skoi revoliutsii', *Morskoi sbornik*, 1922, no. 1/2, 59.

2 L. S. Gaponenko (ed.), *Oktiabr'skaia revoliutsiia i armiia: 25 oktiabria 1917 g. – mart 1918 g.: Sbornik dokumentov* (M, 1973), 394.

3 B. Gorev, *Anarkhizm v Rossii (ot Bakunina do Makhno)* (M, 1930), 111; *IKS*,

no. 23 (31.i.18), 1, no. 30 (22.ii.18), 1f, no. 31 (23.ii.18), 2.

4 *IGS*, no. 36 (26.ii.18), 2.

5 Mordvinov, 62f; *BMBVS*, 94, 96.

6 Izmailov and Pukhov, 254f; *BMBVS*, 96f; Stasevich, 'Ledovyi pokhod', 130.

7 *IRS*, no. 266 (20.ii.18), 1; *Der Weltkrieg 1914 bis 1918*, XIII, 369; H. Kaupisch (ed.), *Die Befreiung von Livland und Estland*, 70–3.

8 *BFORGV*, 67–73; Kroviakov, *Ledovyi pokhod*, 81–5; N. N. Azovtsev, et. al. (eds.), *Direktivy komandovaniia frontov Krasnoi armii (1917–1922 gg.): Sbornik dokumentov . . .* (4 vols, M, 1971–), vol. 1, 51f; *BMBVS*, 98; A. L. Fraiman, *Revoliutsionnaia zashchita Petrograda*, 109–11; A. A. Gromyko, *et al.* (eds), *Dokumenty vneshnei politiki SSSR* (M, 1959–), vol. 1, 122f; Kaupisch (ed.), 73f; *Weltkrieg*, XIII, 369.

9 *BFORGV*, 73–5.

10 Khomchuk, 123; Mordvinov, 62f.

11 *Izvestiia VTsIK*, no. 93 (357) (12.v.18), 5; Fraiman, *Revoliutsionnaia zashchita*, 231f; Izmailov and Pukhov, 265f; Mordvinov, 50, 64.

12 Kaupisch (ed.), 76–8, 83f; *Weltkrieg*, XIII, 370; *Izvestiia VTsIK*, nos. 91, 93, 94, 97–100 (355, 357, 358, 361–4) (10, 12, 14, 17–19, 21.v.18), 5; Fraiman, *Revoliutsionnaia zaschita*, 227, 230–6; Mordvinov, 52–7.

13 *Izvestiia VTsIK*, no. 91 (355) (10.v.18), 5f, no. 99 (363) (19.v.18), 5. Various rumours appeared in the press about Dybenko. One report said that in April he and Kollontai had gone into hiding, despite a promise not to leave Moscow (*IKS*, no. 75 (18.iv.18), 3). According to another report he was expelled from the party as 'an adventurer of the very lowest kind' (*IKS*, no. 87 (3.v.18), 2).

14 Kaupisch (ed.), 86f.

15 *IKS*, no. 43 (9.iii.18), 1, no. 44 (10.iii.18), 4, no. 46 (13.iii.18), 4, no. 47 (14.iii.18), 3.

16 Kroviakov, *Ledovyi pokhod*, 72.

17 *Protokoly*, 412, 414, 455n108; Avtukhov, 'Ruzhek', 58; *BMBVS*, 123f; *BFORGV*, 87.

18 V. Sokol'nikov, 'Plavanie vo l'du', *Krasnyi flot*, 1927, no. 23, 9f; Kroviakov, *Ledovyi pokhod*, 108f; Bykov, 16f.

19 D. Fedotoff White, *The Growth of the Red Army* (Princeton, 1944), 72; Lukin, 3f; Rengarten, 'Oktiabr'skaia revoliutsiia', 51.

20 *Ostsee*, III, 347–83. The Germans were provided with information about minefields and swept channels by a renegade Russian officer, Lieutenant I. I. Roos.

21 Kroviakov, *Ledovyi pokhod*, 117, 120, 126–9.

22 Ibid., 133f.

23 Ibid., 147f, 153; *Ostsee*, III, 345, 387; *BMBVS*, 133–5. According to the German account the two ratings, pleading ignorance, let the former officers do all the negotiating at Gange.

24 Kroviakov, 138–44; Bykov, 19–21; V. S., 'Nedelia vo l'dakh', *Russkii vestnik*, no. 2 (24.iv.18), 2, no. 3 (25.iv.18), 2.

25 Kroviakov, *Ledovyi pokhod*, 124f, 134–6, 155–7; *BMBVS*, 123f. The British were apparently involved with these plans. In February the naval attaché reported, 'I have every hope of organizing destruction of valuable ships with the aid of Admiral Razvosoff and Admiral Bacherev' (F.O. 371/3315, Lindley to F.O., no. 557, 22.ii.18).

26 Kroviakov, *Ledovyi pokhod*, 109, 168; V. I. Sapozhnikov, *Podvig Baltiitsev v 1918 godu*, 58.

27 Cromie, 'Documents (IV)', 555; Bykov, 16, 21, 23; Stasevich, 'Ledovyi pokhod', 133f, 141; I. Shpilevskii, 'Pokhod iz Gel'singforsa v Petrograd v aprele 1918 goda' *Krasnyi flot*, 1922, no. 3/4, 148; Sapozhnikov, 52; Kroviakov, 166.

28 S. P. B., 62; Shpilevskii, 'Pokhod', 147.

29 Graf, 351. One Soviet source alleged that Graf, for his part, was trying to buy 'Noviks', destroyers, and mine craft for the White Finns (N. S. Kroviakov, 'K istorii "Ledovogo pokhoda" Baltiiskogo flota v 1918 g.', *Istoricheskie zapiski*, vol. 52 (1955), 37f).

30 Khomchuk, 123f; Sapozhnikov, 61–3; Kroviakov, *Ledovyi pokhod*, 169–180; Bykov, 23–8; Shpilevskii, *Bratva*, 93–100; I. Iakovlev, 'Ledovyi pokhod torgovogo flota', *Morskoi sbornik*, 1935, no. 4, 106–9; P. Romanov, 'Ne ostavili vragu (Vospominaniia o perekhode plavuchei masterskoi "Angary" iz Gel'singforsa v Kronshtadt v 1918 g.)', *Krasnyi flot*, 1922, no. 8, 127–30; P. Stasevich, 'Vos'mero spasli esminets', *Krasnyi flot*, 1925, no. 9, 101–3.

31 *Ostsee*, III, 394–9; E. Dymman, 'Na kanonerskoi lodke "Groziashchii" v dni padeniia Gel'singforsa', *Krasnyi flot*, 1925, no. 3, 97–9.

32 M. D. Bonsch-Bruevich, 262f.

33 Monasterev and Terestchenko, *Histoire de la Marine Russe*, 326; Graf, 353.

34 Kroviakov, 97; S.P.B., 62; Khomchuk, 122f.

CONCLUSION

1 A number of Baltic veterans died in the purges, although information is scanty. Data on 181 sailors is given in *Pervyi den' novogo mira* (ed. V. F. Sulin), and of the 159 who were still alive in the late 1930s, 23 (14.5%) died in 1937 or 1938.

2 A large proportion of Russian naval officers emigrated. One survey, published in 1929, found that of 2,019 military branch officers, 792 (39.2%) were living abroad in 1929; this figure should be taken as a minimum, since 668 were untraced (*Morskoi zhurnal*, 1929, no. 5 (17), 15). According to a 1944 survey of 931 graduates of the Naval Cadet Corps classes of 1914–18, 233 (25.0%) were émigrés, 163 were dead, 133 were known to be in the U.S.S.R., and the fate of 402 was unknown (Tarsaidze, 32).

3 Dybenko, *Miatezhniki*, 33f.

4 *Priboi*, no. 41 (30.ix.17), 1.

5 Cromie, 'Documents (II)', 371.

6 Fedotoff White, *Survival*, 176f.

APPENDIX 1

1 Petrash, *Moriaki*, 15, 17f.

2 Ibid., 15; Garkavenko, 'Sotsial'nyi sostav', 48; Khesin, 'Nakanune Oktiabria', 95.

3 Garkavenko, 'Sotsial'nyi sostav', 49.

4 Petrash, 'Sostav'; Khesin, 'Lichnyi sostav'.

5 Garkavenko, 'Sotsial'nyi sostav'.

6 Ibid., p. 56.

7 Khesin, 'Nakanune Oktiabria', 82.

8 Data for 1899–1905 from Garkavenko, 'Sotsial'nyi sostav', 40. Data for 1914–16 from Khesin, 'Nakanune Oktiabria', 84f.

9 Garkavenko, 'Sotsial'nyi sostav', 52.

10 Khesin, 'Nakanune Oktiabria', 86.

APPENDIX 2

1 This is primarily based on a Royal Navy printed list, 'Organization of the Russian Baltic Fleet' (Adm.116/1862), which gives the situation in mid-summer 1917. The list was supplemented with information from other sources, especially Graf (458–74) and Greger (36, 70–4). Whether vessels survived in Soviet hands was determined by checking the 'Provisional Order of Battle of the Fleet of the Baltic Sea for 1918', dated 16 May (*BMBVS*, 166–71).

APPENDIX 3

1 *IKS*, no. 108 (29.vii.17), 3; *Trud i zemlia*, no. 80 (28.vii.17), 1, no. 81 (29.vii.17), 2. The naval vote is derived from the naval vote of Kronstadt proper plus the vote from Biorko-Tranzund, where the training ships were based. The votes cast represent only 61.1% of the 46,051 electors.

2 *IKS*, no. 43 (10.v.17), cited in Petrash, *Moriaki*, 73. The E.C. of the Workers' Section in the 2nd Session included 3 B, 3 SR, 3 M, and 7 NP (*IKS*, no. 44 (11.v.17), 3). The E.C. for the whole soviet was presumably chosen on the basis of 10:1, i.e. 1 B, 11 SR, 7 M, 8 NP.

3 *IKS*, no. 121 (13.viii.17), 1.

4 *IKS*, no. 21 (28.i.18), 2. This is based on the initial results (131 B, 60 SR, 5 M, 20 NP, 14 A, 53 Mx) plus delegates nominated by the party organisations (one for each 15 delegates, and at least one for each party). On 7 March it was stated that there were 302 delegates in the soviet (*IKS*, no. 46 (13.iii.18), 4). The E.C. was presumably chosen on the basis of 10:1.

5 *IKS*, no. 62 (3.iv.18), 1. This is based on the initial result (53 B, 39 SR, 14 M, 24 NP, 10 A, 41 Mx) plus delegates nominated by party organisations on the basis of 10:1. The E.C. was presumably chosen on the basis of 10:1.

6 Kiuru, 52. In April it was reported that the soviet contained 600 deputies of whom 29 (4.8%), all workers, were in an organised Bolshevik fraction (*7-aia konferentsiia*, 279).

7 Zalezhskii, *Bor'ba*, 88; *IGS*, no. 48 (13.v.17), 1, no. 97 (12.vii.17), 1; *Golos Sotsial-Demokrata*, no. 1 (30.vii.17), 16; Raskol'nikov, *Kronshtadt*, 100. At the 6th Party Congress Zalezhsky claimed 70–80 Bolsheviks (17.5–20.0%) and 125 'Internationalists' (31.2%) out of 400 members (*6-oi s"ezd*, 74).

8 Kiuru, 53; *IGS*, no. 42 (7.iii.18), 2.

9 Kiuru, 55. An alternative figure for the committee of 7 soldiers, 7 sailors, and 2 workers can be cited (*IGS*, no. 49 (14.v.17), 4).

10 Kiuru, 76f; *IGS*, no. 58 (26.v.17), 4. The LSRs were 'S.R.-Internationalists'; of the Mensheviks 2 were listed as 'S.D. non-fraction'.

11 Kiuru, 130, 132; *IGS*, no. 158 (24.ix.17), 3.

12 *IGS*, no. 214 (30.xi.17), 2f. The Regional Committee dissolved itself on about 3 March 1917.

13 Petrash, *Moriaki*, 74.

14 *IRS*, no. 52 (17.v.17), 4. Petrash gives figures of 9 NP and 13 from other parties, with a total of 196 (*Moriaki*, 74).

15 *IRS*, no. 131 (22.vii.17), 3. On the eve of the October rising the delegates comprised 102 B, 97 SR, 15 M, 23 NP, 2 A, and 19 In., for a total of 258 (*Zvezda*, no. 23 (19.x.17), 3).

16 *IRS*, no. 217 (4.xii.17), 2; *Bor'ba*, no. 1 (22.xii.17), 4. SR are Left S.R.s.

17 *Revel'skii nabliudatel'*, no. 176 (11.viii.17), 2. About 65% of the electorate voted.

18 V. V. Petrash, 'Vybory v Uchreditel'noe sobranie po Baltiiskomu izbiratel'nomu okrugu', *Gorod Lenina v dni Oktiabria i Velikoi Otechestvennoi voiny 1941–1945 gg.*, eds S. N. Valk, *et al.*, 72, 78. Naval units and army units subordinate to the C.-in-C., Baltic Fleet, had their own electoral regulations. The votes cast were nearly double the number of ballot papers because each elector could cast two votes. The two candidates with the largest number of votes were elected. The left S.R. candidates (List 1) were Prosh'ian and Shishko, the Bolshevik candidates (List 2) were Lenin and Dybenko, the 'Union of Officer-Republicans' put forward Rengarten and V. N. Demchinsky (List 3), the Right S.R. candidates were S. A. Tsion and S. L. Maslov (the Minister of Agriculture) (List 4), and the non-partisan candidate (List 5) was G. A. Lopatin, an aged *narodnik*.

Naval units in the capital voted with civilians in the Petrograd Electoral District. The 42nd Corps was part of the Northern Front district. The 48,727 registered soldier-electors cast 35,145 valid ballots (72.1%); the Bolsheviks received 59.2% of the vote, the Left S.R.s 31.7%, the Right S.R.s 1.6%, the Mensheviks 0.9%, and others 6.6% (Kiuru, 167).

19 *Golos pravdy*, no. 118 (23.xi.17), 1, 4; *Trud i zemlia*, no. 177 (23.xi.17), 4. 'Normal' voting for the assembly, as practised in the civilian vote, was on the basis of proportional representation; voters voted for a list rather than for individuals.

20 *IRS*, no. 203 (17.xi.17), 1.

Index

Abo, 20, 143
Admiralty Council, 129
Aland Is., 87, 121, 139, 142–3, 146
Aldaisky, Sr. Lt., 36
Alekeev, Ia. Z., 122
Alekseev, Gen. M. V., 46, 84
Al'tfater, Capt. V. M., 19
anarchists, 23–4, 53–4, 59, 121, 126–7, 135, 142
Antipov, N. K., 30, 49, 153
Antonov-Ovseenko, V. A., 25, 35, 49–50, 60, 82–3, 119–20; biography of, 29–30, 153; in July, 65, 70–1; in October, 99, 103, 106–7, 109–10, 197 (n. 38)
Anvel't, Ia. Ia., 30, 75, 102, 127, 153
army units, German: 8th Army, 143; Northern Corps, 143–4; Baltic Div., 147
army units, Russian: Northern Front, 95, 143; 12th Army, 93, 141; 3rd Cav. Corps, 99; 42nd Corps, 76, 205 (n. 18); 1st Ussuri Cossack Div., 76; Caucasian Native Cav. Div., 77; 1st Machine-Gun Rgt., 55–6; 3rd Ekaterinodar Rgt.; 71; 3rd Kronstadt Artillery Rgt., 13; 469th Arzamas Rgt., 76; Reval Bn. of Death, 75, 90
Artamanov, Maj. L. K., 68
Averichkin, F. S., 80
Avksent'ev, N. D., 70
Avsaragov, 102

Bakhirev, V.-Adm. M. K., 46, 87, 130–1, 202 (n. 25); biography of, 90, 154; at Moon Sound, 91–3, 95
Balakin, I., 153
Baltic Fleet, strategy for, 3, 85–6, 94; matériel in, 84–6, 193 (n. 3); losses, 193 (n. 4); Artificers School, 14; Torpedo and Mining Training Detachment, 13–14; 1st Baltic Fleet Depot, 2, 4, 13–14, 54, 68; 2nd Baltic Fleet Depot, 2, 12, 77, 97, 109, 112; 116; Naval Guards Depot, 2, 12, 97–8, 103, 109, 112; Mine Defence Depot, 16; 1st Battleship Brigade, 3, 47, 88, 95, 146–7; 2nd Battleship Brigade, 16–7, 43, 146; 1st Cruiser Brigade, 19, 25, 88, 120, 124, 131, 139; 2nd Cruiser Brigade, 48, 88, 128; Destroyer Division, 25, 75, 88, 95, 125, 139; 6th Destroyer Flotilla, 87; 11th Destroyer Flotilla, 91; Submarine Division, 25, 47–8, 87–8, 95; 1st Submarine Flotilla, 87; 3rd Submarine Flotilla, 43, 48; 4th Submarine Flotilla, 134, 147; 1st Patrol Boat Flotilla, 23; Mine Defence, 18; Minesweeper Division, 88; Minelayer Detachment, 88; Patrol Boat Division, 88; Aviation Division, 88; Abo Air Station, 72–3, 76; see also committees, officers, sailors, warrant officers, warships
Baltic Staff, 11, 42–6, 72, 81–2, 86, 95, 111, 130–1, 184 (n. 35)
Baranov, A. V., 124, 135, 154
Behncke, V.-Adm. P., 92
Berens, Capt. E. A., 129, 154–5
Berg, E. A., 74, 152
Berliand, V. I., 30
Berzin, R. I., 120
Biorko Sound, 3, 77, 204 (n. 1)
Black Sea Fleet, 20–1, 49, 94, 157
Blokhin, E. S., 82, 127, 136–7, 140, 201 (n. 33)
Board of the NKMD (Supreme Naval Board), 129, 132–4, 136, 138–40, 143, 148–50
Boitsov, 31
Boky, G. I., 125
Bolsheviks, 23, 79, 154–5; in February, 9; cadres and organisation, 28–31, 186 (n. 17); ideology, 31–5; and democratisation, 49–50; and Kronstadt Republic, 52–3; in July, 57–8, 64–6, 74; in October, 102–7, 111, 114;

and Constituent Assembly, 117;
after October, 123, 126–7, 142, 201
(n. 23); C.C., 30, 53, 56–60, 65, 74,
82–3, 104, 106, 108, 112, 121, 151;
Petersburg Committee, 8, 29–31, 53,
57, 68, 106, 112, 114, 197 (n. 39);
Military Organisation, 53, 56–8,
107; Vyborg District Committee, 29;
Helsingfors Committee, 34, 49, 60,
74, 186 (n. 17); Kronstadt Com-
mittee, 30–1, 53, 58–9, 108, 186
(nn. 17, 20); Reval Organisation, 30,
76; Conference of Party Workers
(Mar–Apr), 32, 186 (n. 17); 7th
Conference, 186 (n. 17); 6th Con-
gress, 74, 186 (n. 17); 7th Con-
gress, 125, 186 (n. 17); *see also* Social
Democrats
Bonch-Bruevich, Gen. M. D., 146, 151
Bregman, L. A., 30, 58, 69, 108, 127
Breslav, B. A., 30, 109
Brest-Litovsk, Peace of, 127, 140, 145–6,
149
Brushvit, A., 53–4, 59, 123, 146
Brusilov, Gen. A. A., 46, 68
Bunakov, I. I., 70
Bykov, P. D., 150

C.E.C., 45–6, 70–2, 75, 77–9, 82, 97, 190
(n. 33); and July, 55–7, 59, 62–6;
after October, 105, 114, 118, 129,
143–4
Central Position, 3, 85, 94, 142–4, 151
Cheka, 90, 122
Cheremisov, Gen. V. A., 95
Cherkassky, Capt. Prince M. B., 78, 81,
88–9, 154
Chernov, V. M. 55–6, 118
Chkheidze, N. S., 28
Chudakov, P. D., 41
Committee for the Salvation of the Motherland and the Revolution, 99, 104
committees, 12, 36, 41, 155; Maksimov
regulations on, 38; government regulations on, 38; Lebedev Commission and, 39, 44–5, 71; Tsentrobalt
regulations on, 45, 71; and operations, 87; 1918 regulations on,
132–3
Conference, All-Russian Naval, 132, 200
(n. 18)
Congress of the All-Russian War Fleet, 79,
129
Congress of the Baltic Fleet: 1st, 41, 43–9,

73, 81–2; 2nd, 79, 81–3, 100, 110,
130; 3rd, 124
Congress of Peasants' Soviets, 52
Congress of Soviets, All-Russian: 1st, 25,
53–4; 2nd, 75, 79, 82, 97, 99, 101–6,
108–10, 197 (n. 39); 3rd, 118, 126–7;
4th, 201 (n. 33)
Congress of Soviets of the Northern
Region, 106
Constituent Assembly, 44, 67, 130–1;
elections to, 26–8, 34, 105–6, 154,
168–70, 205 (nn. 18–19); closure
of, 117–18, 126
Council of the Republic, 79, 82, 98
Cromie, Cmdr. F. N. A., 36, 46–7, 87, 93,
95, 131, 149–50, 155

Dago Is., 89–90, 93, 143
Daniels, R. V., 196 (n. 34)
death penalty, 67, 73, 76
Declaration of Servicemen's Rights, 38–9,
43–4, 47
Demchinsky, Sr. Lt. V. N., 81, 203 (n. 18)
Democratic Conference, 79–81
Deshevoi, V. I., 30
Detached Naval Cadet Classes, 6, 29, 40
Dmitriev, Lt., 36
Dolgov, V., 136
Dovkont, Cmdr. F. Iu., 184 (n. 35)
Dudorov, Capt. B. P., 40, 61–5, 69, 75,
154
Dukhonin, Gen. N. N., 119
Dutov, Col. A. I., 119
Dybenko, P. E., 74, 118, 121, 154, 205 (n.
18); biography of, 42, 153; in Tsent-
robalt, 30, 45, 49, 72, 80, 82, 188 (n.
26); in July Days, 62, 64–5, 70; in
October, 99–100, 103, 107–11, 195
(n. 8), 197 (n. 38); in Civil War, 124,
198 (n. 5); as Naval Commissar, 129,
131, 134–5, 139, 142–6, 202 (n. 13)

Emel'ianov, 102
Entin, S. L., 30
Essen, Adm. N. D. fon-, 3, 47, 85–6
Estonia, M. R. C. of, 108; E.C. of, 108,
127, 143–4; nationalists in, 120, 144;
German invasion of, 140, 143
Ezel' Is., 89–91, 96, 143

February Revolution, 12–21, 155
Fedotov (-White), Lt. D. N., 9, 11, 147,
154–5

Filippovsky, Eng. Cmdr. V. N., 11
Finland, nationalists in, 15, 77, 107, 120; Civil War in, 121; evacuation of, 101, 146; Lenin in, 112, 197 (n. 45)
Finnish Regional Committee, 26, 34, 70, 146, 205 (n. 12); radicalised, 80, 111; in October, 102; composition of, 166, 204 (n. 9), 205 (n. 10)
Flerovsky, I. P., 30, 53, 58, 66, 68, 79, 102, 108–9, 153
Forward Position, 3, 85, 88–9, 93, 95, 147
Fraiman, A. L., 120

Galler, Cmdr. L. M. fon-, 154
Gange, 20, 80, 147–8, 202 (n. 23)
Garin, S. A., 32, 34
Garkavenko, D. A., 157–9
Gerasimov, V.-Adm. A. M., 19
German Navy, losses of, 93, 193 (n. 4)
Gnedin, V. A., 131
Goltz, Gen. Graf R. von der, 147–8
Graf, Cmdr. G. K., 11, 69, 90, 131, 134, 136, 139, 150, 154, 203 (n. 29)
Grediushko, S. S., 108
Gromov, F. V., 58
Grundman, Lt. R. R., 70
Guchkov, A. I., 38
Gurvich, I., 59

Helsingfors, March mutiny in, 1, 9, 11, 14–21, 118, 184 (n. 39); political activity in, 21–35; in July, 61–6; after July, 70–1, 74; and Kornilov, 77, 83; in October, 99, 101, 105, 109–10, 112, 114; after October, 118, 121, 125, 142, 148–9; captured, 151
Helsingfors Revolutionary Committee, 77–9
Helsingfors Soviet, composition, 22, 25–6, 34, 126, 165, 204 (nn. 6–7); and fleet, 38–9, 41, 47; early moderation of, 59–61; after July, 70, 74–5; in October, 100–2, 111
Helsingfors Soviet Sailors' Section, 40–1, 48, 61, 73–4, 81

Iakovlev, Sub-Lt. N., 120
Iarchuk, Kh. Z., 54, 78, 146, 152; in July Days, 46, 58–9; in October, 102–4, 109
Ice Crossing, 146–52
Il'in-Zhenevsky, A. F., 30, 54, 56, 119

Ivanov, Cptn. M. V., 128–32, 154
Ivanov, Gen. N. I., 13
Izmailov, N. F., 82, 127; biography of, 135, 153, 201 (n. 33); in October, 104–5, 196 (n. 23); as head of Vobalt, 127, 131, 135f; as Main Commissar, 136–9, 143, 145

Kabanov, A. N., 136
Kadets, 24, 55, 75, 77, 79, 117
Kaledin, Gen. A. M., 119, 124
Kallis, K. M., 102, 119, 124
Kallistov, Cmdr., 86
Kamashko, S., 136
Kamenev, L. B., 57, 109, 128
Kandyb, Sub-Lt. D. M., 78
Kanin, V.-Adm. V. A., 3, 86
Kapnist, Capt. Count A. P., 37, 129
Kedrov, R.-Adm. M. A., 38, 88
Kerensky, A. F., 20, 33, 54–5; as Justice Minister, 11, 17–18, 24, 51; as Navy Minister, 26, 38–9, 44, 46, 48, 188 (n. 26); in July Days, 56, 64; as Minister-President, 67–8, 89, 91, 194 (n.34); and Kornilov, 76–7, 79; in October, 97–101, 106, 195 (n. 8)
Khesin, S. S., 157, 159
Khokhriakov, P. D., 122, 153.
Khovrin, N. A., 20, 23, 44, 72, 75, 83, 154; and underground, 8, 30, 42; in July, 62–5, 70; in October, 103, 110; in Civil War, 119, 123
Kingissepp, V. E., 30, 127, 153
Kireev, G. P., 153
Klado, Capt. N. L., 96
Klembovsky, Gen. V. N., 88
Kokoshkin, F. F., 126
Kolbin, I. N., 31, 58, 122
Kolchak, Admiral A. V., 21
Kollontai, A. M., 28, 42, 137–8, 202 (n. 13)
Kolosov, 68
Kondrat'ev, Sub-Lt. M. E., 78
Kornilov, Gen. L. G., 54, 68; attempted coup by, 76–9, 83
Koval'sky, Capt. A. A., 81
Krasnov, Gen. P. N., 99–100, 113–14, 195 (n. 8)
Kronstadt, 34, 41; pre-revolutionary, 1–5, 8–9; February Mutiny in, 12–14, 20–1, 183 (n. 31), 184 (n. 32); Town Duma, 23, 25, 34, 68, 103, 204 (n. 1); Republic, 51–3; in June, 53–4; in July, 55–9, 61, 68–9; and Kor-

nilov, 76; in October, 98–9, 107–10, 113–15, 197 (n. 38); and Civil War, 119, 123–6; and Brest-Litovsk, 142, 146; and Constituent Assembly, 169
Kronstadt Military-Technical Commission, 77–8, 101–2, 107–8, 198 (n. 49)
Kronstadt Soviet, composition of, 25–6, 164, 204 (nn. 2, 4, 5); early moderation of, 22–3, 25, 51–2; and Provisional Government, 39, 52–4; in July, 55–9, 61, 68–9; and Kornilov, 77, 79; in October, 98, 100–2, 104–5, 107–9; after October, 123–7, 142, 146
Kroviakov, N. S., 151
Krylenko, N. V., 119, 143
Krylov, 126
Krymov, Gen. A. M., 76
Kukel', Capt. S. A., 40
Kurkov, P. I., 103, 153
Kurosh, V.-Adm. A. P., 13
Kvasov, 124

Lamanov, A. N., 153
Lamanov, Sr. Lt. P. N., 55
Lapvik, 80, 88
Lashevich, M. M., 196 (n. 32)
Lebedev, M. D., 32, 52
Lebedev, V. I., 27, 40, 87, 128; biography of, 39, 153; and Lebedev Commission, 39–41; and Tsentrobalt, 44, 48, 71; in July Days, 61–2, 69
Left S.R.s, 27–8, 64–5, 71, 102–5, 117, 127, 141–2, 154
Lenin, V. I., 123, 125, 153, 194 (n. 34); doctrine of 32–3, 49; and Kronstadt Republic, 53; and July Days, 57, 67–8; in October, 99, 104–7, 109–10, 112, 114, 195 (n. 8), 197 (n. 45); and Constituent Assembly, 117–18, 198 (n. 5), 205 (n. 18); and naval organisation, 128–9, 142–3, 151, 155–6
Leskov, R.-Adm. P. N., 19
Liberty Loan, 27, 52, 60, 75
Liubovich, A. M., 58, 146, 153
Liven, Adm. Prince A. A., 1, 5, 38
Lodyzhensky, Cmdr. I. I., 43, 50, 81–2
Loos, A. S., 63, 153
Lopatin, G. A., 205 (n. 18)
Ludri, I. M., 138
Lunacharsky, A. V., 28, 57
L'vov, Prince G. E., 67

M.R.C. of Petrograd Soviet, 97–101, 108 10, 114–16, 196 (n. 32)
Magnitsky, S. S., 71–3, 80
Main Naval Staff, 40
Maksimov, V.-Adm. A. S., biography of, 37, 154; as C.-in-C., 18–19, 37–8, 43, 96; dismissal of, 46–7, 49; as Chief of Naval Staff, 46–7, 68, 86
Mal'kov, P. D., 116
Markin, N. G., 152
Marusev, V. M., 135
Marushevsky, Gen. V. V., 113
Maslov, S. L., 205 (n. 18)
Mel'gunov, S. P., 114, 184 (n. 35)
Mensheviks, 28, 80; and Helsingfors, 25, 33, 59, 71, 75, 79; and Kronstadt, 53; see also Social Democrats
Menzhinsky, V. R., 116
Meurer, R.-Adm. H., 147–8, 151
Mikhailov, Sub-Lt. K. D., 78
Military Commission of the Provisional Committee, 13, 184 (n. 32)
Miliukov Note, 52, 60
Moon Is., 89–91
Moon Sound, 1, 20, 48, 89, 91–2; Battle of, 89–96
Moscow State Conference, 86
Muranov, M. K., 32
Murav'ev, Cmdr. L. P., 43, 45
Murav'ev, Col. M. A., 114

Nagorny, 9
Naval Cadet Corps, 6, 40, 203 (n. 2)
naval courts, 40
Naval Engineering Academy, 14
Naval General Staff, 19, 40, 61–2, 85–6, 91, 129–30, 146, 148–9
Naval Revolutionary Committee, 101, 104–5, 114, 116, 129, 195 (n. 14)
Naval Section of the C. E. C. (Legislative Council), 129, 132, 137
Nebol'sin, R.-Adm. A. K., 16
Nepenin, V.-Adm. A. I., 1, 3–5, 14–20, 88, 184 (n. 35)
Nevsky, M. A., 195 (n. 14)
Nevsky, V. I., 107
Newspapers: *Golos pravdy*, 31, 68, 108, 124, 127; *Izvestiia Gel'singforsskago Soveta*, 124, 127; *Kiir*, 75; *Moriak*, 46, 105, 117; *Narodnaia niva*, 26; *Narodnoe slovo*, 114; *Obshchee delo*, 24; *Pravda*, 32, 34, 56; *Priboi*, 74; *Proletarskoe delo*, 68; *Sotsialist-revoliutsioner*, 27, 71; *Svobodnoe*

slovo soldata i matrosa, 76; *Svobodnyi flot*, 49; *Trud i zemlia*, 24; *Utro pravdy*, 31, 75; *Volna*, 31, 33, 47, 71; *Vol'ny Kronshtadt*, 24, 142; *Za zemliu i voliu*, 26; *Zvezda*, 75, 106.
Nikolai II, 9–10, 12, 15, 52, 61, 122
Nikolaishtadt, 20
non-partisans, 23, 53, 102
Nordman, Lt. Col. A. N., 111

Octobrists, 24
offensive of 18 June, 27–8, 54, 60–1, 67, 75
officers, naval (command staff), class origin of, 5; training of, 6, 40; political attitudes of, 10–11, 16, 24, 183 (n. 24); murders of, 14, 16–17, 78, 155, 183 (n. 31); authority of, 36–7, 48, 86–7, 150; election of, 47–8, 83, 111, 130, 133, 138–40; and Kornilov, 77–9; number of, 86–7, 156; capitulation of, 131–2; become command staff, 132–3; desertion of, 150; emigration of, 154, 203 (n. 2)
Olich, F. V., 195 (n. 14)
Onipko, F. M., 40, 43–4, 46, 63–4, 71, 78, 118, 188 (n. 15)
Order No. 1, 39
Orlov, K. N., 8, 30, 32, 53

Parsky, Gen. D. P., 145
Pechnikov, 102
Pepeliaev, V. N., 52–4
Perepelkin, P. M., 153
Pereverzev, P. N., 56
Pervushin, F. Kh., 126
Peters, Ia. K., 196 (n. 32)
Petrash, V. V., 157, 183 (n. 31), 184 (n. 39), 185 (n. 47), 198 (n. 49)
Petrograd, naval units in, 1–3, 12, 76–7, 97–8, 103, 112, 116–17, 197 (n. 47)
Petrograd Soviet, 12, 18, 45, 52–4, 76–7, 82, 100; and fleet, 45, 52, 188 (n. 15); in July, 58, 60–1
Petrov, Capt. M. A., 95
Pilkin, R.-Adm. V. K., 19–20, 36, 69, 81, 154
Podgursky, R.-Adm. N. L., 188 (n. 30)
Podvoisky, N. I., 122–3
Pogodin, 102
Polovtsev, Gen. P. A., 56
Polukhin, V. F., 135
Possony, S., 114

Pronin, A. G., 108–9, 154
Prosh'ian, P. P., 27, 64, 71, 102, 127, 153, 190 (n. 40), 205 (n. 18)
Provisional Committee of the State Duma, 11–12, 14–16
Provisional Government, 43, 50, 94; first steps, 15, 18, 51, 60, 188 (n. 38); and Tsentrobalt, 44; and Kronstadt, 52–5, 68–9; 1st Coalition, 51, 60; and July Days, 57, 63–4, 66; 2nd Coalition, 67, 69, 74–5; Directory, 79, 80; overthrown, 98–101, 103, 111
Pukhov, A. S., 93, 198 (n. 52)

Rabchinsky, I. V., 30
Radzikovsky, 34
Rashin, A. G., 158
Raskol'nikov, F. F., 25, 43, 53, 121; biography of, 29, 153; in July Days, 56–8; 68; in October, 99; and Constituent Assembly, 118; at Naval Commissariat, 123–4, 129, 132, 135, 139, 145
Razvozov, R.-Adm. A. V., 49, 137, 202 (n. 25); biography of, 69, 154; appointed C.-in-C., 69–70; position as C.-in-C., 71–3, 80–1, 83, 87; and Kornilov, 77–8; and Moon Sound, 90, 94–5; in October, 108, 111; dismissals of, 130–1, 135, 139; election of, 138–40
Rengarten, Cmdr. I. I., 16, 19, 77, 81, 89, 130–2, 147, 153–4, 205 (n. 18)
Reval, 1, 3, 23, 34; March revolution in, 19–21, 185 (n. 47); moderation of, 34, 75; radicalisation of, 76; Town Duma of, 76, 168, 205 (n. 17); and Kornilov, 78; United E. C. of, 78–9; in October, 106, 108, 120, 196 (n. 32); capture of, 143–4, 150; and Constituent Assembly, 170
Reval Soviet, 41, 78, 102, 118, 126–7, 144; composition of, 22, 25–6, 34, 167, 205 (nn. 14–16); moderation of, 75
Riamo, P. Ia., 194 (n. 14)
Rivkin, N., 102, 104
Rodichev, F. I., 18–19
Rodzianko, M. V., 14–15
Romanov, Grand Duke M. A., 12, 15–16, 18
Roos, Lt. I. I., 202 (n. 20)
Roshal', S. G., 53; biography of, 29, 153; in July, 57–8, 68

Royal Navy, 87, 95, 194 (n. 34)
Rubanin, L. K., 43
Rusin, Adm. A. I., 36, 46, 55, 86, 154
Ruzhek, Capt. A. A., 88, 131, 135–6, 138, 146

S.R.–Maximalists, 23, 126–7, 142
sailors, conscription of, 2; pay of, 2, 39–40, 134; food of, 2, 86, 134; leave for, 2, 41, 67, 73, 134, 157; petty officers, 2, 40; training of, 2–4, 54–5, 134; morale of, 3–4, 150; discipline of, 4, 14, 125, 136–7, 150; restrictions on, 5, 17–18, 37–8; class origins of, 6–7, 157–9; age of, 7, 183 (n. 17); pre-revolutionary views of, 7–10; political attitudes of, 22, 35, 50, 59, 66, 73, 78–9, 100–6, 122–7, 154–5; desertion and demobilisation of, 121, 123–4, 143, 146, 149–50, 199 (n. 21); numbers of, 156
Sakman, A. F., 17–18
Sapozhnikov, I. P., 195 (n. 14)
Savich, N. V., 39
Savinkov, B. V., 77
Schmidt, V.-Adm. E., 89, 92, 141
Seckendorff, Lt. Gen. Frhr. von, 143–4
Shchastny, Capt. A. M., 140, 147–52
Sheinman, A. L., 30, 34, 80, 101–2, 104, 110–11, 127, 153, 165
Shingarev, A. I., 126
Shishko, P. I., 120, 136, 142, 205 (n. 18)
Shpilevsky, I. F., 150
Shtarev, A. S., 135–6
Shteinberg, I. Z., 145
Shubin, Col., 64
Shul'gin, V. V., 183 (n. 24)
Shushara, 31
Skobolev, M. I.,18, 28
Skurikhin, P. M., 126, 136
Sladkov, I. D., 8, 30
Smilga, I. T., biography of, 30, 74, 153; chairman of Finnish Regional Committee, 80, 121, 127; in October, 101, 103, 106–7, 110–12, 197 (nn. 38–9)
Smirnov, 102
Smirnov, P. I., 30, 107, 127, 153
Social Democrats, 7–9, 28–35; *see also* Bolsheviks, Mensheviks
Socialist-Revolutionaries, 33, 61; underground of, 7–9; position in 1917, 24–8, 31; and Kronstadt Republic, 53; and July Days, 59, 75; in

October, 117, 126f; *see also* Left S.R.s, S.R.-Maximalists
Sokolov, N. D., 28, 70
Sovkombalt, 138–40, 149–50
Sovnarkom, 117, 137–8; in October, 104–6; naval measures of, 129, 133, 136, 139–40, 142, 146, 149
Sovokin, A., 197 (n. 38)
Spiridonova, M. A., 59
Stal', L. N., 68
Stalin, I. V., 56, 153
Stanley, Adm. Sir V. A., 36
Stark, R.-Adm. G. K., 90–1, 154
Stark, L. N., 71, 153
Stasevich, P., 150
State Duma, 11–13, 15, 61, 76
Stavka, 3–4, 12–13, 46, 68, 85–6, 111, 119
Stepanov, A., 102
Sukhanov, N. N., 29, 56, 58–9, 113, 190 (n. 33)
Sutyrin, P. S., 123
Sveaborg, *see* Helsingfors
Sverdlov, Ia. M., 57, 106, 108, 110, 197 (n. 38)
Sveshnikov, R.-Adm. D. A., 90
Sviridov, K. P., 197 (n. 38)

Tereshchenko, M. I., 54
Timirev, R.-Adm. S. N., 5, 16, 46, 69, 77–8, 92, 129, 131, 154, 188 (n. 30)
Tizenko, Lt. B. P., 78
Trotsky, L. D., 28–9, 52, 77, 128, 140–1; in July Days, 56–7, 66–7; in October, 100–1, 105–6, 109–10, 113–14
Trudoviks, 24, 27
Tsentrobalt, origins of, 38, 41–2, 49; charters of, 42–5, 82; and Baltic Staff, 43, in July, 61–4, 70–1; post-July moderation of, 71–2; radicalisation of, 77, 79–81; and operations, 43, 48, 86, 89, 108; in October, 99–105, 107–8, 110–11, 196 (n. 23); and Constituent Assembly, 117–18; and demobilisation, 123; takes power, 130–1, 133; crisis in, 126, 134–8, 142–3, 146, 201 (n. 23)
Tsentroflot (Naval Section of Petrograd Soviet) 71, 129; formation of, 44–6, 48; and Kornilov, 77; crisis over, 80
Tseretelli, I. G., 28
Tsion, S. A., 205 (n. 18)
Tupikov, A. I., 153
Tyrkov, Capt. N. D., 68

Ul'iantsev, T. I., 30
Usarov, G. A., 98
Ustinov, A. M., 27, 190 (n. 40)

Vakhrameev, I. I., 132, 149, 154
Vasilevsky, Sr. Lt. K. I., 133–4
Verderevsky, V.-Adm. D. N., in
March, 19, 21, 36; biography of,
47, 154; appointed C.-in-C.,
45–7; in
July Days, 61–2, 65, 69, 73; as Navy
Minister, 16, 21, 79, 81, 83, 86, 128
Viren, Adm. R. N., 4, 12–14, 20, 182
(n. 9)
Vladislavlev, R.-Adm. P. P., 95
Vobalt, 83, 131, 135–6, 142–3, 146
Vul'f Is., 125, 144

warrant officers, 2, 6, 17, 38, 41, 86, 157,
184 (n. 34)
warships, German: *Equity*, 121, *König*,
92; *Kronprinz*, 92; *Posen*, 147, 151;
Westfalen, 147, 151; U-boats, 3, 89,
121
warships, Russian: *Admiral Makarov*, 20,
41, 43, 68, 75–6, 83, 90, 144, 147;
Amur, 98, 102, 113, 197 (n. 38); *Andrei
Pervozvanny*, 15–17, 21, 43, 60, 74, 88,
117, 119, 148; *Avrora*, 12, 77, 97–9,
103, 108–9, 111–13, 135, 197 (n. 47);
Baian, 5, 19, 78, 92, 148; *Bditel'-
ny*, 140; *Boevoi*, 78; *Bogatyr'*,
19, 47, 71, 75–6, 83, 147; *Deiatel'-
ny*, 99; *Diana*, 5, 27, 74, 128, 135;
Edinorog, 144; *Ermak*, 144, 147–8;
Gangut, 3, 5–6, 9, 74; *Grazhdanin*
(*Tsesarevich*), 20, 41, 88, 90, 92, 124,
130, 135; *Grom*, 91, 93; *Gromiashchy*, 63; *Gromoboi*, 74, 124,; *Iastreb*, 113; *Iziaslav*, 36; *Khoper*, 113;
Khrabry, 91, 124; *Krechet*, 1, 17–18,

62, 69, 131, 149–50; *Metky*, 99, 110;
Minesweeper *No. 14*, 98, 113; Minesweeper *No. 15*, 113; *Novik*, 11, 47;
Oleg, 19, 34, 76, 83, 99, 111, 130, 148;
Orfei, 63; *Pamiat' Azova* (*Dvina*), 10,
36, 149; *Petropavlovsk*, 17, 33, 47, 61–
2, 64, 70–1, 74, 78, 119, 136, 190
(n. 40); *Pobeditel'*, 90, 99, 111, 130;
Poliarnaia zvezda, 61–5, 72; *Poltava*, 17, 83, 200 (n. 18); *Pripiat'*, 91,
194 (n. 21); *Prozorlivy*, 198 (n. 52);
Raziashchy, 78; *Respublika* (*Imp. Pavel
I*). 8, 16–18, 21, 23, 30, 33, 42, 61–2,
64, 70, 74, 88, 139, 145, 148;
Riurik, 19, 74, 76, 83, 122, 124, 145,
147–8; *Rossiia*, 17, 60, 74, 135;
Sampo, 147, 151; *Samson*, 99, 103,
110, 113; *Sekret*, 32; *Sevastopol'*, 33,
60, 74; *Shcha*, 42; *Shdandart*, 130,
138; *Slava*, 16–17, 48, 51, 64, 70–1,
88, 90, 92–3; *Strashny*, 9, 110;
Tarmo, 147–8; *Truvor*, 147; *Turkmenets Stavropol'sky*, 75; *Verny*, 147;
Viola, 42; *Volkhov*, 4; *Volynets*, 147;
Zabaikalets, 149; *Zabiiaka*, 99, 110,
113; *Zaria svobody* (*Imp. Aleksandr
II*), 14, 68, 98, 109; *Zarnitsa*, 113
Williams, A. R., 87

Zalezhsky, V. N., 25–6, 30–1, 49, 74, 153
Zarubaev, R.-Adm. S. V., 47, 130, 147
Zelenoi, Capt. A. P., 70, 81
Zhelezniakov, A. G., 54, 82, 125; bio-
graphy of, 118, 153; and Constituent
Assembly, 118, 198 (n. 5)
Zhemchuzhin, B. A., 30, 65, 112, 153
Zherve, Capt. B. B., 93, 144
Zhitkov, Cmdr. K. G., 11, 184 (n. 35)
Zinoviev, G. E., 57
Zverin, 105

DATE DUE